STUMBLING BEAR

Soviet Military Performance in Afghanistan

Also from Brassey's

BAXTER
The Soviet Way of Warfare

BELLAMY
Red God of War:
Soviet Artillery and Rocket Forces

GHAUS
The Fall of Afghanistan:
An Insider's Account

HALL
Soviet Military Art in a Time of Change:
Command and Control of the Future Battlefield

HEMSLEY
The Lost Empire:
Perceptions of Likely Soviet Policy Shifts in the 1990s

LAFFIN
War Annual series

STUMBLING BEAR

Soviet Military Performance in Afghanistan

by

Scott R. McMichael

BRASSEY'S (UK)
A Member of the Maxwell Macmillan Group
LONDON · OXFORD · WASHINGTON · NEW YORK

UK	Brassey's (UK) Ltd.,
(Editorial)	50 Fetter Lane, London EC4 1AA, England
(Orders, all except North America)	Brassey's (UK) Ltd., Headington Hill Hall, Oxford OX3 0BW, England
USA (Editorial)	Brassey's (US) Inc., 8000 Westpark Drive, Fourth Floor, McLean, Virginia 22102, USA
(Orders, North America)	Brassey's (US) Inc., Front and Brown Streets, Riverside, New Jersey 08075, USA Tel (toll free): 800 257 5755

First edition 1991

Library of Congress Cataloging-in-Publication Data
McMichael, Scott R. (Scott Ray), 1951–   Stumbling bear: Soviet military performance in Afghanistan / Scott R. McMichael. -- 1st ed.
p. cm.
1. Afghanistan--History--Soviet occupation, 1979–1989.
2. Soviet Union--History, Military--1917- 3. Soviet Union--Armed Forces.
I. Title.
DS371.2.M46 1991 958.104'5--dc20   91-13713

British Library Cataloguing in Publication Data
McMichael, Scott R.
Stumbling bear : Soviet military performance in Afghanistan
1. Afghanistan. Military operations
I. Title
958.1045
ISBN 0-08-040982-2

Printed in Great Britain by B.P.C.C. Wheatons Ltd, Exeter.

Contents

List of Illustrations

List of Tables, Figures and Maps

Glossary

Abbreviations and Terms Used in the Text

AA   Anti-Aircraft

AP   Anti-Personnel

AT   Anti-Tank

Afganets/Afghantsy singular and plural term for an Afghan war veteran

blokirovka a blocking position

blokirovaniye the concept and practice of using blocking positions

BMD   a light, armoured vehicle used by airborne and air assault forces

BMP   a light, armoured fighting vehicle used by motorised rifle units

BRDM a light, armoured, wheeled reconnaissance vehicle

BTR   a light, armoured, wheeled vehicle used by motorised rifle troops

chars   an opium product sometimes used by Soviet troops

CI   Counter-Insurgency

dedovshchina term used to describe the unofficial and sometimes brutal system of privileges and seniority through which second-year soldiers exercise power over more junior recruits

desant   an assault landing by parachute or helicopter

desantnik term used for soldiers in *desant* units

DRA   Democratic Republic of Afghanistan

dushman pejorative term for the insurgents meaning bandit

eco-war economic warfare

FAC   forward air controller

GS   General Staff

grach   rook. Soviet slang for the SU-25 Frogfoot

HE   high explosive

KHAD the Afghan secret police

kishlak Afghan village

LAW   light anti-tank weapon

LCSFA Limited Contingent of Soviet Forces in Afghanistan

mayak   beacon. Slang term for a ground forward air controller

medevac medical evacuation

mg   machine gun

MD   military district

MR   Motorised Rifle

MRD   Motorised Rifle Division

MRL   Multiple Rocket Launcher

mujahedin   holy warrior. Name chosen by the Afghan insurgents. In use throughout the Arab world.

NVD   night vision device

OO   enveloping detachment

OOD   engineer mobility detachment

OP   observation post

pchela   honeybee. Slang term for the Mi-8 helicopter

PDPA   People's Democratic Party of Afghanistan. The ruling socialist party.

plamya   flame. The name for the AGS-17 grenade launcher

plan   hashish

razvedchik   reconnaissance soldier

recon   reconnaissance

retrans   retransmission

RPG   Rocket-Propelled Grenade

RTO   radio telephone operator

SA   Surface-to-Air

SAM   Surface-to-Air Missile

shmel'   bumblebee. Slang term for the Mi-24 Hind helicopter

SOP   Standard Operating Procedures

sqn   squadron

TVD   *Teatr voennykh deistvii* (theatre of war)

VDV   airborne and air assault force

VVS   air forces

zelenka, zelenaya zona   green zone. A vegetated area possibly occupied by *mujahedin*. Used to denote any danger area.

Abbreviations Used in Chapter Notes

AIC   Afghan Information Centre, Monthly Bulletins

AK   *Aviatsiya i Kosmonavtika* (Aviation and Cosmonautics)

AS   *Asian Survey*

IA   *International Affairs*

IDR   *International Defence Review*

KR   *Kryl'ya Rodiny* (Wings of the Motherland)

KVS   *Kommunist Vooruzhennikh Sil* (Communist of the Armed Forces)

KZ   *Krasnaya Zvezda* (Red Star)

JDR   *Jane's Defence Review*

JDW   *Jane's Defence Weekly*

RFE/RL Radio Free Europe/Radio Liberty

SR   *Sovetskaya Rossiya* (Soviet Russia)

SShA   *SShA. Ekonomika, Politika, Ideologiya* (USA. Economics, Politics, Ideology)

SV   *Sovetskii Voin* (Soviet Soldier)

ViZh   *Voyenno-Istoricheskii Zhurnal* (Military History Journal)

VV   *Voyennyi Vestnik* (Military Herald)

WUFA   Writers' Union of Free Afghanistan

Foreword

THEY should have known better than to let themselves become embroiled in Afghanistan, 'they' being the anonymous Brezhnevite leadership now shrouded in convenient obscurity or else hidden behind an impenetrable veil of obituaries. All the historical portents and precedents not only shouted but shrieked against it, warnings writ large for all to see, save for those unwilling to take note and pay heed. It was only necessary to look at British experience and the Third Afghan War begun in 1919 — not so remote — which caused Sir Henry Wilson, Chief of the Imperial General Staff, to note in his diary that 'the whole thing is unsatisfactory as I really have not enough troops to cope with possible difficulties'. The British even turned to the idea of chemical warfare, gas which might be 'more merciful' than high explosive. So wrote Churchill, convinced that 'if it is fair for an Afghan soldier to shoot down a British soldier behind a rock and cut him to pieces as he lies wounded . . . why is it not fair for a British artilleryman to fire a shell which makes the said native sneeze?' This question of 'fairness' had the strangest ring. Gas might conflict with the traditional notion of the 'chivalry' of frontier warfare. Brigadier General Foulkes laughed the idea to scorn. The tribesmen were utterly barbaric. British officers considered them 'as vermin fit only for extermination'. In any event, using gas was hardly 'unfair' when the tribesmen could command greater number, enjoyed tactical initiative, greater mobility and should be accounted better marksmen than the average Indian sepoy. It is certainly true that even in this latest war the Afghans made good use of their tried and trusted zeroed-in Lee Enfield rifles, causing Soviet commanders to wonder at the overwhelming prevalence of fatal head wounds and an unexpected proportion of dead to wounded. So the 'black tulips', those Soviet transport aircraft carrying cargoes of zinc coffins, continued their flights back to the Soviet Union, first for months and then for many long years.

Not that the Soviet leadership, whether civilian or military, needed to moil through the British archives or turn up such hair-raising accounts as *The Russians at the Gates of Herat* published in the late 1880s, for much of the material which was pertinent to their Afghan adventure lay to hand in their own archives. Simply by making recourse to their own Central State Military-Historical Archive, under Archive No. 445, folio 55, they would have found the voluminous holdings from the Imperial Russian Army on Afghanistan covering the years 1835–1917, or yet again the massive material published by and for the Imperial Russian General Staff, in four score volumes and more in the last quarter of the nineteenth century, *Sbornik geograficheskikh, topograficheskikh i statisticheskikh materialov po Azii*,[1] briefings on the fortifications of Afghan towns not entirely without relevance to forthcoming modern Soviet operations. They might even have turned up the notes of Colonel Matveyev, *Poezdka general'nogo shtaba Polkovnika Matveyeva po Bukharskim i Afganskim vladeniyam v fevrale 1877 g,* [2] though leaving out the implications of an Anglo-Russian clash in Asia and its possible ruinous consequences for British rule in India. Rather more pertinently, none other than General Kuropatkin contributed his own special study which might have commended itself to the Soviet command, *Zapiska ob obozakh dlya voiska Turkestanskogo voennogo okruga.* [3]

But if the Soviet command shied away from utilising the expertise of its imperial predecessors, it could at least turn to one of its own, or certainly identified as one within Red Army ranks, a graduate of the General Staff Academy in 1899 and an officer with first hand experience of Afghanistan, Lieutenant General Andrei Yevgen'evich Snesarev, a senior Red Army commander during the Civil War and subsequently chief of the General Staff Academy, before becoming both dean of and a professor at the Institute of Oriental Studies (*Institut Vostokovedeniya*). In 1921 he published his book *Afganistan,* nothing less than a warning for all to read, though few, if any, seem to have known of it, much less to have heeded its injunctions.

General Snesarev uttered a clear and wholly unambiguous warning — keep the Red Army out of Afghanistan, which represented only a stop-over on the way to India. The country itself was as inhospitable as it was dangerous, its population bordering on the barbaric, ingrates to a man where any outside help was concerned, bent on warring amongst themselves, but let the infidel outsider come, then in the name of Islam they would offer unified resistance. Any Soviet military involvement in Afghanistan could only be foolhardy as it would be calamitous. This prescience, candour, prejudice or jaundice is finally and fully, albeit retrospectively, vindicated in Colonel McMichael's comprehensive study of this most recent Soviet military performance in Afghanistan.

Not unnaturally, there has been a massed flight from any hint of responsibility for what Artyom Borovik in his book *Afganistan eshche raz pro voinu*[4] (now in English as *The Hidden War*) has called the obliteration of an entire Soviet generation of 18-year-olds. As Colonel McMichael points out, in true Soviet fashion 'blame' is lodged where it most conveniently belongs, to a dead and, therefore, mute leadership — Brezhnev, Gromyko, Ustinov, Andropov, with Gorbachev and Shevardnadze quite properly abed and blissfully unaware of the fateful decision. The Soviet military makes a curious case. The inconsistency seems to lie in the fact, as Colonel McMichael shows, that while the Soviet High Command and the General Staff argued against a heavy commitment of ground forces, nevertheless by early autumn 1979 very substantial military preparation, involving two Military Districts, was set in motion, even as Soviet military advisers in Afghanistan became more immediately involved with operations against the *mujahedin*. Major General Ivan Ryabchenko, commander of 105 Airborne Division, had already received his operational orders in September 1979, to render assistance to friendly Afghanistan in a struggle against counter-revolution, while Suslov 'prepared' a new government for Kabul at the end of December 1979, five Soviet motor rifle divisions were on the move into Afghanistan. If General Ryabchenko's 'boys' thought they would be home by 23 February, 1980, they were soon sadly and brutally disillusioned. When I was in Moscow shortly after the Soviet invasion, talking with senior Soviet officials, it appeared that the dread idea of not only a long haul had begun to dawn but also the impression of being drawn into a political quagmire.

Soviet operations involving 40th Army, meticulously retailed and analysed by Colonel McMichael, developed in several distinct phases, the first involving a certain reorganisation of the Soviet forces from the armour-heavy formations equipped with everything including the proverbial 'kitchen sink' into combined-arms brigades and divisional task forces, with a growing need for helicopters. The second phase of the operations of the Limited Contingent of Soviet Forces in Afghanistan (LCSFA) involved divisional offensives against guerrilla forces, followed by a recourse to air power and something of a stalemate. In the mid-1980s Soviet casualties mounted steeply with at least six very substantial Soviet offensives, but with the arrival on the scene of Gorbachev, defensivism was in the air and retrenchment, heralding ultimate withdrawal.

At the cost of 13,310 killed in action, 35,478 wounded and 311 missing in action — figures officially affirmed by Army General Varennikov interviewed by *Sovetskii Patriot*[5] — the Soviet Army learned lessons which it should have digested at a much earlier stage, particularly with respect to training, a subject to which Colonel McMichael devotes an important and illuminating section of his book — Soviet training which proved unsuitable either to prepare troops for basic combat operations or for the special nature of counter-insurgency operations. With the motor rifle troops, the problem lay with the failure to continue systematic unit training once the men were in Afghanistan, leaving the individual soldier to 'fit in' and 'catch up' as best he might with the more experienced fellows of his unit. The counter-insurgency force, as opposed to the motor rifle troops, trained harder and rehearsed its small-unit operations, with airborne and air assault units carrying out training patrols under combat conditions. But what emerges from Colonel McMichael's analysis is that the senior command failed to institute a systematic training programme to keep abreast of the special requirements imposed by operations in Afghanistan: this may have been in one respect a counsel of despair, a recognition that it was quite impossible to train the motor rifle component effectively in order to execute decentralised, independent operations.

The weaknesses of junior command and poor morale, drug-abuse, atrocities, the brutality of the 'old soldiers' towards the fresh conscripts — *dedovshchina* — had their counter-part, one might even suspect their deepest root cause, in the monumental muddle of what passed for 'command and control' in Afghanistan. This was a lamentable state of affairs bitterly criticised by Major General Ivanov of the General Staff Academy, where 40th Army came directly under the army commander himself, under the 'operational group' of the Turkestan Military District as well as under the 'operational group' of the Defence Ministry which included personnel attached from practically every arm and service, none of which contributed to flexibility of command. Quite the contrary.

What is quite horrible but accurately delineated by Colonel McMichael is the catalogue of medical mismanagement and ineptitude displayed not only throughout the campaign but also in its aftermath. The poor living conditions present Soviet soldiers complain of were magnified and complicated in Afghanistan: even in the early days of the war in Afghanistan I was told in Moscow that the greater hazard was hepatitis, to which had to be added dysentery, jaundice, parasitic infections and skin diseases — acute misery made worse by the shortage of water and the prospect of cure or treatment diminished by the abysmal hospital or medical evacuation facilities. Colonel McMichael supplies in strictly factual form what Borovik and others have sketched in journalistic guise or what can be gleaned from the bitter comments of the *Afgantsy*, the veterans even now bereft of after-care.

If the sights and sounds and sufferings of the war were as of old, Colonel McMichael draws attention in his evaluation of the scope of the war in Afghanistan to what was new in terms of weapons and technology. Of particular note was the introduction of the SU-25 Frogfoot ground-attack aircraft and the 'bloodying' of the Mi-24 Hind helicopter, while on the ground Soviet forces introduced the BM-27 220-mm rocket launcher, a tracked BMP-2, the AGS-17 automatic grenade-launcher, the RPO-50 flame rocket launcher, the distinctive RPG-22 light anti-tank rocket, the AK-74 automatic rifle and a whole catalogue of anti-personnel mines and mine dispensers.

This is a highly professional, fully documented appraisal of the nature of the Soviet Army's performance in the course of the 10-year war in Afghanistan, with much of the material drawn from Soviet sources. The 12 chapters cover the decision to invade, the restructuring of 1980, the nature of *mujahedin* resistance, the shortcomings of Soviet doctrine — indeed, the absence of a counter-insurgency doctrine — the armed forces of Afghanistan as such, the creation of a Soviet counter-insurgency force, the war in the air, Soviet combat and troop support and a final evaluation. With respect to the latter, there can be little argument that this was military venture which ultimately bordered on the disastrous. But what is even more compelling is the inescapable conclusion that those shortcomings of Soviet military organisation and deficiencies in Soviet military performance, shown up so harshly in the Afghan clime, were not 'little local difficulties' but rather rooted deep within the system as a whole, one which had fed too long on its own conceits and obdurate self-delusion. They were not shortcomings and deficiencies which could be overcome by improvisation, of which there was a deal, or by tinkering. So, as Colonel McMichael very aptly puts it, here was a bear which could not but stumble. It was and is still a bear, badly mauled, which has also been for all to see, not least the Soviet population itself long held in ignorance of the circumstances, manifestly and undeniably humbled.

JOHN ERICKSON

Edinburgh, January 1991

Notes

1 Collection (or Digest) of geographical, topographical and statistical materials concerning Asia.
2 Trip by Colonel Matveyev of the General Staff through the Bukhara and Afghan Domains in February 1877.
3 Report on Troop Trains of the Turkestan Military District
4 Afghanistan, Once More About the War.
5 Soviet Patriot.

Preface

WHILE taking a course in 1989 on the subject of Soviet military views of local wars under the able direction of Natalie Gross at the US Army Russian Institute, I became interested in, or rather intrigued by, the Soviet–Afghan War. How was it that a relatively small number of ill-equipped, ill-trained *mujahedin* managed to hold a well-equipped Soviet Army at bay for so long? After a moderate amount of research into the war, it became clear to me that the Limited Contingent of Soviet Forces in Afghanistan (LCSFA) suffered from major systemic deficiencies. However, it also became clear to me that the treatment of the war in Western publications suffered from two serious shortcomings.

Firstly, few sources devoted any significant attention to a professional analysis of Soviet tactical operations and military performance, except in a macro sense. Although many outstanding works on the war are available, the majority of authors have stressed the social, political, economic, regional and international aspects of the war at the expense of the military. Thus a serious gap exists: there is no single work in English which develops the most important themes of Soviet military performance in Afghanistan: preparation for war; the force mix; operations by the various arms of service; integration of Soviet and national Afghan forces in combat; air–ground co-ordination; training for combat in Afghanistan; tactical innovations and, perhaps most importantly, questions of leadership, adaptation and the applications of lessons learned in Afghanistan to the Soviet Armed Forces as a whole. This book is intended to fill that gap. Each chapter provides conclusions on various discrete aspects of Soviet military performance, with a final chapter summarising the most important conclusions.

Secondly, most Western commentaries on the Soviet–Afghan War rely more or less exclusively on Western or Afghan sources, including, of course, authoritative eyewitness accounts and personal experiences in the country. What has been lacking, however, is a comprehensive exploration of Soviet sources, particularly the Soviet military press. Soviet press accounts of the war, though veiled, are not opaque. Used in conjunction with other sources and studied carefully for what they do not say as much as for what they do say, Soviet reports in the military press provide important information on how Soviet military experts viewed the war. Where Soviet sources have previously been used, in general there is too much reliance on articles rendered into English by translation services.

In contrast, this book is based largely on an exhaustive study of the Soviet military press during the 1980s, complemented by research into Western and Afghan sources which focus on Soviet military operations. As such, I believe that *Stumbling Bear* provides a unique viewpoint not available in most other works on the war. In particular, it reveals how the Soviets themselves analysed and modified their operations during the course of the war and how the experience of Soviet arms has been internalised within the Soviet Army and Air Force.

The bulk of this book was written while I was a postgraduate Research Associate at the Centre for Defence Studies, University of Edinburgh, under the supervision of the eminent Professor John Erickson. I take the opportunity here to express my gratitude to Professor Erickson for his counsel and assistance, not least of which is the excellent Foreword he has contributed to this work. I am also grateful to Dr Jana Pavlova, Chief Librarian, and her staff at the library of the US Army Russian Institute. Finally, I would like to acknowledge the graciousness of the National Defense University Press in permitting me to use some of the photographs and drawings from a previous NDU publication.

SCOTT R. MCMICHAEL

Vienna, Virginia,
February 1991

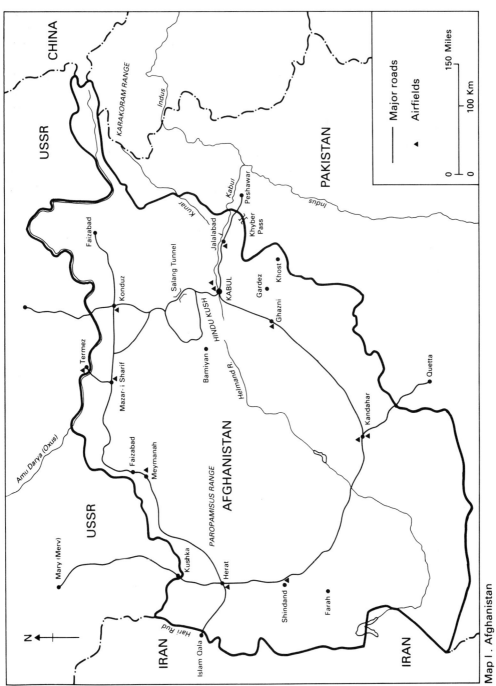

Map I . Afghanistan

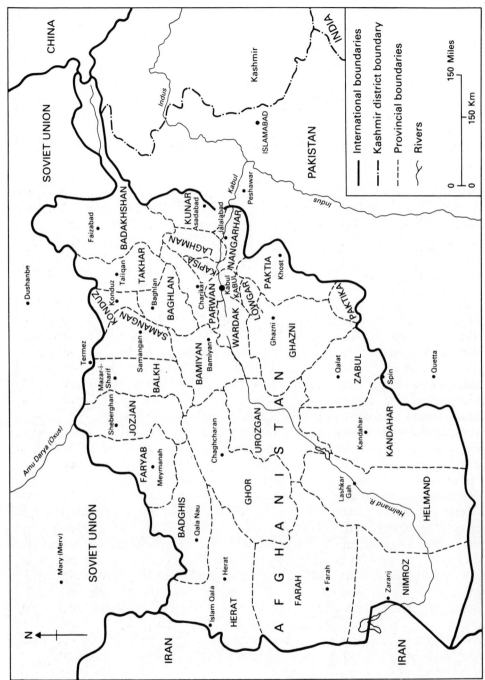

Map II. The Provinces of Afghanistan

CHAPTER 1

The Invasion

COMMUNIST power was established in Afghanistan in April 1978, in the usual way — by force of arms through a bloody coup, assisted by the Soviet Union. The new president, Nur M Taraki, leader of the Khalq faction of the People's Democratic Party of Afghanistan (PDPA), was a highly unpopular leader. His announced programmes of land redistribution, emancipation of women, and the construction of a new 'egalitarian' society through the destruction of the old, found little support among the largely traditional, Islamic people.

The stability of the new Soviet client régime began to deteriorate virtually from the first days of its existence. Almost immediately, the small armed resistance groups in the countryside attracted new members and increased the size and frequency of their attacks against the government. Simultaneously, the Army of the Democratic Republic of Afghanistan (DRA) began to disintegrate, helped along by a Taraki-directed purge of military officers from the Parcham faction of the PDPA. Soviet elation over the establishment of another fraternal socialist state on its frontier turned to deep concern and doubts about the survivability of Taraki's government. As these concerns mounted, military involvement increased. Soviet advisers started to pour into the country soon after the coup; within 18 months, their numbers had reached several thousands, under the direction of General Major L. Gorelov.[1]

Conditions worsened dramatically during the course of 1979. In March, the city of Herat flared into revolt with the bulk of the 17th Infantry Division rising in mutiny. The bitter fighting to restore order lasted a week. Army units loyal to Taraki advanced and occupied the city while the Air Force bombed the headquarters and garrisons of the 17th Division. About 5,000 people died before control was re-established, including nearly 100 Soviet citizens in mob violence. This event probably stimulated the Soviet General Staff to start planning for military intervention.

Desertions in the DRA Army increased with many senior officers leaving their posts. An entire brigade of the 7th Mechanised Division is said to have defected to the side of the resistance in May, taking their arms and combat vehicles with them. Additional mutinies by other Army units, including the better trained paratroopers and commandos, took place during the summer and fall. The 5th Brigade, 9th Infantry Division, revolted in August and joined in a rebel attack in the Kunar Valley. By the end of the year, the strength of the Army had fallen by more than half from 90,000 to about 40,000. Moreover, half the officer corps had either been purged or had defected to the rebels.

Prelude to Invasion

His security deeply threatened by these events, Taraki turned repeatedly to his Soviet benefactors for help. According to Soviet sources, the Afghan President made 18 separate appeals for Soviet military assistance during the year, even to the point of requesting two Soviet divisions, paratroopers, and helicopters with crews.[2]

Although the multitude of Soviet military and political advisers in-country were providing periodic reports on the status of the Kabul Army and its capability to deal with the *mujahedin* threat, a closer look was deemed necessary. In April, 1979, Army General A A Yepishev (Chief of the Main Political Administration of the Soviet Armed Forces) led a delegation of several generals in a visit to the country. Yepishev had made a similar visit to Czechoslovakia in 1968, prior to the invasion of that country by Soviet forces. There is no question that the two visits had the same mission — to assess the internal military-political situation and advise on suitable actions to be taken.

Shortly after this visit, the Soviet Union increased its direct military aid. Two hundred T55 tanks, possibly as many as 100 T62 tanks, an undetermined number of lighter armoured vehicles, 12 Mi-24 Hind helicopter gunships, and some later model MIG-21s were delivered to Afghanistan during the summer.[3] The first Soviet unit, a paratroop battalion, secretly deployed to Bagram air base, 40 miles north of Kabul, on 7 July. The paratroopers took over the base, consolidating it as a secure airhead for future intervention if needed.

In the middle of August, Army General I Pavlovskii (Commander-in-Chief, Soviet Ground Forces) was notified by then Defence Minister D Ustinov that he would head a second high-ranking military delegation to Afghanistan. Like Yepishev, Pavlovskii must have experienced *déja vu*, since he had commanded the Soviet invasion force into Czechoslovakia in 1968. Pavlovskii spent several weeks travelling around the country with 50–60 officers, among which were a number from the Main Staff of the Ground Forces. Undoubtedly, this group of officers included the principal members of the planning and operations staff for an expeditionary force, should the decision be taken to commit one.

For a number of reasons, it seems indisputable that a decision to prepare for intervention had been made by the time of Pavlovskii's visit. The most significant indicator is the fact that several divisions in Soviet Central Asia were ordered to a higher readiness level and began to mobilise at the same time that Pavlovskii was touring the DRA. Thus, Pavlovskii's visit provided an extraordinary opportunity for the completion of the invasion plans through an actual, on-site inspection of the operational area and the key objectives.

The Decision to Intervene

During the 1980s, most Western analysts and observers assumed that the Soviet military had strongly influenced the Politboro decision to invade their southern neighbour; the inspection trips by Yepishev and Pavlovskii are cited as compelling evidence for this view. After all, military solutions had proved their effectiveness in the past — in Hungary in 1956 and Czechoslovakia in 1968.

Little was known about the mechanics of the decision until 1989, when the Soviet generals began to tell the story themselves. By 1989, common wisdom in the Soviet

Union held that the decision to intervene had been a mistake, a gross mistake paid for in the blood of Soviet men. Foreign Minister Eduard Shevardnadze characterised the decision as a disaster 'both for the people of the USSR and the people of Afghanistan'. He and Gorbachev cleverly distanced themselves from any responsibility, claiming that, despite their membership of the *Politboro* in 1979, they had heard about the introduction of Soviet troops into Afghanistan like any other Soviet citizen — on the radio. In keeping with the hallowed Soviet tradition of heaping blame on deceased leaders, responsibility for the decision has been fixed on a small group of *Politboro* members — Brezhnev, Ustinov, Andropov, and Gromyko — all of whom are now dead and unable to defend themselves.[4]

Nevertheless, given the opprobrium falling on anyone associated with the decision, the Soviet generals began to speak out in 1989 in order to make sure that they would not be found guilty of complicity. General Lev Gorelov, the chief of the Soviet military advisory group in-country, has stated that when he was called before a *Politboro* commission in August 1979, he reported that it was 'inadvisable' to strengthen the Soviet military presence in Afghanistan. He considered the DRA Army to be capable of maintaining the régime in power without any additional help. Gorelov further stated, however, that General Lieutenant B Ivanov, the KGB Chief in Kabul, presented an opposing view, which the commission found more convincing.[5]

Upon his return to the Soviet Union, General Pavlovskii, according to his own testimony, also reported to Ustinov that 'there is no necessity to introduce our troops into Afghanistan', but Ustinov, apparently, was not inclined to heed his advice. Allegedly, Pavlovskii's assessment was shared by high-ranking members of the Soviet General Staff, including: Marshal Ogarkov, then the Chief of the GS; his First Deputy, Army General S A Akhromeev; and, another Deputy, Army General V Varennikov. According to Varennikov himself, they all expressed opposition to intervention.[6] [*Varennikov's statements are especially interesting in that it has been speculated that he was appointed Chief of Staff of the theatre command established to prosecute the war.*]

The proposal being put to the General Staff at that time (the key question is by whom) suggested the introduction of 75,000 troops, a force which the General Staff considered to be inadequate for the tasks intended for it. Ogarkov and his deputies argued that the introduction of Soviet troops would lead to an increase in the numbers of rebels and that the Soviet troops would become the objects of their attacks. However, should the political leadership nevertheless decide to introduce troops, the General Staff advised that they should be used only to establish garrisons and not in direct action against the rebels.[7]

[*The full story on who was responsible for the 'Afghan decision' will not be brought to light for some time. In the meanwhile, the limited information provided in the Soviet press must be digested with care, particularly when the individuals providing the information have self-serving reasons for doing so, which is clearly the case above. These attempts by the Soviet generals to depict themselves as wise, reasonable, prescient advisers must be viewed with scepticism.*]

From the Soviet point of view, the crisis reached its peak in September 1979, when Afghan Prime Minister Hafizullah Amin, also of the Khalq faction and second to Taraki in the government, led his own coup to seize power. President Taraki, who had just returned from a state visit to Moscow, was executed. Taraki's ruthless execution by his rival and fellow communist may have shocked Brezhnev into the conclusion that only direct Soviet military intervention could save its client from degeneration into total chaos. Amin's policies alienated the population even more than had those of Taraki. Moreover, his previous ties to the United States and his obvious disinclination to follow the advice of the Soviet Ambassador and the other Soviet advisers throughout the governmental machinery sealed his doom.

Definite preparations for invasion can be traced to the late summer and early autumn. The forces designated for employment were drawn from the military districts adjacent to Afghanistan, i.e. the Central Asian and the Turkestan districts, commanded respectively by General Colonels P Lushev and Yu Maksimov.[8] The low-readiness divisions here had to be brought up to strength and retrained. Phased mobilisation of the 360th and 201st Motorised Rifle divisions (MRD) from the Central Asian MD began in September, followed by the 66th and 357th MRDs in Turkestan in November/December. Local reservists were called up, resulting in an invasion force composed largely of Central Asian nationalities. It appears that some difficulty may have been experienced in staffing the divisions with the required number of technical specialists, such as artillerymen, engineers, and signallers.[9] This unusual massing of men and materials was carried out under the predictable guise of a large, routine mobilisation exercise, which fooled only those who wanted to be fooled.

The operations obviously would require the services of airborne forces, so the 105th Guards Airborne Division was alerted. Transport aircraft to provide the airlift shuttled into the marshalling areas established at the end of the Soviet rail lines at Termez and Kushka on the Soviet-Afghan border. Fuel, ammunition, and other stockpiles of necessary war supplies built up over several months, duly noted by spy satellites.

Overseeing these preparations was a theatre headquarters established (with satellite and special communications links to Moscow) under the command of Marshal Sergei Sokolov, First Deputy Minister of Defence. An operational headquarters for ground forces, designated the 40th Army, General Lieutenant Yu Tukharinov (First Deputy Commander, Turkestan MD commanding), took shape at Termez.[10] Tukharinov was replaced after a few months by General Lieutenant V Mikhailov. General Colonel S. Magometov replaced Gorelov as senior Soviet military adviser in the country.[11]

Meanwhile, on Afghan territory, Soviet military advisers became more and more involved in the operations against the *mujahedin*. The domineering influence of the huge Soviet advisory group was such that, after Taraki's assassination, all significant operational orders to Afghan units had to be approved with a Soviet signature. In addition, Afghan access to the new Soviet military equipment was severely restricted. At the end of October, the Soviet contingent planned and commanded, through the Afghan officers, a 10-day anti-guerilla operation in Paktia Province, complete with air support flown by Soviet pilots. This kind of direct management of events was a presage of things to come. In addition, the loss of control by the Afghan officers led to another sharp drop in morale within the army of the régime.[12]

The Invasion Plan

The final, no-turning-back, decision to invade Afghanistan was undoubtedly taken in late November, because early December saw a major leap in Soviet military activity. At the end of the first week of December, one regiment of the 105th Guards Airborne Division flew into Bagram airbase and promptly dispatched sub-units to occupy the military side of Kabul International. It appears that the 105th was also augmented at this time by the addition of two regiments, one each from the 103rd and 104th Guards Airborne divisions. In the middle of December, a battalion of paratroopers moved from Bagram up to the Salang Pass Tunnel in order to secure this vital choke point on the main highway from Termez to Kabul. Throughout the rest of the month, Soviet military traffic into Kabul by road and air remained at a high level. Afghan officers and ministers concerned about the obvious build-up were quieted by the declaration that the movements were connected with preparations for an impending military exercise.

The Soviet invasion plan, quite properly, was focused on Kabul. Here it was planned to airland a sizeable force over a compressed period of time into both Bagram and Kabul airbases, a force which would move into the city on signal and occupy the key centres of power. The Kabul Army garrison was neutralised ingeniously. Soviet advisers to the unit guarding the radio station informed its leaders that their tanks would soon be replaced by newer models. However, because diesel fuel was in short supply, the fuel from the present tanks would have to be removed and used in the new vehicles to bring them forward. The ruse worked; the tanks were immobilised.[13]

The commanders of the 7th and 8th Mechanised divisions were also duped. In one case, an inventory of 'faulty' ammunition was conducted so that the tanks turned in their rounds for safety reasons. In the other, crews were instructed to prepare their vehicles for winter by, among other things, removing the batteries for storage. Similar deception, such as the directed turn-in of live ammunition for training rounds, took place at other garrisons.[14]

In addition to the main objective of Kabul, the rest of the country's urban centres would have to be neutralised according to the Soviet plan. In particular, it was imperative that the Soviet invasion force should immediately obtain control of the main highway arc encircling the country and the other major airbases. Accordingly, they planned to conduct the ground invasion from two directions, the points of origin being Termez and Kushka. The western arm would proceed via the main highway to occupy Herat, Shindand, Farah, and Kandahar in sequence. The eastern strike force would move from Termez to Kabul, again along the main highway. While the ground elements were on the move, airborne contingents would occupy and neutralise DRA airbases at Herat, Shindand, Kandahar, and Jalalabad. The plan was simple, yet complete. Executed properly, it stood a good chance of success.

Coup de Main

Late at night on Christmas Eve, the first of what would become a continuous stream of Soviet aircraft began to touch down at Kabul and Bagram airports. Simultaneously, Soviet soldiers began to disembark from transport aircraft landing at Shindand, Kandahar, and Jalalabad. The *coup de main* had begun. By the morning of 27 December, approximately 5,000 troops were present in the vicinity of Kabul. Little did the Soviet leadership realise at this point that nearly ten years would go by before the 40th Army would return to the Soviet Union.

Soviet ground forces moved from their airfield bases into the capital city on the evening of 27 December. At 7:00 pm, Kabul's main telephone exchanges were blown up. By 7:15, the Ministry of the Interior had been occupied. The radio station fell a few hours later. Paratroopers from the 105th Guards Airborne Division occupied key intersections, ammunition depots, the post office, and other key ministries and government posts.[15]

At approximately 9:15 pm, Afghan citizens who were tuned in to Radio Kabul heard the voice of Babrak Karmal, leader of the Parcham faction of the PDPA, in a pre-recorded statement being broadcast from a Soviet transmitter across the border but on Radio Kabul frequency. In the statement, Karmal announced that he had taken over the government and had appealed to the Soviet Union for military assistance.[16]

President Amin may still have been alive at the time that Karmal's announcement was being made, but, if so, he did not survive it by much. Earlier in the month, Amin had changed his residence from his headquarters in the city to the fortified Darulaman Palace on the outskirts, having been advised to do so by the Soviet Embassy for his own protection. Having thus isolated their prey, a Soviet strike force of several hundred Soviet 'commandos', including a KGB assault team, attacked the palace at the same time that the city was being invested. Dressed in Afghan Army uniforms and using vehicles with Afghan markings, the assault force overcame the palace guard in a battle which lasted for four hours.

Reports on the storming of the palace are contradictory and incomplete, no doubt because the assault force was allegedly instructed to leave no witnesses alive. Apparently, Amin was located drinking in a bar in the building and killed on the spot. Also killed during the *putsch*, according to some reports, was General Lieutenant V S Paputin, a First Deputy Minister of Internal Affairs, who may have been charged with the mission of taking Amin alive for a subsequent show trial and execution. Another source reports that the actual leader of the commando assault, Colonel Bayerenov (head of the KGB terrorist training school) was also killed during the attack, by his own men, ironically, as he emerged from the palace to call for additional help.[17] Speculation has been made that one or both of these deaths could have been intentional. What certainly seems clear, in the midst of this confusion, is that the storming of the palace and the capture of Amin did not go as smoothly as planned, although the ultimate objective — the removal of Amin — was achieved.

While the paratroopers were strengthening their grip on the capital, elements of five Soviet motorised-rifle divisions (MRD) crossed the border in the north. The 357th and 66th MRDs advanced from Kushka to Herat, Shindand, Farah, and Kandahar, leaving garrisons in each city as it proceeded. The 360th MRD crossed the border at Termez and moved through Mazar-i Sharif towards the Salang Pass Tunnel, reaching Kabul by the morning of 26 December. Further east, the 201st MRD, followed later by the 16th MRD, occupied the provincial capitals of Konduz, Badakhshan, and Baghlan. Looking up, the tank crews of the ground columns could see the jet streams of the aircraft from the two Soviet air divisions which made up the air component of the invasion force. General Mikhailov moved up to establish

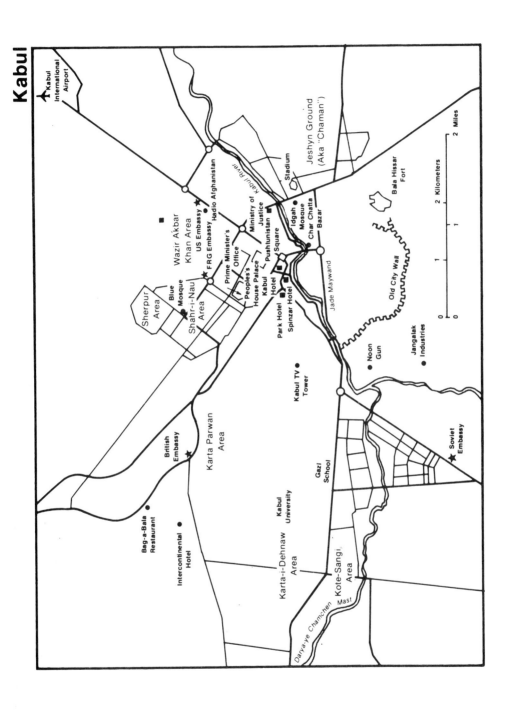

Kabul

the forward command post of the 40th Army at Bagram, with its Lolos satellite ground link station; later the headquarters would be moved to Kabul itself.[18]

Support units followed in the wake of the armoured columns in order to sustain the 1,750 tanks and 2,100 infantry combat vehicles brought in by this first wave. The dust had not long settled at the border, when Soviet pipe-laying battalions began constructing a fuel pipeline southwards.

Although the invasion force achieved its primary objectives promptly, resistance by the Afghan Army was considerable. The 8th Infantry Division near Kabul resisted until 5 January; perhaps 2,000 of its ranks were killed. Major fighting also took place in Herat, Jalalabad, and Kandahar, where the 15th Division revolted. Kandahar was reportedly bombed and strafed by the DRA Air Force, although the pilots are said to have taken pains to avoid hitting any of their own people. Numerous Afghan units, particularly those officered primarily by Khalqis, were simply disarmed by the Soviets before their resentment developed into open resistance. Curfews were imposed in all the major cities and Soviet soldiers took care not to venture out of their cantonments at night. Soviet control of Afghan airbases was sure-handed; there were no reports of Afghan pilots attacking Soviet units at this time.

Several weeks were required before Soviet and loyal DRA units asserted control in all provincial capitals. Several other brigade-sized revolts by DRA Army units had to be put down. (In July, the 14th Mechanised Division burst into mutiny.) It appears that the army mutinies had as much to do with the Khalqi/Parchami factional battles as with the Soviet presence. 'Loyal' DRA units were employed as much as possible to suppress the military revolts. Major riots and uprisings broke out frequently, including a three-day battle in Kabul itself in the last week of February. The Soviets also had to deal with *mujahedin* attacks and highway ambushes in almost every region.

During January, additional Soviet units flowed into the country and the airlift into the various airbases continued. By the end of the month, Soviet strength pushed over the 50,000 mark. The coup had been a stunning military success, but the Soviets now discovered that executing a coup and installing a hand-picked ruler were only the first and easiest steps. Stabilising the régime would prove to be a task beyond their means and strength.

CHAPTER 2

The Second Phase of Soviet Occupation, 1980–82

THE Soviet invasion of Afghanistan can be compared in several respects to the Soviet invasion of Czechoslovakia in 1968. Both invasions were carried out under the 'so-called' Brezhnev doctrine, the declarative policy of the Soviet Union that it possessed the right, duty, and willingness to intervene in neighbouring, socialist countries to preserve socialism if it were threatened. The plans and invasion forces were similar in concept. Certainly the goals were identical — the (re) establishment of a stable, orthodox socialist state through the ousting of a wavering, unstable régime which was losing its way — as were the expectations that combat operations would be quite limited in scope and duration. Here the parallels begin to break down, although the 'Czechoslovakia mentality' undoubtedly influenced Soviet thinking for some time.

In support of the primary goal of the establishment of a stable socialist government, properly subservient to Soviet leadership, several sub-objectives had to be met more or less concomitantly:

▶ The PDPA had to establish itself as an effective and legitimate ruling party under Karmal.
▶ The armed forces of the DRA had to be built up into an effective force capable of defending the régime.
▶ The resistance had to be crushed.
▶ The non-supportive population had to be won over, at least to passive acceptance of socialism.

Initial Problems

Ironically, the immediate effect of the Soviet invasion ran counter to the achievement of all of these goals. The PDPA, already weakened by the Khalq-Parcham factional strife, split yet more deeply; neither Karmal nor the PDPA as a whole could claim legitimate right to rule as long as they depended on Soviet military power to keep them in place. The Afghan Army became totally demoralised and unreliable to the point of being unable to respond to *mujahedin* attacks. In contrast, the Soviet invasion invigorated and emboldened the resistance and led to an immediate increase in rebel activity and influence. Finally, the great majority of the Afghan population reacted to the invasion in the same way that they had reacted in

9

the past to every foreign invader — not with cowering fear and shattered will, as the Soviets had hoped, but with outrage, resentment, and characteristic Afghan implacability. In the course of the entire period of Soviet occupation, none of the fundamental Soviet objectives were achieved. These failures critically affected the effectiveness of the Soviet military effort.

From a military point of view, the Soviets probably expected that its occupation forces would remain in the country for a short period, up to two years perhaps, although a permanent advisory and security presence was envisioned. Five main points comprised the military concept behind the intervention.

▶ Soviet forces would stabilise the country by establishing garrisons along the major transport routes and in the major cities, airbases, logistical centres.

▶ DRA Army units would thus be relieved of the burden of maintaining garrisons and freed to move into the countryside to eliminate the resistance.

▶ Soviet forces would support the Afghans logistically and with combat support (air, reconnaissance, artillery).

▶ In general, however, Soviet forces would maintain a low profile and refrain as much as possible from too much contact with the local population and from direct operations against the *mujahedin*.

▶ Once the DRA Army had been strengthened and the resistance defeated, the bulk of the Soviet forces would be withdrawn.

This concept broke down immediately because the assumptions on which it was based were without foundation. In short, in what must be considered to be gross failures of intelligence and strategic assessment, the Soviets completely underestimated the strength, vitality, and resilience of the resistance and vastly overestimated the feasibility of regenerating the Afghan Armed Forces. Within two months, the Soviets found themselves forced to conduct major operations against the guerillas using their own forces.

That the Soviets intended to remain only a short period of time, holding combat activity to a minimum, is borne out in the first place, by the testimony of high-ranking Soviet generals closely connected with the war in Afghanistan. Consider, for example, the testimony of Army General V I Varennikov in an interview in December, 1989, with the newspaper, *Soviet Patriot*:

> *Soviet Patriot*: And how did it happen that a troop commitment planned to last several months turned into 10 long years for us?
>
> *Varennikov*: After the decision to commit was made, the Army was obligated to carry it out. But the matter of time, or more precisely, the 'from and to' dates, was not addressed. It was also important that we did not intend to involve ourselves in combat activities. And we did not pose such goals to ourselves. Our mission was to enter the country, establish garrisons and thus stabilise the situation, and prevent opposing forces from disturbing the tranquillity of the country and the people, including transferring their detachments out of Pakistan.
>
> *Soviet Patriot*: But didn't we get involved in combat activities nonetheless?
>
> *Varennikov*: Yes, because the forces of the opposition began raiding our units, and naturally we had to defend ourselves in such a situation. And after that, all this began growing like a snowball, and events began developing in an undesirable direction.[1]

General Lieutenant Gromov is on record with similar statements that Soviet forces were intended to establish garrisons, stabilise the situation, and refrain from significant combat operations, withdrawing at an early opportunity.[2]

This position is further supported by the fact that the ground forces introduced were of very low quality and no plans existed to replace them quickly with better trained units. Military planners knew that the MRDs used in the invasion force were poorly trained and unused to working together. They knew that the equipment complements of the divisions encompassed old, obsolescing systems. They knew that the Central Asian soldiers called up to fill out the divisions, by and large, had very limited military training and experience in actual combat skills, since it has long been (unofficial) Soviet policy to use Central Asian minorities only in construction battalions and non-combat support duties (such as cooks, transport and supply etc.).[3] They also knew that mobilisation had not gone smoothly and that the more technical units in the force (combat engineers, artillery, communications, in particular) were deficient.

For a temporary occupation force, intended to conduct what amounted to a show of force, these deficiencies were troubling but not debilitating. Certainly, combat operations over an extended period of time were not envisioned. Thus, as armoured columns thundering down the highway, Soviet invasion forces were most impressive; as combat units engaged in battle in difficult terrain against guerrilla forces, they turned out to be inept.

In contrast, the airborne regiments which were deployed displayed a high level of capability. On the other hand, they had completed their primary mission of taking Kabul and seizing the airfields. Their post-invasion role was quite limited — providing security for the facilities which they had seized. There were too few of them and they were needed much too much as reliable, security troops to send off into the countryside chasing rebels.

It is not surprising, therefore, that the Soviet motorised rifle divisions stumbled badly when they were forced out of their garrisons by the necessity to put a stop to the incessant rebel attacks against highway convoys and static government posts. The first of these initial, anti-guerilla operations took place in March 1980, in the Kunar Valley. After a large-scale air and artillery preparation against suspected rebel concentrations, regiments of the 201st MRD pushed up into the valley and relieved the Afghan Army posts which had been under pressure by the *mujahedin*. Forewarned by the preparation but confounded by the advance of Soviet forces, the *mujahedin* evacuated the valley floor for the safety of connecting canyons and the mountains. The armoured columns met no determined resistance except for repeated ambushes which, however, they showed no expertise in handling. The operation temporarily reduced insurgent activity in the area. Similar operations were carried out in Paktia and Nangarhar provinces, achieving insignificant results. These operations followed a crude pattern, conveying the image of a clumsy, lumbering bear stubbornly making its way through a network of canyons, beset by more nimble jackals and dogs nipping it at every opportunity.

The Soviet Army received a severe shock in June 1980, during a large operation intended to clear the route from Gardez to Khost in the vicinity of Irgun. A strong *mujahedin* force managed to isolate and immobilise an entire motorised rifle battalion on a section of tortuous road. The guns of the Soviet armoured vehicles could not elevate to reach the *mujahedin* positions, while the narrow confines hemmed them in. Surrounding, unable to manoeuvre, and unwilling to dismount, the battalion panicked. The men huddled in the safety of the armoured sides of their combat vehicles until their ammunition ran out, after which they were massacred. The performance of this unfortunate battalion was not untypical in the early days of the war.

Facing Up to the Insurgency

The repetition of events like this one, but on a smaller scale, coupled with the recognition that crude sweep operations were having no effect on the military situation, led the Soviet leadership to the realisation that eliminating the *mujahedin* was going to be a far more complex and time-consuming task than they had envisioned. It was already clear that significant changes needed to be made to both the structure of the occupation force and to its method of operations.

By the summer of 1980, therefore, the Soviet Army had completed the first phase of its occupation. No progress had been made on the achievement of the pre-invasion political and military objectives. In fact, the most important result of this first phase of Soviet involvement in Afghanistan was the decision to increase the level of commitment and to press forward with a military solution to the problem of the resistance. The idea of passively holding garrisons and cities while the Kabul army met the *mujahedin* in the field was given up as a failed approach.

During the next two years of its occupation, the Soviet Army passed through a period of build-up of military infrastructure and combat forces, coupled with some experimentation with tactical operations. The general idea seems to have been to bring in more forces, raise the level of violence, increase the intensity and frequency of operations against the insurgents, and see what might happen as a result. Simultaneously, the Soviets studied their operations closely seeking an answer to the question of how best to organise and conduct their military operations.

Restructuring in 1980

The first step taken by the Soviet command to come to grips with counter-insurgency war in the DRA occurred in February 1980, when soldiers of Central Asian ethnicity began to be sent home. These men had posed problems from the start; first, because they had unexpectedly began to fraternise with the Muslim soldiers of the DRA Army as well as with the populace, including the *mujahedin*. Their political and military reliability thus cast into doubt, the only solution was to replace them with soldiers from European Russia. By June, virtually all the Central Asians in Afghanistan had returned home and those who had been mobilised in the Soviet Union in a stand-by status were released back to civilian life.[4]

The first major effort to restructure the force took place in the summer of 1980. By this time, the occupation forces comprised elements of seven MRDs, possibly as many as five airborne regiments (from three airborne divisions), and one MRD in reserve across the border.[5] The number of aircraft and helicopters in the country was still quite small; the precise organisation of the air component at that time is not known. In June, the 40th Army sent home unessential elements of the ground forces: SA-4 and FROG missile battalions, some heavy artillery, and a tank regiment, all of which had little or no utility in the counter-insurgency situation. The AT and AA batteries in the divisions were also withdrawn in order to prevent the loss of their weapons to the *mujahedin*, who had far more need of such weapons than the Soviets.

The Soviet command then took several steps to decentralise the military effort. Afghanistan was divided into seven military districts.[6] Each district had its own senior military commander, brigade or division-level headquarters, and dedicated helicopter and ground forces. It is quite likely that the establishment of these regional districts meant that the regional headquarters assumed a greater, more detailed role in the actual planning of operations, the 40th Army giving up some of its responsibility in this regard.

Several division headquarters were sent home. In their places, two independent regiments and two independent brigades were established, all having regional operational responsibilities. Supporting arms (such as engineers and rocket artillery) were detached from army or divisional level and provided to these independent formations to upgrade their combined arms capability and self-sustainment.

The independent brigades (66th at Jalalabad and 70th at Kandahar) are quite interesting from an organisational point of view because the brigade is used in Soviet force structure in two ways only: for army- and front-level combat and combat support units such as air assault, artillery, anti-tank, and SAM brigades; and for experimental organisations. These 'Afghan' separate brigades were definitely hybrids. They included four battalions of mechanised infantry, at least one tank battalion, an increased number of artillery sub-units, plus their own dedicated helicopter assets. They were one-of-a-kind units designed especially for decentralised regional operations.[7]

The airborne establishment was also reorganised. A centralised '*desant*' headquarters (103 Airborne Division HQ) remained in Kabul, but several regiments and battalions were deployed to other regions where needed. These changes were entirely appropriate, since a division of airborne troops in counter-insurgency war has no operational significant. It is the companies, battalions, and regiments which can be used as discrete, operational entities.

Decentralisation of air force assets also took place. Realising that the 45–60 helicopters in Afghanistan in June 1980 were insufficient, the Soviet command accelerated the deployment of additional helicopter units.[8] By mid-1981, the number of helicopters in country was approaching 300. Independent air regiments established permanent bases in the primary regional centres of Bagram, Konduz, Kandahar, and Shindand, while a number of independent and detached squadrons were placed in more remote locations under the operational command of ground force commanders.

Naturally, the Soviets increased and spread out their fixed-wing assets, but not to the same extent as the rotary-wing units, since high-performance jets require larger basing facilities and long runways. Moreover, command of these elements did not devolve to regional commanders, it remained at 40th Army and at theatre level.

In this way, Soviet forces in Afghanistan increased from a level of about 80,000 in 1980 to approximately 110–120,000 by mid-1982, a strength which the Soviets maintained until withdrawal of their forces, under the Geneva Accords, began in 1988. Table 2.1 describes the general organisation of Soviet forces.

Pol-i-Khomri, located between the Salang Pass and Kabul became the main loglistical support base for the LCSFA. A fuel pipeline, which originated in the Soviet Union, terminated there; beyond Pol-i-Khomri, fuel had to be trucked or

---

Table 2.1

Limited Contingent of Soviet Forces in Afghanistan (LCSFA)

General Strengths:
   85,000 ground troops
   25,000 support troops
   10,000 air force troops

Ground Units:
   40th Army Headquarters (Kabul)
   4 motorised rifle divisions
   4–5 separate motorised rifle brigades or regiments
   3–4 airborne regiments
   2–3 air assault or airmobile brigades
   1–3 brigades of special operations troops (*spetsnaz*)
   1 engineer regiment/brigade
   1 army artillery brigade

Note: The total of 110–120,000 is misleading because 30,000 additional soldiers and airmen across the border in the southern USSR also took part in operations on a regular basis. The composition of the LCSFA varied from year to year, but the figures above are representative of the kinds and numbers of units in country at any one time. Deployments were geographically balanced, with about one-third of the force in the Kabul area. Other major deployments were located in Jalalabad (east), Konduz and Mazar-i-Sharif (north), Herat and Farah (west), Shindand (southwest), and Kandahar (south). Smaller garrisons were situated in Gardez, Ghazni, Khost, Faizabad, and Bamiyan.
   Helicopter and aviation assets are shown in Table 9.1.

---

airlifted to users. The location of this base near the entrance to the Panjshir Valley, a powerful guerilla stronghold, made it a frequent target of mortar and rocket attacks.

Soviet forces took over complete operational responsibility from Afghan forces for several areas in the country. Because so many of their headquarters and support forces were based in Kabul, the Soviet Army gradually assumed full control of the exterior security of the capital. The Soviet command was similarly unwilling to commit the security of its airbases to régime forces, so they were protected by MR and airborne units. The Soviets also assumed responsibility for the Wakhan Corridor in the far northeast, in order to close it off as a conduit of supplies from China to the resistance. Finally, it should be understood that the 40th Army headquarters, with guidance from the Southern TVD and Moscow, retained authority to direct the entire war effort. All DRA Army and Air Force operations were approved before execution by the Soviet command.

Strangely enough, the Soviets brought in combat contingents from many of its allies, including Bulgaria, East Germany, Czechoslovakia, Vietnam, and Cuba. The contingents were small and unadvertised; certainly the Soviets did not introduce them for the purposes of demonstrating international solidarity. The Cubans may well have been invited to provide advice on counter-guerilla operations, given their experience in Angola and Ethiopia, a country not unlike Afghanistan. The Bulgarians were the most numerous. Apparently they functioned as a security force at selected sites, such as the airports at Jalalabad and Mazar-i-Sharif[9], and natural resource sites.

Periodic, Conventional Offensives

Despite the quite obvious fact that the 'enemy' of the Soviet invasion forces was an irregular guerrilla force practising an unconventional style of warfare, the Soviets persisted in using conventional military methods during the first two to three years of its occupation. Periodic, conventional-style offensives, generally on a divisional or brigade scale, became the early staple of Soviet and DRA Army operations against the insurgents. These large offensives were usually conducted sequentially on a regional basis, although simultaneous offensives were not unknown. They were intended to last from one to several weeks. The forces for the offensives were assembled from different garrisons into one task force normally under a divisional headquarters which was responsible for the planning, preparation, and execution of the general orders worked out by the 40th Army headquarters. The offensives always included régime army and air forces under separate Afghan command, but subordinate to the designated Soviet division commander. Typically, then, these operations would involve 6–12,000 troops (sometimes more) and 500–1,000 combat vehicles, supported by hundreds of aircraft.

Because of the difficulty of conducting operations in such inhospitable terrain, logistical preparations often took from several weeks to a month or more. The Soviets had difficulty in supporting continuous operations by all of their forces at once. The logistical infrastructure was too fragile and the air and ground lines of supply and communications too weak.

The offensives were most often directed against the most active rebel strongholds. The bolder and more effective a regional rebel organisation became, the more likely they were to experience an operation aimed at their destruction (or at least their temporary suppression). The Soviets also conducted many such offensives to break through to garrisons cut off by the *mujahedin* (many of these were unsuccessful) and in periodic drives to seal off infiltration routes in certain border areas. In the border operations, militia and DRA units usually played a larger role than the Soviets.

Offensives always began with an extensive bombardment of the objective area, lasting from several days to as much as a week, by fixed-wing aircraft, helicopter gunships, rockets, and artillery. Then, mechanised columns (tanks and armoured infantry vehicles) moved along the major roads into mountain valleys, under constant fire support. Soviet units often demonstrated dangerous tactical rigidity, inflexibility, and lack of aggression.

> The columns, finding comfort in technical superiority and obsessed by their adherence to traditional firepower as the principal supporting means of advance, were normally firing to the front and flanks (sometimes at random) to suppress suspected *mujahedin* positions and to force their advance. The lack of ground probes and the absence of tactical reconnaissance and security elements to operate on the ridges and high ground, which often closely dominated the axis of advance created an uncertain situation as the columns moved on.[10]

Such manoeuvres exposed Soviet units to surprise attacks at close quarters by the lightly armed rebels. Slow to react to contact and unable to exploit their heavy direct fire weapons, the Soviet troops were, nevertheless, quite reluctant to dismount and engage in close combat.[11] In general manoeuvre was restricted to valley floors; Soviet units hesitantly entered the restricted side valleys and canyons. Moreover, they seldom ventured out of the range of supporting artillery.

Despite these flaws, Soviet forces usually managed to establish temporary control in disputed territory, at least in the larger villages, by virtue of their superior numbers and firepower. The *mujahedin* elected not to try to meet them in force until they were fully spread out and venturing into side canyons. However, these operations had no lasting effect. The local population and the resistance usually learned about them ahead of time, giving them the opportunity to disappear into mountain hideouts, although significant casualties often occurred.[12] Unable to sustain a continued presence, Soviet forces eventually left the area to return to their permanent cantonments, at which time the resistance came down from the hills and was reconstituted. Sometimes, security posts were left behind to extend government control in the region as long as possible, but it usually did not take the *mujahedin* long to drive out the outposts one by one.

In general, the *mujahedin* commanders were unimpressed with the Soviet commanders. They considered the Soviet officers to be inflexible, mechanical in their tactical responses, and committed to cookbook warfare. A Rhodesian journalist who spent time with the *mujahedin* on operations considered the Soviets to be 'tactical zeros'. An American journalist graded the Soviet troops 'third-rate'. Trained for conventional war, Soviet MR commanders lacked the skills needed for decentralised combat in mountainous terrain.[13] [*We will consider these failings in more depth later*].

Beginning in 1981–82, the Soviets introduced some more effective modifications to these offensives. They started to emplace light troops — airborne, air assault, and, sparingly, dismounted motorised rifle units — by helicopter along the axes of advance used by the ground force through the mountain valleys. Use of these airmobile elements to pre-empt *mujahedin* occupation of key terrain helped to restrict the number and effects of their attacks on the ground columns. Later, growing use of heliborne elements evolved into a kind of blocking tactic aimed at fixing and destroying the *mujahedin*:

> ...with the increased use of heliborne units and teams, a new form of combined arms operation has been developed featuring a heavy infantry advance along the major ground axis supported by local militias and permanent military posts and outposts, and heliborne detachments landed deep in the rear and flanks of the *mujahedin* strongholds with a tactical mission of isolating the resistance strongholds, destroying *mujahedin* bases, and cutting their supply and infiltration routes.
>
> The heliborne action phase normally involves 50–60 and sometimes even more helicopters (in groups), landing commandos, militias, air assault units or infantry troops at keypoints in the rear and flanks of *mujahedin* concentrations and passes in combined operations. The action normally starts when mechanised and tank columns charged with the mission to destroy the resistance forces in the areas are in a position to link up with the heliborne elements at the appropriate time suitable for tactical interaction of both elements. At the tactical level, it is apparently 15–20 kilometres since the land forces have to support the heliborne teams by their artillery. However, on more than one occasion, the Soviets have been forced to withdraw the airborne elements by air where a timely link up was not possible and the heliborne troops were in danger of being destroyed by *mujahedin* forces.[14]

These new tactics demonstrated growing sophistication on the part of the Soviets and a capability for combining heavy and light forces. They also reflected the dawning realisation that conventional operations alone would not have the desired effect on the resistance. However, the overall effectiveness of these operations is borne out by two significant facts, the first being that the Soviet Army had to conduct such operations over and over again in the same areas, even when the rebels suffered significant casualties. The Panjshir Valley, perhaps the strongest guerrilla stronghold, was the object of at least 10 such offensives, yet it remained almost continuously under *mujahedin* control. Secondly, these large offensives received very little attention in the Soviet military press (from an analytical point of view). Isolated tactical facets of an operation, such as, e.g., engineer support to dismounted troops, the use of airmobile blocking forces, or actions by a reconnaissance detachment, were often highlighted, but the offensive itself as an operational entity was seldom described. This lack of self-analysis is a tacit acknowledgement of the indecisiveness of the conventional offensives.

There were several reasons why the offensives failed to achieve lasting results. First, the small size of the Soviet contingent and the ineffectiveness of the DRA army and militia excluded the possibility of maintaining strong garrisons in all the locations where they were needed. Second, the nature of the offensives and the general Soviet approach to operations failed to take into account fully the problems presented by the terrain and climate. Third, the Soviets also were unable to solve the riddle of how to neutralise the special capabilities of the *mujahedin*. Fourth, the Soviets were hampered by an ideological and military blind-spot, that is, a complete lack of counter-insurgency doctrine which might have better guided these initial efforts. Before discussing how the Soviet Army in Afghanistan dealt with these obstacles, it is advisable to investigate the obstacles themselves in more detail in the chapters which now follow.

CHAPTER 3

The Physical Environment

EVERY military professional knows that all campaign planning begins with an analysis of the physical environment. From the military point of view, Afghanistan's topography and climate present a forbidding prospect to the invader. Spectacular, sharp-peaked mountains dominate the eastern and central regions of the country, giving way to deserts and high plateaus to the west and south. Severe extremes of temperature stress men and machines. In every region, a dearth of water threatens life. The passage of large bodies of armed men on foot or in vehicles is a nightmare for both the commander and his logisticians. The fact that Afghanistan has been invaded as often as it has, in spite of these conditions, is not so much a reflection of its value as a country rich in natural resources (which it is), as it is a function of its strategic location between competing empires. Through the ages, Afghan tribes have had to contend with the Russian colossus to the north, China on the east, Persia/Iran on the west, and the rich Indian sub-continent to the south.

The Terrain

From a satellite's-camera view, 'the country resembles an irregularly-shaped leaf' attached by a thin stem (the Wakhan Corridor) to China, with whom it shares a tiny border. The longest border of this land-locked state, 1,500 kilometres, is with Pakistan to the east and south. Afghanistan comprises approximately 640,000 square kilometres (250,000 square miles). Its length from east to west runs to 1,240 kilometres (770 miles) at the longest part and 565 kilometres (350 miles) from north to south. In size, it approximates to the American state of Texas or the country of France.

The Afghan mountain mass, an extension of the vast Himalayas, is oriented south-west to northeast. The Hindu Kush (translated as 'Hindu Killer') is the major component range. Its highest peaks exceed 7,000 metres (21,700 feet) and are found in the eastern provinces (Badakhshan, Kunar, Laghman). The mountains diminish in height as they extend to the west for almost 1,000 kilometres (620 miles). In the vicinity of Kabul, mountain elevations range from 4,500 to 6,000 metres (14,000–18,600 feet), although the capital city itself is lower. By way of comparison, it can be noted that the highest mountain in Europe is Mt. Blanc at 5,100 metres (15,800 feet) and in the continental United States, Mt. Whitney reigns supreme at 4,680 metres (14,500 feet). North to south, the Hindu Kush measures 240 kilometres (150 miles). The average altitude of the range is 4,500 metres.

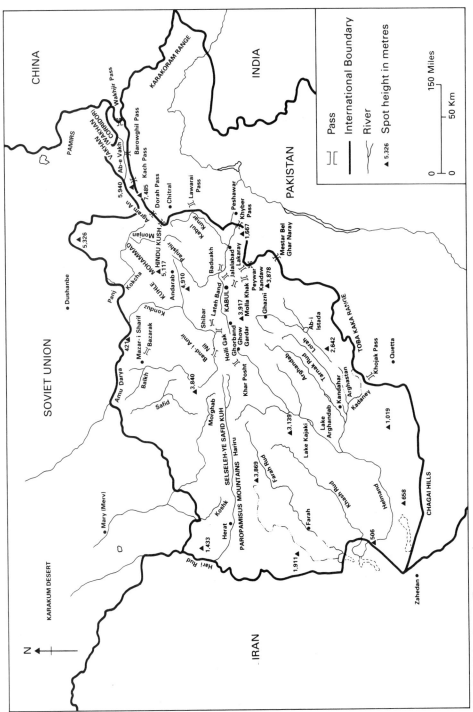

Map IV. Afghanistan - Topography

Geologically, this is a young mountain range, characterised by sharp peaks, steep slopes, intermittent but rapid streams and rivers, and deep, rugged valleys, the larger ones of which have been the site of many of the campaigns directed against the *mujahedin* during the war. Smaller mountain systems spread out north, south, and west from the central core of the Hindu Kush. Of the total land area, almost 50 per cent lies above 2,000 metres (6,200 feet) elevation.

A number of significant passes permit voyagers to cross this mountain barrier, beginning with the Kowtal-i Shabar northwest of Kabul. Ten major passes in the East lead from Pakistan into Afghanistan, including Killik Pass (4,255 metres), Wakhjir (4,923 metres), Dorah Pass (4,511 metres), Agram An (5,069 metres) and Afsik Pass (3,749 metres). Further west, passes of lower elevation permit transit, e.g. Molla Khak (3,548 metres) and Bazarak (2,713 metres) passes. The famous Khyber Pass, at 1,027 metres, leads eastward out of Nangarhar Province to Pakistan and is located quite near the main *mujahedin* and refugee centre at Peshawar. Over 300 lesser, unmarked passes in the east and south exist; these passes provided secure entry into the country for *mujahedin* during the periodic campaigns by the Soviets to close infiltration routes from Pakistan. Only the major passes are suitable for (all-terrain) vehicle passage.

In the north, the mountains diminish into rugged foothills, thence to the fertile, pre-steppe of Russian Central Asia. The largest deserts and desert plateaus are located in the extreme west and south west. The five provinces in this area — Kandahar, Helmand, Nimroz, Farah, and Herat — are often plagued with intense heat, drought, and sandstorms.

Afghanistan's rivers do not have major military significance. The largest ones are the Amu Darya (Oxus), which forms part of the country's northern border with the Soviet Union, and the Helmand, Hari Rud, and Kabul rivers.

Forbidding terrain is matched by an equally harsh climate, a climate typical of arid, continental régimes. The mountainous areas see dry, cold winters and dry, warm summers, although the summer nights can also be quite cold and frosty. The highest peaks never lose their snow cover. Annual precipitation in the mountains, much of which is snowfall, averages up to 40 centimetres (16 inches), with July to September being the moistest months of the year. Some northeastern sections, such as the Wakhan Corridor, have less than 10 centimetres (4 inches) a year. Winter temperatures in the high mountains drop very low, of course, (15–21°C), but summer temperatures are usually no higher than 30°C. (Dependent on altitude).

In the desert regions, summer temperatures rise as suffocatingly high as 35–45°C and annual precipitation falls below 15 centimetres (10 inches). Rivers through these areas originate in the mountains, but simply peter out in the rocks and sand. Summer sees an extended period of fierce, northerly winds which are sometimes transformed into dust-storms of near-hurricane force. Overall, precipitation varies widely. As in any mountainous country, the sound and sight of thunderheads in the mountains warn the wary traveller to be prepared for flash-floods through the valleys and even into the plains.

Transportation Nets

Given the nature of the topography and climate, it is not surprising that the road and rail nets of Afghanistan are severely underdeveloped. For many years, Afghan rulers resisted any improvements to the transportation system because they recognised that the difficulties of movement in the country enhanced its defensive capabilities. [*Scottish clansmen destroyed roads and bridges built in their glens and hills for a similar reason — to keep English soldiers out of the Highlands.*] However, in the post-war period, both the United States and Soviet Union have spent large sums of money to develop the Afghan road network in order to enhance the country's economic development and political integration.

By 1975, Afghanistan had 17,000 kilometres (10,700 miles) of roads, of which 9,200 kilometres (6,600 miles) are considered to be all-weather. However, only 2,500 kilometres (1,550 miles) of this total consist of paved roads. Interestingly, the Soviet Union built the northern sections of asphalt highway and the United States the southern.

Map V clearly shows how the main highways of Afghanistan extend in a U-shaped arc from Herat in the west, south to Shindand, thence west to Kandahar, and finally northward from Kandahar to Qalat, Ghazni, and Kabul. Kabul is connected by highway to Jalalabad to the east and to Konduz, Mazar-i-Sharif, and Balkh to the north. The high-speed ground route from the Soviet military headquarters and marshalling centre at Termez to Kabul was greatly improved by the construction by the Soviets of the critically-important Salang Pass tunnel. The tunnel stretches 2.7 kilometres in length at an elevation of 11,000 feet. A few major towns and province capitals, such as Faizabad (Badakhshan Province) and Meymanah (Faryab Province), are still not connected to the central arc by paved highways. Practically all the trunk roads into Afghan's major cities are unsurfaced roads. Within provinces, there are few secondary and tertiary roads; many of these are little more than rocky, unimproved tracks, suitable only for all-terrain vehicles.

Afghanistan's virtually non-existent railroad system is concentrated in the northern provinces of Balkh and Jowzjan. The few kilometres of track were built by the Soviets in order to handle military and commercial traffic moving on the Amu Darya river and through Termez. Plans to extend the railroad further south to Pol-i-Khomri, thence to Kabul have been held up by the war, the difficult terrain, and the high cost. An earlier plan to build a railroad paralleling the highway circle died when Iranian financing collapsed in 1978. The Soviets also built a bridge across the Amu Darya (known as the Oxus to Alexander the Great), completing it in 1982.

Supplementing this rudimentary ground transport system is a network of airports and airfields. In 1985, approximately 40 airfields were in operation, the most important of which, from a military point of view, was Kabul International, with Shindand a close second. All the major airfields have been ungraded by the Soviets since December, 1979, in order to accommodate large, military jets. Many new strips were built in the 1960s and 70s at politically and militarily significant locations such as Mazar-i-Sharif, Bagram, Jalalabad, Konduz, Meymanah, Faizabad, and Ghazni and a large number of heliports have been constructed to support the Soviet garrisons spread throughout the country. The air facilities most important to the Soviet war effort, other than Kabul and Shindand, were the large bases at Kandahar, Bagram, and Herat. Overall, this network of airbases, airfields, and heliports provides a great deal of basing and operational flexibility to Soviet air forces in the country. On the other hand, not a single installation was able to secure

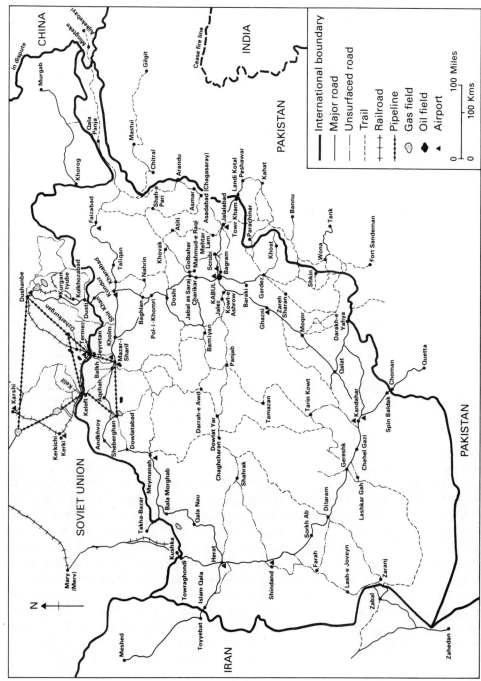

Map V. The Transportation Network

itself from rebel attacks during the war, although the Shindand base had a good deal of natural protection, due to its location on the western plain.

Consequences for Military Operations

The problems which the natural environment and undeveloped transportation system present to the military adventurer in Afghanistan are multiple and daunting. First, from the point of view of the ground commander, military operations are naturally fragmented by the sculptured terrain. Massive columns of forces move out of cities and soon become separated and physically isolated from each other as they plunge into the mountains. Most mountain valleys will not permit the movement of more than a division-sized formation. As the main valley narrows or as units move off into side-canyons, the command is split and there is no room for manoeuvre. Flanks are very difficult to secure; it is all but impossible to maintain contact with units to the left and right. Observation and fire from valley floors are severely restricted. Communications between adjacent valleys just a few kilometres apart fail unless special measures are taken. Furthermore, navigating in mountains can be a bewildering experience for the inexpert.

The few roads that exist make surprise impossible, since a ground unit must pass over routes which are easily kept under observation. Often there is only one vehicular approach to an objective, or two at best. Thus, movements are quite predictable once begun. Knowing the routes which ground units must use simplifies the efforts of the enemy to mine and interdict. With only one way in and one way out, once a ground element has been blocked, it has nowhere to go until it is relieved. Off road movement is not possible in many places because of the steep slopes and sheer drop-offs. Roads easily become traps and killing zones.

Maintaining ground lines of communications and supply through such terrain is extremely difficult, even when movement is restricted to the paved highways. Any section of road not secured by posts or patrolling is inherently unsafe and subject to interdiction. Every sharp turn invites an ambush. Only one section of the road needs to be blocked or mined for traffic to come to a halt. Destroyed bridges can hold up traffic for days. Secondary and tertiary roads are also vulnerable to natural blockages — such as avalanches, and washouts. Deliveries of goods over a few hundred kilometres which could be done in a few hours in Europe or the United States require several days in Afghanistan. All emergency deliveries must be made by air.

From the air, a sprawling mass of mountains has a confusing regularity. Everything tends to look the same; many flights are often necessary to determine suitable landmarks for orientation. Ground attack aircraft have a difficult time both in locating the target and in choosing an appropriate approach for attack. Aircraft must fly low in order to 'acquire' the target, making them vulnerable to hidden anti-aircraft weapons. Area munitions are often ineffective. Finally, unexpected and varying weather conditions affect mission capability in an unpredictable manner.

Operating characteristics of weapon systems and machines are also affected by the physical environment. Military equipment is normally designed to function best in normal operating conditions, i.e. moderate temperatures and mean elevations. In the hostile setting of Afghanistan, vehicles often suffer mechanical breakdowns:

engines overheat, tyres go flat, suspensions break, and differentials crack and spill the fluid out into the ground. Combat vehicles throw tracks as they traverse rocky, uneven ground. An entire column can be halted while one vehicle is being repaired or moved out of the way. Helicopters flying at the extreme limits of their operating tolerances become unsafe. Even the firing characteristics of weapons are affected. Swirling winds deflect the trajectories of mortar bombs and artillery shells. Rapid changes in weather invalidate firing data. Furthermore, distances are difficult to judge; rounds fall long or short as a result.

Finally, the human body and mind are also subject to the environment and must be acclimatised to extreme heat or cold, low oxygen density of the air, etc. Physical endurance is severely stressed in mountains and desert whether one is driving a vehicle, operating a radio, or searching for rebel bases. Personnel not used to such conditions sometimes require weeks or months to get used to them. A great many Soviet soldiers were unprepared for the physical requirements of combat in Afghanistan; they simply lacked the necessary level of physical fitness.

CHAPTER 4

The *Mujahedin*

THE origins of the armed resistance in Afghanistan can be traced back to the 1960s, but the movement did not present a significant military threat until the reign of Sardar Daoud (1973–76). The communist coup of 1978 led by Taraki with the immediate implementation of hated social and economic reforms galvanised the resistance and broadly increased its support among the population. When the Soviets intervened and installed Karmal as their hand-picked choice for ruler, popular outrage and resentment were such that the ranks of the *mujahedin* swelled immensely as more and more Afghans entered into *Jihad* — holy war — against the atheistic, foreign invaders and its illegitimate puppet, the ruling PDPA.

General Characteristics of the Insurgency

From the very beginning, the resistance was extremely fragmented, diverse, spontaneous, and unco-ordinated. Eventually a number of separate organisations emerged, each with its own aims and structure. (See Appendix A for a description of the most important organisations.) The seven major groups established headquarters in the refugee camps in Peshawar, Pakistan. Over time, these headquarters became important as logistical conduits for the fighting groups inside the country and as representatives to the outside world. In general, however, the Peshawar offices exercised little or no influence on military operations inside Afghanistan and relations between the fighting commanders on the inside and their 'representatives' on the outside were not always the best. The most important leaders of the *mujahedin* were the fighting commanders on the interior.

It would be wrong to characterise the entire resistance movement as religiously motivated and ideologically committed to throwing out the foreign invaders. Opportunists and adventurers also existed. There are sufficient examples of *mujahedin* groups which defected to the régime or which operated more like bandits than freedom fighters to dispel the notion that the entire movement was pristine and holy. Still, the large majority of the *mujahedin* fighters and leaders joined the fight for the right reason, i.e. the right to determine their own future without the heavy foot of the Soviet Union on their necks.

Estimates vary in regard to the scale of the resistance and distinction is often made between the permanent fighters and those that could be mobilised for special operations. It is safe to say that during the course of the war, the strength of the cadres and permanently fighting detachments averaged from 80–100,000, with the

25

mobilisable strength about double that. (Of course, at no time would the entire reserve potential of the rebels have been called out. Non-permanent fighters participated in operations somewhat infrequently and then only on a regional basis. It would be quite incorrect to think of the *mujahedin* in terms of 'fielding' large forces like a conventional army.) The *mujahedin* came from every class of society. His leaders, generally, came from traditional élite classes, from the small university-educated population, and from the diverse corps of defecting officers from the Armed Services.

As a rule, the separate rebel groups co-operated rather poorly with each other, conflicting tribal allegiances, differing levels of Islamic fervour, and class structures being significant obstacles to unity. In fact, some rebels appeared to have spent almost as much time fighting other rebel groups as they did against the régime and occupation force. During the first two years of the war, there were almost as many clashes among the *mujahedin* as against Soviet and régime forces.[1] These clashes occasionally resulted in severe battles where hundreds lost their lives.[2] Hezb-i Islami, under the command of Engineer Gulbuddin Hekmatyr, was the most unco-operative, insular and intolerant of the groups; its leadership demanded that all other *mujahedin* groups accept their goal of establishing an Islamic state or face extinction. Many times, Hezb-i Islami groups eschewed attacks on the régime in favour of attacks against fellow insurgents. The groups also competed with each other for recruits and arms provided by outside sources. Gradually, the intensity of the inter-group hostility abated and military co-operation rose. Within a few years, relatively large-scale *mujahedin* attacks (several thousand participants) were being conducted by groups from different factions uniting to achieve a common objective. Military co-operation was also common during the large Soviet offensives.

The Afghan Secret Police, the KHAD, recognised the intra-*mujahedin* hostility as a weapon which could be used against the rebels and they exploited it ruthlessly. This lack of unity also had a negative influence on the willingness of foreign sympathisers to provide aid to the insurgents.

The insurgent leadership also recognised that lack of unity was a major weakness; sincere efforts were made to achieve some degree of co-operation and to create an appearance of a united front. The first loose alliance was formed as early as 1980 but it quickly broke down. The next year, two separate coalitions formed, one of three 'moderate' groups and the other of three 'fundamentalist' groups. The moderates shared the goal of establishing what might be called representative government with traditionalist features, while the fundamentalists were striving to install an Islamic state based on Islamic law. Finally, in May 1985, the seven Peshawar-based groups formed the 'Islamic Union of Afghan *Mujahedin*', a coalition which generally held together through the end of the Soviet occupation. This alliance helped to reduce competition and conflict and increased military co-operation. Still, it cannot be said that a national leadership acceptable to all parties emerged nor did the coalition produce anything resembling a consolidated, national strategy. The five major goals of the Islamic Union during the Soviet Occupation were:[3]

1. To co-ordinate military strategy and weapons distribution.
2. To develop a programme to protect supply routes.

3. To prevent infiltration by régime agents.
4. To establish joint training and raise the quality of training.
5. To work out joint responses to major Soviet military moves.

Most of the major groups were organised quite loosely, being composed of hundreds of small bands of 10–30 men, which operated more or less on a regional basis. Strict discipline and centralisation were notably absent as organisational and operational principles. Command hierarchies could be quiet indefinite; local commanders of small rebel bands often were reluctant to recognise a higher authority. These deficiencies manifested themselves operationally. In general, there was no particular logic to the selection of targets or to the timing of attacks. Thus, the effectiveness of the local bands was normally a function of the personality and ability of the commander.

Some provincial groups were structured along fairly rigid military lines, the most prominent example being the forces led by Ahmad Shah Massoud, the famous *mujahedin* leader in the Panjshir Valley. Known in the country as 'The Lion of Panjshir', Massoud was generally considered to be one of the best, if not the best insurgent commander. Because the valley is located not far to the north of Kabul and configured in such a way that rebel groups residing in the valley could easily interdict the route from Kabul to the Salang Pass, the Panjshir Valley was the object of more large ground offensives by Soviet/DRA forces than any other region. Despite this tremendous pressure, Massoud retained virtually continuous control of the valley.

By 1983, Massoud had divided his force (approximately 3–4,000 men at that time) into three functional groups: the Mantaqa groups were regionally stationed for local defence; the Motahrak groups were mobile commandos which could be described as reaction forces; the Zarbati groups functioned as strike forces against designated objectives. Massoud further organised the territory under his control into districts (*Qaragah*), each of which possessed its complement of permanent fighters, 'mobilisable' reserves (men working the fields), plus mobile and strike groups. Each *qaragah* consisted of several villages; the villagers rotated into and out of permanent duty. Massoud also established special groups to operate the more sophisticated weaponry and he developed his own training programmes with indigenous experts who were sometimes sent to other provinces to assist other rebel organisations.[4]

Other regional commanders, perhaps having taken note of Massoud's successes, began to adopt more of a military structure in the middle 80s. For example, the northern province of Mazar was organised into 73 small military sectors, each with its own fighting force of up to several hundred men. Each sector had its sector commander and the province, a general commander. A similar organisation developed in the Ghazni region under commander Qari Baba. The 'militarisation' of the rebel organisations permitted the conduct of larger operations over a wider territory.[5] It also improved the frequency of inter-group co-operation, making it possible for large régime installations to become the objectives of *mujahedin* attacks.

Arms, Ammunition, and Equipment

Among the major initial problems faced by the *mujahedin* was the scarcity of modern arms and ammunition. Because of the warrior caste of the society, most rural Afghan males possess their own personal arms. However, such personal weapons were of ancient vintage in most cases and the quantity of ammunition available was quite low. For example, the individual weapon most commonly carried was the Lee-Enfield .303, a nineteenth-century bolt-action rifle of British manufacture used extensively in the First World War. Better and more arms were urgently needed if the *mujahedin* were to accomplish anything more than harassment against an enemy possessing all of the weapons of a modern conventional army. The insurgents developed three primary sources: arms obtained from the régime through capture or defection; arms purchased locally at bazaars and weapon shops; arms provided by foreign countries supporting the *mujahedin*.

The first source turned out to be the richest and most consistent. The many defections from the DRA Army, both individual and by units, provided an initial source of heavy weapons and ammunition to the *mujahedin*. Hundreds of DShK heavy machine guns, for example, were taken off T55 tank cupolas and handed over by sympathisers or defecting crews. One scenario, repeated many times over, was that of the isolated outpost surrendering itself and all its stores to the local insurgents rather than be attacked. In some cases, outposts did not surrender; they remained in place and simply funnelled supplies and arms to the *mujahedin* on a periodic basis.

Western journalists on location with the rebels have sometimes reported how the rebel bands took shelter at such government outposts, sharing meals and sleeping quarters. Others describe live-and-let-live arrangements:

> In early 1982, I came across no fewer than three Afghan forts with which the *mujahedin* had come to an understanding. Outside one of the garrisons, manned by 15–20 men, a group of bored conscripts were kicking an empty can about. We met several soldiers hauling water from a nearby desert well. We shook hands and they watched as dozens of guerillas marched by, leading strings of pack horses loaded with arms, ammunition, and other supplies.[6]

> We ended up stopping for the night in the open within 50 yards of an Afghan government militia post. The militiamen, in reality working with the resistance, gave us each water and a hard-boiled egg for dinner. And when it started to rain around midnight, they let us come inside the hilltop post and sleep in the corridor.[7]

An Afghan source described how a defecting Afghan officer in Herat dressed a local *mujahedin* group in Afghan army uniforms and escorted them into a supply depot seven times, each time bringing out truckloads of materials.[8]

The *mujahedin* also captured enormous amounts of materials in their military operations. Each time an outpost was taken, it was stripped of anything valuable. The same was true for vehicles or aircraft destroyed by the rebels, leading to the practice of Soviet aircraft routinely destroying by fire any Soviet/régime equipment left on the field of battle in order to deny its use by the *mujahedin*.

Sometimes entire convoys of military supplies were spirited away into the mountains after a successful attack. For example, in 1987 in Faryab Province, the *mujahedin* captured the following stocks: 5,700 individual weapons, nine machine guns, six mortars with 5,000 mortar rounds, 17 radios, three armoured personnel carriers (APC), seven jeeps, 90 trucks loaded with wheat, 700 barrels of oil, seven tanks, and 35 rocket launchers with 1,100 rockets.[9] Another example: on 24 December 1985, *mujahedin* from various groups jointly attacked Zauki outpost which was located on the highway from Kandahar to Spin Baldak. After seven hours of battle, from 1–8 am, the *mujahedin* occupied the post and removed the following military stocks: seven pieces of artillery, two DShK heavy machine guns, 75 light machine guns, one truck, three motorcycles, and a large amount of ammunition.[10] In one more example, the rebels destroyed a convoy in Parwan Province which was carrying, among other things, a huge amount of Afghan banknotes, which they were able to use for some time to come to finance their operations.[11]

In 1983, the *mujahedin* of Paktia Province obtained significant military supplies through airdrops! They had surrounded and cut off a large enemy garrison manned by 1,200 DRA soldiers and 10 Soviet advisers. The outpost was being supplied solely by airdrop, but many of the supplies fell outside the grounds of the outpost (e.g. 300 mortar shells in one sortie), thereby enriching the besiegers.[12] Many other examples of this nature could be cited. Naturally, not all of them provided such large quantities of materials. The larger the objective, the more abundant was the booty.

In many respects, the Kabul régime motorised the resistance through its severe losses of transport. Western journalists have described how they toured the country in Soviet vehicles appropriated by the *mujahedin* and used even in daytime, passing through checkpoints manned by DRA Army soldiers. Many *mujahedin* commanders had their own dedicated vehicle or motorcycle for transportation. In the Panjshir, the *mujahedin* operated a regular bus service using régime vehicles.

Captured stocks of food helped keep the resistance on its feet. For example, in 1987, as much as 60 per cent of the food consumed by the resistance in Farah had been captured from the enemy.[13] A quote from one of the rebel commanders puts this issue in perspective:

> On a regular basis, we take useful items from the enemy: truck loads of wheat, cooking oil, iron roofing sheets, electric heaters, refrigerators, TV sets, etc. We sell them to traders from Kabul or Mazar and with the cash we buy what we need.[14]

Weapon markets also formed a steady, useful source of arms for the *mujahedin*. Merchants and weapon manufacturers in Pakistan did a steady business over the course of the war, demanding and receiving high prices for the more exotic weaponry (for example, $31,000 for a SAM-7 missile, $9,000 for an RPG-9). Weapons, ammunition, and other goods could almost always be found for sale in Afghan bazaars in all the major cities and in areas where garrisons were located. DRA and Soviet soldiers frequently sold such items or traded them for illicit goods such as hashish. Soviet and DRA patrols conducted periodic searches of suspected suppliers in order to cut off this flow, but there simply were too many different streams to staunch.

Arms suppliers from foreign countries sympathetic to the *mujahedin* assumed significant levels beginning about 1982. Quite a number of countries participated in this support. Most important were the supplies of sophisticated arms (which could not be copied by local manufacturers) such as rocket launchers, rocket-propelled grenades, recoilless rifles, mortars, heavy machine guns, and anti-aircraft missiles. China was a major supplier, providing its own copies of Soviet designed weaponry: AK-47 automatic rifles, 12.7- and 14.5-mm AA machine guns, 107- and 122-mm rocket launchers, mortars, and anti-tank (AT) and anti-personnel (AP) mines. The other major suppliers of munitions, equipment, or financial support were Egypt,

Saudi Arabia, Japan, Iran, and of course the United States, the latter most notably for SA-7 (obtained through third parties) and Stinger AA missiles. France and Sweden provided funding, supplies, and personnel (France only) for medical support to the resistance.[15]

Some of this outside support passed into Afghanistan directly from Iran and China, but the majority entered through Pakistan. A large portion of the supplies disappeared in Pakistan as it changed hands, or else, payment of some kind was demanded, even though the goods were being provided free of charge from the donor countries. Apparently, the Peshawar resistance organisations themselves were not free from this sort of graft and greed. Problems with the distribution of arms often led to accusation and hostility between the Peshawar cadres and the fighting organisations in country. The formation of the 'Islamic Alliance' in 1985 somewhat eased this source of hostility and distrust. Pakistan authorities, sensitive to charges from the Soviet Union that they were harbouring and sponsoring insurgents, did place some restriction on the arms flow to keep it from becoming too blatant.

Getting the munitions from the border to the users was an operation of some difficulty, since the Soviets and the régime expended a great deal of effort to cut the infiltration routes. At first the *mujahedin* were able to use motor transport day and night. However, Soviet ambushes, bombing, air-strikes, air assaults, interdiction operations, use of air-dropped mines in vast quantities, and employment of militia patrols forced the *mujahedin* off the major routes and out of the best passes into slower, higher, longer routes. As a result, supply runs could easily take weeks. The trip from Peshawar to the Panjshir Valley, for example, crossed four passes averaging 15,000 feet in altitude and required as much as 30 days by animal pack.[16] The Soviets were able to make the transport of arms more difficult and time-consuming, but they were unable to close the border to such traffic; the border was simply too long and too difficult to police.

By the last three or four years of the war, the *mujahedin* were operating with an astonishing array of weaponry of Soviet and foreign manufacture. In fact, virtually every system in use by the Kabal Army, less aircraft, was also in use by the resistance. A listing of the kinds of weapons and equipment in their hands is shown in Table 4.1 below.

All of this is not to say that the rebels solved their supply problems. In the first place, weapons tended to be distributed quite unevenly, with some groups being favoured by certain sources. Iran, for example, was most interested in helping out the fundamentalist *mujahedin* groups. Rebel groups in western Afghanistan suffered more difficulty in obtaining arms because it was much harder to smuggle materials in the open terrain of that region. Herat, for example, experienced chronic shortages of heavy weapons. In addition, Soviet sweeps aimed at suspected cache sites recovered or destroyed substantial quantities. In November 1986, a Soviet operation against a major base in Nangarhar Province recovered an enormous amount of material: 5,000 mortar bombs, 3,500 RPG rounds, 1,200 AT mines, 1,764 AP mines, dozens of heavy machine guns, and eight tons of explosives. (The Soviets had to fight through two lines of defence with minefields, defended by an estimated 700 rebels from 20 different groups.[17]

Even as late as the middle 80s, Western observers reported that not all the members of certain insurgent groups possessed a modern rifle. The most serious persistent shortages were in the areas of AT and AA weapons and long-range systems. In 1982, for example, Panjshir guerrillas disposed only 13 heavy AA machine guns in the entire valley. Lack of training also resulted in wastage and inefficiency in the employment of some systems. The more complicated the system, the less likely it was to be employed properly. Finally, many times captured Soviet weapons or older models obtained from the outside simply failed to work, a problem also experienced by the Kabul Army.

Table 4.1

Mujahedin Arms and Armaments

Rifles
Lee-Enfield .303 (bolt-action, First World War vintage)
AK-47 (of Soviet, Chinese, and Egyptian make)
AKM carbines
AK-74 (in limited quantities)
Dragomirov 7.62 sniper rifles
Shotguns
M1 carbines and rifles (Second World War vintage)

Machine guns
12.7-mm DShK heavy machine guns
RPD M-53 (Degtyarev) light machine guns
7.62-mm PKM light machine guns

Indirect Fire Weapons
51-, 60-, and 82-mm mortars
AGS-17 automatic grenade launchers
D30 122-mm howitzers
107- and 122-mm rocket launchers (Chinese make)
BM-13 132-mm MRLs

Anti-tank Weapons
RPG-7
SPG-9
D85 recoilless rifles of Soviet and Chinese make
82-mm B-10 recoilless AT guns
Some rifle-mounted AT grenades

Anti-aircraft Weapons
12.7- & 14.5-mm (ZPU-1, ZPU-2) machine guns, (Chinese make)
23-mm Chinese AA guns (in northern provinces)
Oerlikon 20-mm AA automatic cannons
SA-7 missiles of various vintage (most quite old)
Blowpipe missiles
Stinger missiles (US)

Combat Vehicles
T55 tank
BTR series APC
BMD (light airborne armoured vehicle)
BMP-1, BMP-2 infantry fighting vehicle
BRDM light reconnaissance vehicle

Transport
Toyota trucks
Motorcycles
Vans
Light utility trucks (jeeps)
Various model cargo trucks of Soviet and E. European make

Miscellaneous Equipment
Hand grenades
Pistols (of various manufacture)
Binoculars
Night vision devices (very limited quantities)
Radios (all captured, used widely after about 1985)
AP & AT mines of assorted make (Chinese, Soviet, Italian, French, etc.)
Clothing and boots

Mujahedin Tactical Operations

The primary features of *mujahedin* tactical operations fit the classic guerrilla mould. Short in firepower and manpower, lacking the mass, mobility, and staying power of a conventional military formation, the Afghan *mujahedin* quite naturally developed a hit and run style. On the plains and in the broad valleys, the superior hitting power of the DRA and Soviet armies was too much for them to handle. However, in the high mountain passes, ravines, gorges, canyons, and ridges, the guerrillas found many places more suitable to them. Here they could lay ambushes, conduct quick strikes, isolate and destroy small bodies of the enemy, interdict traffic routes, observe the enemy's movements, and safely evade advances into the area in force by slipping away into almost impregnable sanctuaries.

If the enemy persisted in following the *mujahedin* deep into the mountains, at some point in time the advantages would turn to the favour of the rebels. First, the terrain separated advancing units into smaller elements. Then, it forced them to dismount and leave behind armour and heavy weapons. Eventually, the Soviet/régime forces would find themselves facing an impassioned rebel force intimately familiar with the terrain and able to exploit it far better, with deadly results, particularly at night.

The *mujahedin* conducted a wide variety of offensive actions which can be divided into six primary categories: direct attacks against régime military installations throughout the countryside; attacks against convoys; ambushes; urban terrorism; attacks against economic targets; and, stand-off rocket attacks. The frequency of insurgent operations dropped off during the winter because of the harsh conditions.

Because Afghanistan is so large and fragmented by mountain barriers, the small numbers of Kabul and Soviet troops could not produce the force density needed to establish large secure areas. As a result, the country was dotted with hundreds of garrisons, bases, outposts, strong points, highway posts, and checkpoints, each of which was essentially responsible for providing its own security. There was no such thing as a fixed front or a secure flank. Wherever the barbed wire ended, *mujahedin* control began. In consequence, any régime military installation in any part of the country was susceptible to attack by the rebels at any point in time.

Typically, in an attack against a government post or garrison, the *mujahedin* would carefully study the layout of their chosen objective. Probing attacks might be conducted to determine the nature of the enemy's defensive scheme, the location of his heavy weapons and fighting positions. Often, information on the size, disposition, and vulnerabilities of the objective would be provided by Afghans inside the installation. Prior to the attack, the operation might be rehearsed on a terrain mock-up laid out on the ground and attended by all key leaders. In many cases, the attack of the *mujahedin* would be accompanied by a co-ordinated attack on the inside by sympathisers. The assault was normally begun with fire from mortars, rockets, RPGs, grenade launchers, and heavy machine guns (assuming that the rebel group had these weapons on hand). If the garrison did not surrender, the attack would be pressed home, by the use of captured armoured vehicles, if available.

Before a large government garrison could be taken, a long siege was usually required. All land routes into the objective would be cut and held by *mujahedin* units. The garrison would be subject to frequent rocket/mortar attacks and constant sniping. There was always the danger that DRA units put under siege would surrender, although often they managed to hold out for months, receiving all resupply and reinforcement by air. No Soviet unit is recorded as having given up. The town of Khost in Paktia, for example, remained cut off and under siege for years. It was kept functioning solely by air supply, except for brief periods when the siege was broken by a determined offensive effort, such as took place in Operation 'Magistral' of November-December 1987.

Naturally, some government installations were too large for the *mujahedin* to overrun and occupy or to destroy *in toto* but this did not deter the rebels. On several occasions, for example, they mounted strong attacks against the huge Balahissar Fort in Kabul. In such cases, the rebels resorted to hard-hitting raids designed to inflict maximum shock and damage before withdrawal. Some of these raids were devastating. On 3 June 1984, Commander Abdul Karim led such a raid against the Bagram airbase. Allegedly, they destroyed or damaged between 60 and 70 aircraft and killed scores of Soviet soldiers.[18] The following month, Jalalabad airport suffered a similar raid, losing nine aircraft and 30 soldiers. A third example: on the night of 21 March 1985, the *mujahedin* of the Harakat organisation conducted a co-ordinated series of attacks in the Kabul area. Beginning at 8:00 pm, the insurgents attacked Bagram airbase, the Kabul airport, the Military Academy, the DRA 15th Division, and the DRA 4th Division. The attackers destroyed approximately 40 combat vehicles and killed 40 soldiers before returning to their mountain stronghold (by vehicle) in Koh-i Safi, the mountainous redoubt to the east and north of Kabul.[19]

[*Figures reported by mujahedin sources are automatically considered to be inflated by at least 100 per cent. Sometimes, the mujahedin received information on damage they had caused from informers on the inside*].

Mujahedin groups also raided into the Soviet Union, penetrating up to 50 kilometres. Such raids on to Soviet territory, which occurred as early as 1982, always drew stiff reprisals in the form of extended, indiscriminate bombing attacks against Afghan villages.

Convoys were especially vulnerable to *mujahedin* interdiction. Even the major highways passed through narrow, constricted areas well-suited for surprise attacks by hidden rebels. The plan of these convoy ambushes was to force all or part of the convoy to come to a stop through the use of mines, obstacles, or the immobilisation of a selected vehicle in a location which blocked movement. Then, the trapped elements could be destroyed in detail or severely damaged until relief arrived. These operations are described in more detail in Chapter 7.

The *mujahedin* conducted ambushes against convoys and against any enemy units which ventured beyond the security of their garrisons. Even large military formations experienced ambushes. If the *mujahedin* were outnumbered and could not count on the complete destruction of the target, they simply disengaged and slipped away to wait for another opportunity. Small Soviet/DRA units which could not be relieved or move through the ambush site quite often suffered complete destruction. The insurgents tried to choose ambush sites where there was little room for manoeuvre and where the trapped elements were forced to face into the sun to locate their attackers above them.

Some *mujahedin* groups proved to be quite imaginative in their ambush techniques. One Soviet source reports that the insurgents would use Japanese bullhorns to unnerve the troops when they had them surrounded.[20] When circumstances permitted it, several ambushes would be set. The first would attack the initial target; the second lay in wait to attack any relief forces which might be sent. Ambushes would be laid in sequence to hit an enemy force several times. Sometimes, if the *mujahedin* were driven off, they would circle around and some time later hit the Soviet troops from another direction while they were relaxing, unwinding, and consolidating.[21]

In one specific example, the *mujahedin* learned in advance of the movements of a military convoy and took position in a thickly vegetated area known as a 'green zone', a term which came to mean any danger area. When the column approached, the rebels released about 200 chickens. Seeing so many chickens running free, the soldiers (Soviets) stopped their vehicles, dismounted, and gave chase. At that moment, the rebels opened fire destroying the nine armoured vehicles and 13 transports at the cost of three of their own wounded.[22]

The insurgents did not restrict their activities to the mountains and countryside; all the Afghan cities became combat zones as well. During the daytime, *mujahedin* attacks were generally limited to the planting of bombs, sniper fire, assassinations, and other forms of urban terrorism. Raids and rocket attacks also occurred, but not as frequently as during the night. After dark, many of the cities, including Kabul, took on the aspect of no-man's land.

Another category of insurgent combat activity was the stand-off rocket attack. The usual target was either an urban facility (garrison, ministry, headquarters), fuel/ ammunition depot, or, perhaps most often, an airbase. Because most of the Soviet/ Kabul major installations were located within a few kilometres of rugged mountain terrain, they were vulnerable to indirect rocket attacks. In preparation, the *mujahedin* often spent several days setting up hidden firing positions because it was an arduous task moving the launchers and rockets into covered locations at night. At the appropriate time, the rockets were launched at the selected target(s). After the last round was fired, the *mujahedin* immediately packed up and moved off in order to avoid the inevitable retaliatory air strike.

The numbers and variety of targets hit by rebel rockets and mortars were dazzling in some cases. Taking Kabul as an example once more, the *mujahedin* struck an enormous variety of targets including: the Soviet Embassy, the Soviet residential quarter, the housing area occupied by PDPA officials, Headquarters 40th Army, KHAD HQ, KGB HQ, the Soviet Friendship House, the Polish Embassy, arms depots, the Police Academy, all the military garrisons, the Central Grain Silo, plus many civilian targets (such as the high school and cinemas).

Damage inflicted during such attacks ranged from negligible to severe. Accuracy of fire varied widely, depending on the quality of the launcher (some launchers received from foreign suppliers had no aiming devices) and the level of training of the operators. Still, the Soviet and DRA air forces suffered many personnel and aircraft losses due to these rocket attacks and they never developed an effective means of preventing them. The Shindand base alone proved to be relatively secure against these attacks because of its favourable location in flat terrain. Even if a rocket attack caused little or no damage, it always had the effect of letting the enemy know that he was vulnerable and disturbing his sleep.

Finally, the *mujahedin* also targeted important economic objectives. During the course of the war, they destroyed dams, fuel pipelines, gas pipelines, power stations, power lines, fuel depots, ammunition depots, grain storage sites, industrial works and gas works. The aims were, first, to disrupt the logistical base for governmental and military operations, and second, to force the régime to spread its forces ever more thinly to protect facilities and to rebuild them.

The *mujahedin* constantly disrupted fuel supplies. Fuel lines at petrol stations often stretched to hundreds of vehicles, including military vehicles. Kabul remained under energy siege with only a fraction of prewar levels of electric power reaching the city. In 1984, Kabul suffered through a six-week power shortage. The oil pipeline to Herat was cut for 25 days during one period. Winters were bleak, cold, and lightless as a result.

The main response of the Soviet command was to bribe local leaders to protect pipelines and power lines from *mujahedin* sabotage. The policy did not work well. After providing a short period of protection, the 'protectors' would frequently blow up the lines, take the money, and run.[23]

An unusual feature of the war was the occasional arrangement of temporary truces between the Soviets and specific *mujahedin* groups. These truces benefited both sides. They permitted the Soviets to shift their military effort to other sectors, to make marginal improvements in local military postures (through forced recruitment, strengthening of guard posts, etc.), and they gave an extended respite to local government forces. The insurgents used truces to sort out organisational problems, gather and store food and supplies, build new sanctuaries and storage sites, recruit new members, and conduct military training without the constant threat of bombing or attack. On the other hand, the more fundamentalist *mujahedin* groups sharply criticised truces, claiming that they violated the sanctity of the *jihad*. Sometimes the truces created or increased contentious relations between rebel groups, a result which the Soviets found beneficial.

Tactical Evaluation — Strengths and Weaknesses

The *mujahedin* were not a professional force, although they included some professionally-trained ex-officers in their ranks. Naturally, they exhibited many deficiencies — such as lack of discipline, poor knowledge of basic tactics and inadequate planning. As expected, their operations suffered because they were badly equipped and could not build up the intensity and weight of firepower necessary for success. They did best when conducting small, simple ambushes and raids. They were at their worst during large-scale attacks (by several groups against large objectives or several objectives), since the latter required a sophistication of planning and co-ordinated execution which untrained rebels lacked.

One of the major strengths of the insurgents, a decisive advantage, in fact, was their excellent intelligence network. The Kabul government and armed forces were riddled with *mujahedin* sympathisers who were willing both to provide a continuous stream of information to the rebels and to support them surreptiously in other ways. According to one report, a majority of workers in the Prime Minister's office were active sympathisers.[24] Significant numbers of sympathisers also worked in the KHAD, militia, and police. Hence many attacks carried out by the *mujahedin* were based on information provided by persons located inside the objective. For example, messages were freely passed in and out of government installations that were under siege. Not uncommonly, as the *mujahedin* mounted an attack against an objective, sympathisers on the inside initiated their own attack, beginning with the killing of DRA and Soviet Army officers.

Usually, the *mujahedin* knew beforehand when and where the Soviets planned to carry out their operations, enabling them to avoid the blow or to position to interrupt it. Some Kabul outposts learned to survive by keeping the rebels informed of significant undertakings. The value of this intelligence to the *mujahedin* cannot be overestimated.

In addition to their intelligence network, the following skills and attributes must be counted as strengths: individual hardiness and physical fitness, giving great resilience; complete acclimation to the climate and terrain; an ability to exploit the terrain for both offensive and defensive purposes; stealth, fieldcraft and aggression which, combined with swift, dismounted tactical mobility, made them masters in the art of surprise; imagination and the creative use of primitive and limited military resources together with the ability to adapt readily to the use of new techniques and weapons acquired from the enemy; their quick exploitation of Soviet and DRA military weaknesses; use of mines and booby-traps.

Like all guerrilla forces, they also suffered from a number of weaknesses: an inability to conduct operations efficiently when the co-ordination of a number of groups, each performing separate functions, was needed; a shortage of experienced tactical leaders and weak tactical communications; a casual attitude towards camouflage and a lack of interest in disciplined training; a lack of heavy weapons and unfamiliarity with complex systems such as surface-to-air missiles and rocket launchers; dependence upon ground-based mobility; vulnerability to air attack and a shortage of air-defence weapons; limited opportunities for high quality training from experts.

As we have already seen, they were vulnerable on a number of the broader aspects of their performance and organisation: an absence of any national leadership and hence a lack of strategic direction to military operations, and the absence of the political and administrative structures needed to provide for the social and economic needs of the people living in the areas under their control; widespread disunity and even outright hostility between groups; an inability to plan and conduct large-scale attacks; sharp variations in the quality of leadership; dependence upon unreliable sources of supply; poor long-range communications and exceptionally poor medical support. These failings and weaknesses, in aggregate, severely reduced the military effectiveness of the resistance.

Training the Resistance

Raising the level of proficiency of the guerrillas was not an easy task because of an inherent cultural resistance to formal training. One beneficial source of military expertise lay in the ex-DRA officers who, having defected, passed on their skills to the irregulars. Officers who had been trained in the Soviet Union knew what to expect from the Soviets, so they were well able to devise tactics which would exploit their characteristics.

Formal training camps for the rebels were established in Pakistan, Iran, China, and even Egypt. An ex-DRA Army colonel who, reportedly, had received commando training in Great Britain and the Soviet Union and had worked with the US Special Forces in Vietnam, established an excellent training camp in Pakistan. He offered four to six week courses for up to 400 trainees at a time.[25] Other reports tell of mobile training teams which travelled inside Afghanistan.

In the Panjshir Valley, Massoud ran his own training courses in the operation of weapons and in basic tactics. He made a conscious effort to develop a cadre of weapons experts trained to handle missiles, rocket launchers, grenade launchers, and mortars. In addition, he also sent some of his trainers and experts to other areas in response to requests for assistance from other commanders.[26] A rebel training base, run by former DRA officers: three majors, two captains, and 35 lieutenants, also existed in Bamiyan Province.[27]

CHAPTER 5

The Doctrinal Dilemma

PRIOR to its invasion of Afghanistan, the Soviet command failed to consider in full the likely effects on its military operations of the harsh military environment and the unconventional nature of the resistance in Afghanistan. There was yet another factor, closely tied to the first two, but which had a deeper, negative effect on the performance of the Soviet Army — a doctrinal obstacle.

The Lack of Counter-Insurgency Doctrine

One of the strengths of the Soviet Armed Forces has always been the military, scientific and theoretical work carried out by responsible, deeply reflective, and often far-seeing officers of the General Staff. Soviet officers are trained and conditioned to approach questions of military doctrine gravely and methodically. Yet, from the very first days of its invasion of Afghanistan, the Soviet Army was hobbled by a serious doctrinal shortfall — it had no counter-insurgency (CI) doctrine to guide and organise its activity.

The Soviet divisions which invaded the DRA were structured and trained for large-scale, combined arms warfare such as would be carried out in the flat, rolling terrain of Europe. According to Soviet military doctrine, this kind of warfare is characterised by deep offensive operations, conducted by heavy tank and mechanised forces, massed and echeloned to breach dense defences, followed by rapid advances into the enemy's rear in order to encircle and destroy his ground forces in detail. These ground operations are accompanied and supported by simultaneous attacks of the enemy throughout his entire depth by means of aviation, missiles, long-range artillery and co-ordinated airborne and airmobile assaults. The enemy is expected to employ the same kind of heavy and deep-striking forces, arrayed in depth and presenting a formidable anti-tank and anti-air barrier. The doctrine places a premium on mass, echelonment, rapid manoeuvre, heavy fire support, high rates of advance and co-ordinated, combined arms action at all levels. Furthermore, the doctrine seeks a quick, decisive victory. The unsuitability of such a doctrine and such forces to the military situation in Afghanistan in obvious, yet it took the Soviet Army years to make the necessary adjustments.

It is difficult to understand why the Soviet Army was not well-prepared to recognise and fight a CI war in Afghanistan. After all, the Soviet Union had substantial numbers of military advisers and trainers in the country a year before intervention, many of whom had participated in or directed operations against the *mujahedin* in

1979. The Soviets also have a rich experience on both sides of the insurgent battlefield: as partisans in the Russian Civil War and the Second World War and as suppressors of partisans in the 1920s (in Central Asia, the Ukraine, and the Caucasus) and again, at the end of the Second World War in the Ukraine and the Baltics. Moreover, Soviet military analysts have studied closely the participation of (primarily) Western powers in local wars.

However, Soviet views on this study and experience have been badly distorted through the prism of Marxist-Leninist ideology, rendering a good deal of it useless. To be precise, the Soviet Army has an ideological blind-spot with regard to CI war. At first blush this might seem to be an unimportant matter but, in fact, the reverse is true, because it affected the readiness of the Soviet Army for war in Afghanistan and it has influenced and will continue to influence, strongly Soviet views on and the uses of their combat experience. A brief overview of Marxist-Leninist principles on the question of war in general will help to put this issue in perspective.

Drawing on the extensive writings of Marx and Engels on war and refining his views to meet the developments of the Russian Revolution and the Civil War, Lenin pronounced his verdict — There are four broad categories of war (each with its own sub-categories), to wit:

1. Wars between states or coalitions of states of the two opposing social systems, i.e. wars between imperialist and socialist states.
2. Wars between antagonistic classes within the confines of one state, i.e. civil war (which could, however, include limited outside support or intervention). This category covers wars of progressive revolutionary movements against ruling traditional or bourgeois classes.
3. Wars between imperialist states and peoples defending their freedom and independence or striving to achieve independence. This category includes wars of national liberation.
4. Wars between different capitalist states.

Although socialist states may have to fight wars, all wars are unleashed by capitalist states, according to Lenin and his disciples. Socialist countries, inherently, are peace-loving and progressive; they enter war defensively when attacked unjustly by their enemies. Just wars are those fought by the progressive forces of world society. Thus, socialist defensive war, anti-colonial war, revolutionary proletarian war, and wars of national liberation are, by definition, just wars, because they advance the march of societies toward the irresistible and inevitable goal of world socialism, as posited by Marxist historical determinism. Capitalist states which fight on the opposite sides are, therefore, initiators of and participants in unjust wars.

This broad framework characterises the Soviet understanding of local war as well as general (world) war. In Soviet military writings on local war, one finds the insistent assertion that local wars are unleashed exclusively by capitalist states. These writers also claim that capitalist states consider local wars to be useful training grounds for testing the newest kinds of weapons and new forms and means of military action.[1]

Counter-insurgency war is a derivative of the broader category, local war. During the 1920s, this subject received some attention in the Soviet military press, but not

much. Surprisingly, Marshal Tukhachevskii, who is best known as a military
theorist regarding questions of strategy and tactics, devoted some attention in the
early 1920s to counter-insurgency operations.[2] However, Soviet military thinkers
of the 1920s and 30s were far more concerned with developing the doctrine and
forces necessary for the coming world war. Tukhachevskii's brief writings on CI war
stand as lonely, ignored beacons of light.

Since the end of the Second World War, the Soviets have maintained that the very
concept of CI war is an imperialist one.[3] In particular, the development of this concept is attributed primarily to the US in the 1960s.[4] The Soviets consider all 'true'
insurgent movements to be socially just and progressive. Consequently, CI war is
seen as a reactionary doctrine which threatens the advance of socialism. Ideology
compels the Soviet Union to oppose CI war and to support national liberation and
revolutionary movements politically, economically, and militarily. If involved in
such wars militarily, the Soviets dogmatically insist that they will always be on the
side of the insurgents.

The equation boils down to a very simple one. Capitalist states unleash war,
including reactionary, CI war, in order to suppress progressive movements. Socialist
states support legitimate insurgencies. They have no reason to expect to confront
an insurgency themselves. In fact, the idea that the Soviet Union needs a CI doctrine
is an ideological anathema.

The attitude that CI war is essentially a capitalist problem is fully reflected in
foundational Soviet doctrinal military writings. The basic Soviet tactical text,
Taktika (Tactics), by Reznichenko, in its 1966, 1984, and 1987 variants makes no
reference at all to CI war. The same is true of the basic Soviet text on operational
art, Savkin's *Basic Principles of Operational Art and Tactics* (1973). In fact, significant discussion of this subject is not found in any of the many tactical and operational texts published in the Soviet Union since the end of the war. The only kinds
of war addressed in these foundational works are conventional and nuclear war.
[*Warfare under special conditions (desert, mountain, and arctic conditions) is addressed
in the 80s versions of* Taktika, *but the context is clearly conventional/nuclear, which is
to say that conventional forces may be forced to conduct operations in special environmental conditions in certain theatres during the course of a general war.*]

As a result, an interesting paradox has arisen. In the 1950s, while fighting a long-
term Chinese Communist insurgency the British Army produced a brilliant tactical
manual known as the *Atom (Anti-Terrorist Operations in Malaya)* manual. In the
1960s, the US Army, engaged in Vietnam, produced a series of field manuals on CI
war and internal defence and development. In the 1980s, the United States further
refined its doctrine on small, local wars and produced new manuals on low-intensity
conflict. In stark contrast, the Soviet Union has not produced a similar manual for
its own use, even after nine years and more of war in Afghanistan.

Soviet aversion to the concept of CI war is also revealed in the absence of an in-
depth analysis of its own anti-guerrilla experience. One has to search diligently to
find tactical analysis in the Soviet military press of military operations against the
Central Asian '*basmachis*' of the inter-war period, or against the post-war Baltic and
Ukrainian partisan movements. Conversely, the experience of Soviet partisans in the
Civil and in the Second World War has received exhaustive, adulatory coverage.
The hindering influence of ideology is further reflected in Soviet reluctance, indeed,

refusal to describe these internal foes of the past as partisans, referring to them instead as bandits, criminals, or counter-revolutionary bands. The same has been true with respect to the *mujahedin* in Afghanistan, which are most often referred to as *dushmen*, i.e. bandits, and occasionally as *dukhi* (spooks). The most complimentary terms used for the *mujahedin* is *miatezhniki* (rebels), but never partisans. To refer to them as partisans would be to confer an honourable status and to insinuate intolerably that the Soviet Union was pursuing a CI war. (By 1990, it was possible to find an occasional reference in a Soviet article to the insurgents using the term *mujahedin*.)

The ideological blind-spot also shows itself in Soviet analyses of bourgeois local wars. The primary Soviet treatise on this subject is the book *Local Wars* (1981), edited by Army General I Ye Shavrov.[5] Like most Soviet works of military history, it is thoroughly researched and well organised. The aim of the book is to distil the primary lessons regarding the conduct of military operations from the experience of local wars since 1945. It includes sections on war in Vietnam, Angola, and Algeria. It identifies the problems faced by Western powers in confronting insurgencies and it describes, in general terms, the primary methods employed. On the whole, however, the presentation of these issues is descriptive rather than analytical. Moreover, there is no separate section in the book dealing with the subject. Little effort is made to synthesise or evaluate these Western operations as a separate form of military activity, requiring a specific doctrine, unique tactical methods, and particular organisations. Notably absent from the book, as well, is any discussion of successful anti-guerrilla operations such as British operations in Malaya against Chinese communist guerrillas (1949–59) or the defeat of the Indonesian-sponsored insurgency in Borneo in the 1960s.

The distinction between a descriptive approach in a discussion of CI war and an analytical approach is an important one, which can be clarified by referring to the treatment given to the Vietnam War by the authors of *Local Wars*. In the course of their appraisal of this war, the following main points were made:[6]

▶ The US had overwhelming superiority in air, sea, and ground power.
▶ The main service employed by the United States were ground troops, particularly in the airmobile role.
▶ Viet Cong and NVA units were forced to fight as partisans: their standard military action was to strike, flee, and hide in the jungles and mountains.
▶ The main operational goal of United States forces was to find and destroy the enemy personnel.
▶ The United States quickly turned from its 'classic' operations of the Second World War and Korea and adopted essentially new tactics.
▶ The tactical methods used flowed from the military situation and the character of the terrain.
▶ The war had a fragmented character spatially, with no fixed front and rear, although both sides had their sanctuaries.
▶ The territory of South Vietnam was divided into separate zones for the conduct of essentially independent, unconnected operations.
▶ Helicopters were employed on a massive scale in a variety of roles.
▶ The United States made limited use of tanks, but artillery found wide use.
▶ The United States developed and deployed new organisations specifically

designed to meet the requirements of CI war.

▶ United States troops often: demonstrated poor night-fighting skills; feared close combat; showed high sensitivity to casualties; and were reluctant to operate without continuous support from artillery and aviation. (These last comments are attributed to Western specialists).

On the surface, these observations give the appearance of reflective analysis. In reality, all but the last are simply descriptive in content. Moreover, at least two (the 4th and 6th) are so general in nature that they could be made to apply to almost any war. Incidentally, all these observations apply equally to Soviet operations in Afghanistan.

What is lacking, above all, is an analysis of effectiveness and utility. The book ignores a number of obvious questions. What worked militarily and what failed to work? What methods would have worked better? What are the basic principles of organisation and tactics required against an insurgency? Why were some parts of the country pacified and others not? What were the differences in methods empl)yed by the US Marines and the US Army? What about the integration of military operations with civil measures? The authors note that the US Army developed a specific doctrine for CI war, but they make no effort to investigate the doctrine analytically or to evaluate as a separate entity.

Elsewhere, Soviet writers have discreetly dissected the United States concept of CI war, taking note of the primary features of this concept: e.g. that CI war required unique types of specially trained forces, employing unique methods; that military operations must be intertwined with political and administrative activity by civilian leadership; that standard, conventional tactics must be replaced by unconventional tactics; that technological superiority is neutralised to a great degree by the nature of partisan warfare.[7] However, again, there is no sense of more than a casual interest on the part of the Soviet military in this question.

The level and quality of Soviet interest in local wars as a source of information regarding the conduct of conventional operations is also reflected in journal articles. The most prestigious Soviet journal, *Voennaya Mysl* (Military Thought, written for generals and admirals) has devoted very little space to the question of local war. From 1937 to 1973, that is, over the space of more than 35 years, this journal printed only five articles concerned with local war or counter-insurgency operations.[8]

Beginning in the middle 1970s, the excellent Soviet publication, *Voenno-Istoricheskii Zhurnal* (Military History Journal), began to run articles under the rubric, 'In Foreign Armies' (*Po Inostranniyam Armiyam*). In 1983, this rubric was replaced by a new category — 'Local Wars'. As a result, the journal's coverage of local wars and foreign armies expanded considerably. However, the main thrust of these articles has been the application of the experience of local wars to the conduct of conventional operations in a possible general war.[9] The same inclination is exhibited in other widely-read Soviet military journals such as *Military Herald* and *Foreign Military Review*. The idea that the Soviet Union itself might become involved in a local war is not admitted in any of these sources. Consequently, there is no apparent effort to use the experience of foreign armies as a source for the evolution of a Soviet doctrine for small wars or CI war. In the few articles which do take a deeper analytical examination of Western CI operations, there is never a call for the Soviet Army to study this experience more deeply and to incorporate the lessons into its own tactical repertoire.[10]

Soviet Pre-War Doctrine for Mountain Warfare

The Soviet bias against CI warfare is also reflected in Soviet doctrine concerning combat operations in mountains. It would be a mistake to say that the Soviet Armed Forces had a separate, highly-developed doctrine of mountain warfare prior to the Afghan War. What existed, in fact, was a highly developed doctrine of conventional and nuclear war which took note of the influence of special environmental conditions on military operations. Furthermore, Soviet military doctrine is strongly buttressed by innumerable in-depth studies of historical operations. With regard to mountain operations, the applicable recent, historical antecedents were the intense, massive operations of the Red Army in the Caucasus, Carpathian, and Manchurian mountain ranges during the Second World War. These operations, particularly the Manchurian campaign, have been analysed *ad nauseam* in the Soviet military press. Soviet analysts have repeatedly attempted to generalise their observations on mountain warfare and apply them to modern conditions, tracing the development of mountain tactics since the end of the Second World War.[11]

However, there is one important catch: with very few exceptions, these historical analyses of mountain operations have been conducted exclusively with respect to their relevance to modern, large-scale operations during general conventional or nuclear war. As a result, they emphasise combined arms offensives using large, mechanised formations, accompanied by strong air forces in a well-developed theatre of operations. The analysts stress factors such as the achievement of high tempo, air defence in depth, use of reserves, mounted (as opposed to dismounted) manoeuvre, deep penetrations, measures undertaken to overcome deeply echeloned defences of mechanised forces, and even defence against chemical and nuclear weapons. These writers acknowledge that a mountainous theatre of operations has its tactical peculiarities — the greater influence of terrain, the need for more reconnaissance, the wider use of outflanking manoeuvre, and the like — but, overall, the doctrine expressed in this body of commentary retains a close resemblance to standard conventional doctrine under normal conditions. Consequently, it does not meet the tactical requirements of the conduct of a prolonged counter-insurgency in severely restrictive mountains.

Training exercises conducted in the Soviet Union in mountainous regions fully reflected this emphasis on conventional operations. It is impossible to find any discussion in the Soviet military press, prior to the Afghan War, of training exercises which included such features as pursuit and neutralisation of guerrilla units, the conduct of long-range patrols or ambushes far from secure bases, the use of motorised rifle troops in air assaults against insurgent bases, defence against dismounted ambushes, or the establishment and defence of isolated mountain outposts. This kind of training was not conducted (or was conducted so infrequently as to have been of no consequence), until after the war began. Even then, the features described above have hardly ever been reported in connection with training exercises carried out on Soviet soil, as opposed to training exercises in Afghanistan.

This is not to say that Soviet analyses of historical operations and training exercises had no value for or relevance to the war in Afghanistan. Some writings on the subject identified many of the key features of mountain warfare which would become painfully evident in Afghanistan, features such as the need for special training in mountain skills; the need for sub-units to operate independently; the need for junior leaders to be creative, flexible, and decisive; the need to decentralise decision-making; the frequent requirement to dismount. However, with regard to the training and preparation of Soviet military cadres, there is little evidence to suggest that these principles of mountain tactics were ever put into practice on a meaningful scale or even with a small part of the Soviet ground forces, with the possible exception of the Soviet mountain training centre.

What then about unconventional warfare? Did the Soviet Army possess doctrine in this area which would have been applicable to operations in Afghanistan? The answer to this question is a very qualified 'yes'. Yes, there is a body of doctrinal literature on this subject in the Soviet Union and there are special formations which train in this field and are reputed to be quite proficient. However, the units tasked with conducting unconventional operations — deep raids, specialised strikes, deep reconnaissance, sabotage and assassinations — are the shadowy *spetsnaz* brigades about which little ever appears in the Soviet press. Standard MRDs have no proficiency at all in this area. Even the 'elite' airborne and air assault units practice only an 'unconventional' form of movement to the objective area. Once delivered by air to their landing zones, their operations conform to the conventional style described above.

Finally, it bears mentioning that the Soviet inclination to overcentralise in military matters, particularly in terms of decision-making, combat support and logistical operations, also represented a doctrinal and practical obstacle to their conduct of operations against the *mujahedin*. As Chapter 2 demonstrated, one of the first reforms put into effect by the Soviet Army in Afghanistan was to decentralise elements of combat power and lower the level of planning and decision-making.

In summary, these doctrinal deficiencies seriously degraded Soviet military performance in Afghanistan. Because of the absence of a CI concept, the Soviet army tried to fight the war with the wrong kinds of forces and the wrong methods. They persisted in taking a conventional approach when it was plain to all objective observers that conventional tactics were doomed to fail. As a result, they repeated many of the errors of the past. Three long years of failure passed before the Soviet army developed and emplaced basic, effective, tactical counter-insurgency techniques (on a wide scale). In 1990, in the first open acknowledgement of this serious deficiency, a Soviet military scholar summed up the dilemma in this fashion:[12]

> Attempts by the command to organise offensives against the detachments of *dushmen* with large troop formations according to the rules of classical war and pursuit did not achieve results; ... Our own significant experience of combat with *basmachestvo* (banditry) in Central Asia through the years of Stalinism was cleanly forgotten ... and the rich, modern experience of other countries in the conduct of partisan and counter-partisan operations in regional wars from 1945–80, in the peacetime combat training of Soviet forces (which was unfortunately directed only toward classical, traditional forms of military operations) was also ignored. Moreover, also missing in our troops was the necessary study of our quite large experience in partisan operations during the Great Patriotic War from 1941–5.
>
> In fact, it was never considered that our army would be used in similar conditions.
>
> That is why our soldiers, officers, and generals sent to Afghanistan were forced to discover, beginning with the wheel, the tactical ABCs of the science of direct combat with small bands of insurgents.

CHAPTER 6

Armed Forces of the DRA

The Afghan Army and Air Force

PRIOR to the communist coup of 1978, the Army of Afghanistan had been a force of 90–100,000 men, with a sizeable number of its officers Soviet-educated. Between the Taraki coup and the Soviet invasion, Army strength fell precipitously to approximately 40,000. It fell even further after the Soviet invasion and thereafter fluctuated widely between 25,000 and 40,000 during most of the Soviet occupation; it finally began to climb towards 80,000 or so in 1989. The Air Force, on the other hand, suffered smaller losses in personnel and remained relatively intact, despite the political turbulence, with a strength of 7–8,000.

Although the manning levels were half what they had been, the basic structures of the Afghan Army and Air Force in the 1970s were retained into the 80s. The Army disposed three Corps headquarters located at Kabul (designated the 1st, then renamed the Central, and finally the 14th Corps), Kandahar (2nd Corps), and Gardez (3rd Corps). These higher staffs functioned as regional headquarters, not as tactical commands. The tactical organisation of the services varied slightly from year to year, but representative structures for the 1980s are shown in Table 6.1 and Table 6.2

Table 6.1

Tactical Organisation of the Afghan Army

11 Infantry divisions
3–4 Mechanised brigades
2 Mountain infantry brigades
2–3 Commando brigades
1 Paratroop brigade/regiment
1 Artillery brigade
Assorted Combat Support and Service Support regiments

Equipment: 5–600 Light and Medium tanks (reduced to about
          200 by 1989)
        4–500 APC/IFV
        450 Artillery pieces, 100-mm or greater
        100 120–, 160-mm Mortars
        50 BM–13, BM-16 MRLs

```
┌─────────────────────────────────────────────────────────────┐
│                         Table 6.2                            │
│                                                              │
│        Tactical Organisation of the Afghan Air Force         │
│                                                              │
│  7 Air regiments consisting of:                              │
│     3  Fighter sqns with MIG-21s                             │
│     3  Fighter-bomber sqns with SU-7s, SU-22s                │
│     4  Fighter-bomber sqns with MIG-17s, MIG-19s             │
│     3  Bomber sqns with IL-28 light bombers                  │
│     2  Transport sqns with AN-2s, AN-26s, IL-14s             │
│                                                              │
│     3-4  helo sqns with Mi-4s, Mi-8s, Mi-17s                 │
│     2  independent helo sqns with Mi-24s                     │
│                                                              │
│     1  Training sqn                                          │
│                                                              │
│  Total aircraft:    140-170 Fighters                         │
│                      45-60 Helicopters                       │
└─────────────────────────────────────────────────────────────┘
```

Never a very effective force, even before the political reversals of the late 70s, the Kabul Army proved to be of small use against the *mujahedin*, for a variety of reasons. To begin with, the Khalq-Parcham factionalism which paralysed the PDPA equally hindered the effectiveness of the Army. Despite a limited purge of Khalqi officers by Karmal (Parchami officers had been purged by Taraki), there still remained a majority of Khalqis in the officer ranks. Some units were almost exclusively officered by one faction or the other, but other units had a mix which invariably led to trouble.

Intra-army clashes sometimes became so severe that Soviet troops had to intervene. In March 1983, factions within the 7th and 8th Divisions clashed during a two-day unity rally. A few months later, units of the 25th Division fought among themselves for two days. Another shocking incident occurred in 1984. A military convoy of approximately 80 vehicles was travelling from Kabul to Gardez when it was ambushed by the insurgents. When the Afghan officer in charge tried to surrender the convoy, fighting broke out between the Khalq and Parcham factions within the convoy. Afghan crews of tanks and combat vehicles began to fire on other Afghan crews within the convoy. The *mujahedin*, of course, were delighted with the situation. When the dust settled, the rebels skipped off with that portion of the convoy still in working condition, having saved a good deal of ammunition to boot. (Ironically, this *mujahedin* convoy was later attacked from the air by the Soviet Air Force. An apocryphal story perhaps, but one fully illustrative of the complex interplay of armed hostility within the country.) Violence between the Khalqis and Parchamis also took the form of assassinations, booby-traps, and bombing.[1]

The Soviets never trusted their Afghan allies, for good reason. Defections of outposts and units occurred monthly. If all or part of a unit planned to defect, the first action normally taken was to shoot the Soviet adviser, if one was present. Occasionally, major defections took place: 1,000 members of a 1,200-man garrison in Paktia defected in September, 1984; a 2,000-man unit in Kandahar defected in July, 1987.[2] Many more examples could be cited.

Afghan officers and troops were also known to conduct sabotage, the most widely-reported case being the destruction of 22 aircraft, 2 helicopters, and 18 oil tankers at Shindand Airbase on 8 June 1985 (accomplished either by actual bombing from the air by Afghan pilots or by sabotage bombs).[3] Similar 'inside' sabotage occurred at the Kabul and Jalalabad airbases. The Soviets normally executed or imprisoned officers involved in sabotage. Allegedly, 80 officers were executed in Nangarhar in November, 1982, because they were planning to assassinate Soviet advisers at the Jalalabad airport. Such executions, violently resented by other Afghan officers, often led to further uprisings and defections within the Armed Forces.[4]

To protect themselves, Soviet headquarters and bases provided their own security and instituted strict control over entry and exit; not infrequently, entire areas were placed off limits to Afghan nationals. Even Afghan generals had to submit to personal searches and surrender their sidearms. Moreover, because the *mujahedin* had so many informers within the régime's forces, the Soviets restricted the release of operational plans and information until the last feasible moment.

Despite a variety of measures to raise manning levels, the régime failed to maintain sufficient personnel strengths. Most Afghan divisions included only 2–2,500 soldiers (all conscripts). Desertion more or less kept pace with conscription. By 1983, all males between 19–39 were declared eligible for the draft and the term of service was increased to three of four years. Draft evasion was so common that impressment of almost any male became the unofficial policy. The Soviet Army conducted sweeps through villages and city neighbourhoods, collecting males as young as 13–14, as well as passers-by and visitors from other regions who happened to be in the area.[5] Nomads also fell victim to these methods. Resistance to impressment could result in execution on the spot.[6] However, despite these draconian measures, impressment failed completely as a manning policy, since such 'recruits' simply defected at the first opportunity, taking their weapons with them if they could. The policy also created a flow of deserters into the ranks of the insurgents.

Given these conditions, it is only natural that the military proficiency of the Kabul Armed Forces was extremely low. Recruits received a maximum of two months training, usually with very little access to their weapons. Officers trained at the Military Academy in Kabul for two years, although some received as little as three months training. Some officers and NCOs, it is reported, were even illiterate. Moreover, the several purges carried out from 1978–80 created a crisis of leadership. Most of the experienced officers fled, died, or were forced out, leading to the elevation of quite junior officers to postings beyond their capabilities. Large-scale or extended training exercises simply were not carried out. The average unit was capable of only the most rudimentary manoeuvres and operations. Reports from rebel sources indicate that they considered Afghan Army units to be easy prey.

Afghan pilots too were poorly trained, spending so few training hours in the cockpit as to make them unsafe by Western standards. Certainly, they often failed to hit their targets, probably due as much to low proficiency as to intentional misaiming. In general, however, the rank and file and officer corps of the Air Force came from a superior manpower pool, that is, citizens with higher education or some kind of technical training. Nevertheless, Soviet pilots considered their Afghan colleagues to be 'worse than the Syrians'. The Soviet command allocated critical air missions to Soviet units and often relegated the Afghan Air Force to convoy escort and indiscriminate 'eco-war' bombing. Afghan pilots were sometimes punished if they failed their missions. In the later years of the war, Soviet 'watchers' accompanied

Afghan helicopter pilots to enforce compliance with mission orders. Despite the clear animosity between the two corps of pilots, there are no known reports of airborne dogfights between Soviet and DRA pilots.[7]

The Soviet command incorporated Afghan formations in all their large offensives, often putting them in the van if *mujahedin* strongpoints were to be attacked or if a string of ambushes were expected, so that the Afghan units would bear the initial brunt of enemy fire. Any attempt to flee or halt would be met by Soviet pressure or fire from the rear. DRA troops manned most of the rural, valley outposts in the provinces, as well as a great many highway checkpoints, security posts outside of cities, and border crossings. Essential outposts were manned by the Soviets themselves. In some respects, the Soviets required the Afghans to man isolated outposts of no real significance simply to give the rebels a multitude of targets, thereby reducing their attacks on the important facilities and Soviet garrisons. Much of the time, the rebels fell for the bait and wasted their energies and resources on insignificant objectives. Both the Kabul Army and the rebels paid the price for this cunning strategy with their blood.

DRA formations also conducted independent offensives. Quite often, Soviet artillery and aircraft would support these operations, but helicopter support to Afghan offensives fell far short of that provided to Soviet units. Beginning in 1985, the frequency and size (up to division-level, keeping in mind that the average division was under 3,000 men) of these independent Afghan operations increased, showing that despite its problems, the Kabul Army was improving marginally.

Within the DRA Army, the commandos and paratroops were considered to be the best and most reliable, although the paratroop establishment dwindled in size and importance as time passed. These units received priority issue of the best available equipment and weapons and they were often trained by Russian instructors, including training in air assault and independent reconnaissance. (Some militia units also received air assault training and were used in that role.) According to a former DRA lieutenant, commando units operated under the direction of the Reconnaissance Department of the Defence Ministry.[8] They were also used as an urban police/security force and in forced recruitment. Morale, generally, was low, just as it was in the regular units; many commando soldiers deserted at the first opportunity.

Paramilitary Forces

In addition to the regular services, there were four other military and para-military forces in the Kabul régime. The Ministry of Interior had its own separate police units, called the *Sarandoy*, organised into standard field units of various branches (infantry, armour, and commandos). *Sarandoy* battalions and brigades were spread throughout the country in provincial commands. They collected deserters, provided route security, interdicted guerrilla supply movements, and joined in the occasional attack. One Western analyst estimated the strength of the *Sarandoy* units to be approximately 20,000 in 1985, but the number of actual 'fighting troops' was probably well below that number.[9] As Soviet offensive operations became more sophisticated, planners incorporated *Sarandoy* units, sending them against specific, separate objectives.

The State Secret Police, or KHAD (*Khedamati i Dalati*, meaning Intelligence and

Security), also possessed separate combat units, as well as irregular units which masqueraded as lawless *mujahedin*, traders, clergymen, or bandit groups, in order to provoke fighting among true resistance groups, to tarnish the image of the rebels in the eyes of the people, and to collect information.[10] Many of the KHAD personnel were trained in the Soviet Union or by Soviet specialists. KHAD personnel were paid up to ten times as much as the average government worker, so they were able to attract a steady inflow of manpower. KHAD agents systematically infiltrated rebel groups in Afghanistan and the refugee camps. There they were able to sow dissension, carry out the occasional assassination, plant false information and keep their masters informed of rebel plans and movements. The *mujahedin* typically took ferocious revenge against any agents they discovered. KHAD units took part in special reprisal raids, impressment, apprehensions, searches, and sanctions against known or suspected enemies of the state. The strength of the secret police averaged about 20,000.

Third, the régime established a number of paramilitary border brigades to patrol the Iranian and Pakistani frontiers. Five such 'brigades', probably numbering no more than 500 men each, existed in 1985; by 1989 there may have been as many as seven. *Mujahedin* reports assign little significance to these units in terms of the threat that they posed either to combat or supply operations. They seemed to have played little part in the war.

The Militia

The last category of military forces in the service of Kabul is the militia. Although the quality and loyalty of these formations varied greatly, the *mujahedin* considered them to be more effective and dangerous than the regular army when they actually had to engage them in combat. Militia forces most often were recruited by the Ministry of Tribes and Nationalities to provide security in provincial areas where the regular military presence was weak. In essence, tribal leaders were paid not so much to lead their people in operations against the *mujahedin* as to secure an area on behalf of the régime, guarding it defensively against *mujahedin* attacks. In so doing, the régime secured at least the neutrality of a sizeable portion of the local population in a given district, a portion which was already organised and led in accordance with traditional tribal discipline. When the leader (*khan*) was bought off, the whole tribe essentially was bought off.

From the point of view of the tribe, joining the militia meant that their district was unlikely to be subject to régime operations or bombardments as long as they kept the rebels out or under control. Thus they could live in relative peace. There was also the financial incentive: members of the militia normally were paid much higher salaries than the regular soldier or average citizen. The régime also provided the militia with food, weapons, and ammunition. From Kabul's point of view, the recruitment of tribes into the militia meant that the local rebel groups would be deprived of recruits into their own ranks.

Tribal militia proved especially useful in protecting power lines and pipelines and in closing off some areas of the eastern border regions to infiltration from Pakistan. For example, Hassan Khan, chief of the Karokhel tribe, controlled a large region east of Kabul in the early 80s. He established outposts, conducted patrols, protected the power lines in the area, and restricted *mujahedin* movement through the area. He co-operated with the resistance to a certain degree by funnelling supplies to them, but he provided a valuable security service to the régime as well. However, in 1984, Hassan came under increasing pressure from the resistance to get off the fence and choose sides once and for all. Faced with the prospect of severe violence, he opted to side with the *mujahedin*. In August 1984, Hassan evacuated his 3,000 tribesmen to Pakistan, taking all his military equipment and supplies with him. Before he left, however, the militiamen and the rebels jointly destroyed almost off the electrical pylons leading to Kabul.[11]

The defection of such a large group of tribal militiamen was not a rare occurrence. Another group, 2,000 strong and under the command of Arbab Ghani Teymuri, had been securing traffic in the vicinity of Herat for two years. In the autumn of 1987, the entire group defected to the rebels, taking a substantial amount of weaponry, including a BM-21 122-mm multiple rocket launcher, two mortars with 5,000 bombs, and two tons of food. The militia then joined the insurgents in attacks against troop convoys in the same area.[12]

Nomad tribes also signed on as militia with the régime from time to time. Militia members were recruited as well from city dwellers who had lost their means of livelihood owing to the economic disruption of the war. Some tribal militia groups are known to have trained as air assault 'commandos'. The militia groups which took their jobs seriously were respected, in a military sense, by the *mujahedin*, because they possessed some of the same guerrilla attributes and skills. However, the quality and reliability of the militia varied widely.

The most effective, reliable, and feared militia group were the 'Jozjanis'. Raised from the population in northern Jozjan along the Amu Darya (Oxus) River, the Jozjani Militia was a unique, mixed force of Soviet and Afghan Uzbeks. Well-paid for their efforts and numbering between 3–4,000, the Jozjanis seemed to have no affinity with the *mujahedin*, yet no love for the Marxist régime either. (At least one source considered them to be some kind of radical Uzbek nationalists.) Perhaps they are best described as a tough, well-organised, coherent, hard-fighting mercenary force.

Soon after their formation, the Jozjanis were sent to southern and western Afghanistan. In Kandahar, where they replaced Soviet soldiers pulled out under the Geneva withdrawal plan, they acquired a reputation for brutality and savagery both during combat in defence of the Kandahar airport and in their relations with the civilian population. They were hard to control and liked by no one, yet respected by both sides for their fighting abilities. It has been suggested that one reason why they fought so hard was because they knew they would receive no mercy from the *mujahedin* if they surrendered.[13]

In summary, the DRA armed forces and paramilitary forces were ill-treated, ill-led, unreliable, untrustworthy, riven with factionalism, and uncommitted to the régime in the rank-and-file. The Soviets had to keep constant watch on them for their own protection. During operations, they provided manpower and mass, but little else. The KHAD and *Sarandoy* units generally were the most effective operationally. By occupying security posts and provincial garrisons, the Kabul Army and militia attracted the attention of the *mujahedin* and so kept some of the pressures off the Soviets and reduced Soviet casualties. The Soviet command grossly miscalculated their ability to carry the fight to the rebels in the opening years of the war and over-estimated the possibility of transforming the DRA Armed Forces into an effective fighting force to defend the unpopular régime. The régime army and air force did not begin to shape up until 1986. Interestingly enough, it was not until the Soviets started their withdrawal that the DRA Armed Forces stiffened and showed a consistent ability to hold off the rebels.

CHAPTER 7

The Third Phase of the War, 1983–89

AFTER two years of military build-up and numerous large offensives against the guerrillas, the Soviet command had little to show for its efforts. The resistance had grown stronger and tactically more proficient. Co-operation between the quarrelling groups was growing. The régime's armed forces had made no progress in developing into an effective force. The power of the puppet régime extended no further into the countryside than it had in 1980; where it did exist it was maintained solely by the physical presence of combat units. The *mujahedin*, in fact, held control or at least denied government control of from 75–90 per cent of Afghan territory, including partial control of several large cities.[1]

The Development of a Counter-Insurgency Strategy

It had become clear that a quick, decisive victory was out of reach. The Soviet Union did not have sufficient military force at its disposal to impose its will and it was unwilling to deploy the number of troops necessary to achieve a military decision within a reasonable period of time. Perhaps 500,000 troops would have been required. The political, economic, and ideological costs of such an approach were unacceptable.

As a result, a military stalemate arose within the country. Because of its technological superiority, the Soviet Army was able to establish temporary control in any part of the country, but it was unable to maintain that presence for more than a few weeks. As soon as the Soviet/DRA forces withdrew, the resistance reasserted its control — until the Soviets elected to conduct another major offensive. This ebb and flow of control between the Soviet/DRA and the *mujahedin* in the Afghan countryside characterised the entire war.

As the realisation sank in that a military stalemate existed and was unlikely to be upset by current methods, the Soviet command shifted its emphasis from military operations to long-term political and economic warfare against the resistance and the population which supported it. In a word, the Soviet command developed an *ad hoc* counter-insurgency strategy of which the military component was only one component, although a very important one. An in-depth analysis of that strategy is beyond the scope of this book, but a review of its main points will serve to place military operations after 1982 in larger perspective. In essence, the strategy had five components: political, ideological, social, economic and military.

Politically, the Soviets had made little progress on the pre-invasion goal of trans-forming the PDPA into an effective, stable, broadly-based ruling party. The Khalq-Parcham schism could not be reconciled either by Soviet demands or mediation. Nevertheless, the Soviet leadership continued its (futile) efforts to broaden public support for the PDPA. Membership drives increased the level of party membership, although total membership probably never exceeded 50,000. Financial incentives were offered to attract the loyalty of tribal leaders. Efforts were made to co-opt religious leaders as régime supporters. Karmal proved, however, to be a stumbling block to many of these efforts. Losing patience, the Soviets replaced him in 1986 with Dr Ahmedzai Najibullah, the former Chief of KHAD.

The Soviet command attempted to create an ideological base for the transforma-tion of Afghanistan into a socialist state through traditional communist agitation-propaganda measures, but especially through the 'sovietization' of the educational system. The old curriculum was thrown out and a new one introduced. Student attendance at all levels dropped so precipitously that children and young adults were actually 'conscripted' into the secondary schools and universities.

In a sense, the Soviet command declared war on the children of Afghanistan from an ideological and spiritual point of view. Thousands of Afghan children, in par-ticular war orphans and children of PDPA members, were sent to the Soviet Union and other Warsaw Pact countries to be educated for as long as ten years and so raised as a new, fully sovietized élite. In 1984, the US Information Agency stated that 16–20,000 children had been sent out of the country by that time.[2] This barbaric policy (the Mongol-Tatars and Ottoman Turks pursued similar ones) horrified the world and created fearful images of fully-grown Afghan men and women returning to their native land as brainwashed puppets ready to ravage their own people. Thankfully, these fears seem to be unfounded; the policy failed to produce fruit. In addition to children, many adults were also sent to the Soviet Union for training, perhaps as many as 52,000 by 1985.[3]

The social and economic components of the Soviet CI strategy were closely inter-twined. The ultimate Soviet aim was the break-up of traditional Afghan society and its re-making into progressive socialism. Various policies, often contradictory to each other, were designed to strip traditional religious and land-owning élites of their authority and influence. Occasionally, the régime moderated its approaches, such as the campaign for national reconciliation under Najibullah. However, no real progress could be made as long as the *mujahedin* controlled so high a proportion of the areas where the rural population lived. To transform the society, the *mujahedin* had to be separated from the people. In short, the Soviet command found itself facing one of the fundamental problems of any counter-insurgency: how to separate the guerrilla from the environment which shelters him. The solution devised by the Soviets can only be described as genocide.

Rather than drive the *mujahedin* from the countryside, the Soviets elected to drive off the population. In practice, this meant the systematic, planned destruction of the rural economy and the deliberate creation of millions of refugees by the most violent means. The execution of this programme depended entirely on the intensive participation of the LCSFA, particularly the air forces, artillery and rocket units. The methods used were brutal and inhuman, yet somewhat detached because they could be implemented from long range:

▶ Bombardment of villages to the point where they became uninhabitable.
▶ Destruction of fields and orchards through incendiary munitions, contaminants, and mines.
▶ Destruction of the extensive, underground irrigation system.
▶ Use of chemical weapons to contaminate water sources, food supplies and living areas.
▶ Burning of crops ready for harvest.
▶ Intentional destruction of livestock by artillery, rockets, mines, and poisons.

By and large, these policies achieved their immediate goals. Entire valleys, such as the Panjshir, Paghman, Kunar, and Logar valleys, were devastated, being left with scarcely a single villager. Harvests rotted in the fields for lack of workers. It is possible to read eyewitness reports from foreign journalists in which they describe how they walked for days without seeing a single farmer, peasant, or villager.

Refugees streamed by the hundred thousands into Afghan cities and across the borders into refugee camps. By 1987, the Soviet eco-war had created 5,000,000 refugees — one million internal refugees in Afghan cities (primarily Kabul) and four million outside the country — which is to say that slightly less than one-third of the pre-war population of Afghanistan was driven into refugee status.[4] Even Soviet historians accept the figure of five million as accurate, although they do not accept responsibility.[5]

On the other hand, the Soviets did not achieve their ultimate objective of eliminating the *mujahedin* by destroying their rural bases of support. Life for the *mujahedin* certainly became more difficult, but not untenable. Without the shelter of villages, the guerrilla had to find or build his own shelter. He had to carry his food with him. The insurgents also had to take care of the few villagers who remained behind. Rebel intelligence sources dried up to a certain extent. However, psychologically the *mujahedin* remained resolute and committed. Soviet eco-war did not have any significant effect overall in inducing a large number of rebel surrenders or in reducing the ability of the guerrillas to conduct operations. On the other hand, it had a devastating effect on the social and economic fabric of the nation which will take long years to repair.

The Soviet CI strategy had a military component as well, which could be described as a stronghold strategy. Unable to subdue the country as a whole, in a sense the Soviets 'fell back and regrouped'. Stymied in their attempts to operate in the countryside, they elected to concentrate their efforts on long-term control of Afghanistan's large cities, provincial capitals, key facilities, economic centres, and the main transportation network, i.e. those elements vital to the general control of the country and the support of military operations. In conjunction with this strategy, they reinforced large garrisons in cities and airbases and established strongpoints and logistical centres along the major arteries. In some areas, a system of outposts and police posts was created to extend a measure of régime control into the provinces. Using these static bases as anchors and refuges, the Soviets continued to conduct periodic, large-scale offensives into guerrilla enclaves. Thus by the end of 1982, Soviet military activity in Afghanistan evolved into four primary kinds of operation: independent eco-war just described, static defence of cities and bases, securing lines of communications and supply, and direct operations against the *mujahedin*.

The motorised rifle formations carried out the first three kinds of operations. They also continued to participate in the large offensives. However, the Soviets shifted responsibility for the bulk of daily, direct operations against the *mujahedin* to a new force, a specialised CI force introduced into the country for the express purpose of anti-guerrilla operations. The process by which the Soviet command realised the necessity of employing a specially trained CI force in qualitatively different kinds of operations is described in the next chapter. Suffice it to say at this point that the Soviet command divided up its effort in this fashion because it realised that the MR force was untrained and ill-suited for counter-guerrilla operations. The remainder of this chapter will describe how the MR force was employed during the third phase of the war.

Operations by the Motorised Rifle Force During the Third Phase of the War 1983–89

The Highway War

The bulk of Soviet military supplies to the LCSFA moved into and around the country by means of the main highway arc, which has been described previously and depicted in Map V (see p. 22). In addition, the economic life of the régime depended on the roads; control of them was vital. Knowing this, *mujahedin* groups in every region concentrated much of their efforts against the frequent targets which came rumbling down the highways. Thus, the Afghan road net existed as one of the main scenes of combat, as evidenced by mile after mile of burned out vehicles, destroyed bridges, and displaced, cratered pavement. West of Kandahar, the destruction was so severe that a 20-mile detour had to be constructed around the battle débris. The Soviets lost literally thousands upon thousands of vehicles in the highway war.

The objectives and methods of the *mujahedin* in their conduct of the highway war have been described in other sections of this book (see Chapter 4), so there is no reason to repeat that information here, except to note briefly that they attacked both the users of the road net and the physical highway system itself. In general, their goal in a convoy ambush was to bring the convoy to a halt through the use of mines and/or RPGs, and then to divide the convoy by fire into small sections which could be destroyed in detail. At other times, they destroyed bridges and undermined sections of roads simply to stop traffic for as long as possible.

The tasks of controlling the highways and protecting convoys were formidable. Great lengths of highway ran through territory dominated by the rebels. There was no alternative other than to force one's way through these areas. The Soviet and Kabul armies lacked the manpower to establish 100 per cent surveillance and security. Ambushes were inevitable, daily losses a fact of life. Like the fighter pilots of the Second World War, Soviet truck drivers painted symbols on their doors and engine covers, one for each successful transit of a given circuit. The Soviet command routinely awarded the drivers decorations, one award for every 20 long-distance trips.[6]

The first and most comprehensive measure taken by the Soviets to secure the highway net was the construction of a large system of security posts distributed over the entire country. Manned by Soviet MR troops and Afghan Army detachments, the posts were spaced every few kilometres, normally not in visual contact with each other, but in positions where they could keep most of the road surface under observation. During the day, security personnel checked all traffic passing through. At night, they retreated into the cover of their fortified positions. In addition to the security posts, the Soviets directed the establishment of platoon strongpoints in key areas.[7]

Along stretches of highway not suitably covered by security posts, the Soviets used independent helicopter patrols. Using loudspeakers to call suspect traffic to a halt, the helicopter would land, dismount an armed search party, and examine the quarry. Elements which refused to stop were attacked by the helicopters from the air.[8]

Some parts of the highway system were repeatedly victimised by the *mujahedin*. Here, the Soviets created a vast no-man's land along both sides of the highway by means of artillery, rocket, and aircraft bombardment. All villages along the road or within the first line of hills from the road were reduced to rubble. In addition, vegetated areas within this belt were destroyed, including gardens, fields, and valuable orchards.[9] A wider area on either side was further subjected to periodic preventive bombardment whenever the road was in use by important convoys. The Soviets endeavoured in this way to make it much harder for the rebels to be harboured in sheltered areas near to the road. If they intended to mount an ambush, it usually meant a day's march to the chosen ambush site and a day's march back to safety. If they were discovered in the devastated area near the highway, they were assumed to be insurgents and attacked automatically.

Most convoys included engineer elements for reconnaissance and mine-clearing, plus combat elements (motorised rifle sub-units) for protection. The Soviets improvised a convoy escort vehicle, consisting of a ZIL-135 (8x8) truck carrying a twin 23-mm automatic AA cannon behind armoured plates. The capability of this AA weapon to fire at high elevation enabled it to engage *mujahedin* positions on the mountain heights.[10] Convoys often included FACs or artillery adjustment teams to call for air and artillery support. The rebels learned to identify these teams, probably from the type of vehicle used and the number of antennae emplaced, and devoted special effort to destroying them first.

As a rule, convoys did not travel at night. Secure bases (traffic control stations) established at intervals along the highway net provided a relatively safe harbour each night.[11] The convoys pulled into the stations before nightfall and moved out the next morning. Occasionally, longer stays in these bases were necessary while sections of the road ahead were cleared of mines and destroyed vehicles, or rebuilt after rebel attacks, traffic being held up for days. The Termez-Salang-Kabul route, a distance of about 300 miles, it often took five or six days to complete the journey. When the rebels were very active, this trip might take as much as two weeks. Whenever an accident occurred in or near the Salang Pass Tunnel, the tunnel would be closed until the damage was repaired.[12]

Under the direction of traffic control officers, smaller convoys were joined together in one large march element and then assigned a convoy commander and a motorised rifle unit for protection. The convoy commander, perhaps an MR company commander, then assumed responsibility for the entire march unit.[13]

Quick minor repairs were taken care of on the road, but any repair requiring more than an hour would be towed to a secure base. Breakdowns plagued convoy operations owing to poor driving skills, harsh operating conditions, and the general wear and tear of daily use.

Standard procedures directed that convoys should move through danger areas as fast as conditions would permit. From time to time, security elements might be sent through danger zones first to clear them of mines or to trigger an ambush if one was lying in wait, before the rest of the convoy entered. If a convoy were attacked, those elements of the convoy not immobilised or damaged accelerated through the kill zone at top speed. Immobilised vehicles would be pushed off to the side if possible to make room for escape.

The Soviets also designed specific airmobile tactics for convoy escort. One or more Hind helicopters, carrying troops, flew in advance of the convoy and landed the troops on key terrain, from which they could pre-empt ambushes and protect the convoy as it passed. Other armed helicopters circled the moving columns on constant patrol. Once the convoy passed, the troops landed for their protection, the troops were picked up and leap-frogged ahead to the next danger area.[14]

Similar methods were used to protect the withdrawal of Soviet forces in 1988–89. In this case, two Hips were observed in use, one loaded with a platoon of troops, the other armed as a gunship. As above, the pair of Hips flew ahead of the march elements, clearing the usual hot spots. Troops might be set down to occupy ambush positions known to have been used in the past by the rebels or, if *mujahedin* were seen, the airborne party would stage an impromptu attack to drive them off. The Soviets also established temporary, platoon-sized blocks on guerrilla approach routes. This kind of operation demanded good co-ordination and communications between the convoy commander and the airmobile parties which were supporting him.[15]

Some Soviet combat units devised their own methods for self-protection while moving. One MR unit located at Narin typically fired their on-board machine guns to either side of the road whenever they left garrison, whether under attack or not. Tanks would fan out off the road into the fields as flank cover, destroying any crops in their path.[16] Recon by fire was also employed in flat, fertile zones of the country (primarily the north). Here the danger zones were not twisty, mountain roads, but thickly vegetated areas, called 'green zones'. Soviet gunners fired into these areas as a matter of routine as they approached and passed them in order to suppress any rebel groups waiting in ambush.

Security and Defence of Fixed Sites

Literally, thousands of Soviet and DRA troops were devoted to the complex task of the security and defence of fixed sites. General Lieutenant Gromov said that this task occupied 30–35 per cent of the LCSFA strength.[17] The task involved a great deal of construction work; defences had to be continuously upgraded and extended. Nevertheless, the *mujahedin* always discovered ways to penetrate urban and airbase security.

Certainly, Kabul was the most important urban site requiring defence; the measures put into effect there are typical of the general approach. Over the space of several years, a triple ring of security posts was built, extending 20 kilometres from the city in some directions. With most important positions manned primarily by Soviet MR troops, because of the importance of the city, the security rings included traffic checkpoints, gun emplacements, bunkers, trenches, obstacles, barbed wire, tank positions and strongpoints.[18] A person or vehicle en route to Kabul might be required to pass through five or six halts and searches before being cleared. Vehicles were searched thoroughly, including fuel tanks and spare tyres.[19]

Within the city, the Soviets established yet additional checkpoints at varying depths. Guardposts overwatched all major intersections. Searches of homes and motor vehicles were carried out at random. Soldiers built defensive fighting positions around and on the grounds of all important Soviet and régime institutions. (The Soviet Embassy had a rocket launcher and a mortar section in its grounds.) Persons entering such facilities were regularly searched. Here and there were scattered reaction forces to respond immediately to any threat. The Soviet quarter of the city was well-protected by MR units and cut off to access by city residents. Homes of VIPs were guarded and sand-bagged against bombs. All police posts were also fortified against ground assault.

Outside Kabul, the Soviets emplaced AP mines to block the approaches leading down from the high mountains, the Koh-i-Safi, to the east. Helicopters flew night patrols to identify rebel rocket and mortar firing positions. Furthermore, by 1985, every village within 10 miles of the city had been razed to the ground and the villagers expelled, so that it could not be used as a jump-off point for *mujahedin* attacks.

Jalalabad had a similar three-ring scheme with a very extensive system of trenchworks close in. The distance between the outer security posts, again manned by Soviet soldiers, was six kilometres. It was reported in 1984 that four gunships flew constant patrol over the city and its environs every night from dusk until 0400 hrs.[20] The security belt at Shindand, also three-ringed, extended 40 kilometres around the airbase.[21]

The Soviets also established these kinds of security systems at natural resource sites, which the Soviets were exploiting economically at the expense of their host country. The Ainak copper mine natural gas works, for example, was so well-defended that the *mujahedin* gave up trying to penetrate it.[22] The Farq-o-Dorq and Dasht-i-Laila natural gas works were also protected by a dedicated Soviet guard unit. Unusually for the Soviet Army, the guard force at these industrial locations conducted heavy security patrols to keep the areas clear.

The authorities increased security measures during 'revolutionary' holidays and special events of political significance. At such times, they barred non-official vehicle traffic, stepped up the number of searches, and augmented the security force. Somehow, the insurgents still managed to disrupt such celebrations. Visits by Karmal, for example, were always marred by bombs, rocket and mortar attacks, or ground assaults.

Despite the enormous efforts devoted to the defence of fixed sites, the Soviet Army never solved the problem. The *mujahedin* displayed a remarkable ability to slip in and out of the security net without major difficulty. The proximity of mountainous terrain to almost all the major cities and airbases permitted the rebels to approach at least within mortar and rocket range at night. Soviet reluctance to conduct dismounted patrols outside the city after dark contributed to the freedom of rebel movement. In addition, infiltration past the security rings posed no major difficulty. Sometimes the rebels bribed their way past guardposts with money or hashish. They were also known to pose as régime troops using DRA vehicles and uniforms. Some guardposts (Afghan-manned) simply let them through out of sympathy or to avoid the consequences of refusal. Once inside any city, the large refugee population present provided food, shelter and support.

As a result, living in Kabul, Jalalabad or Kandahar, for example, was almost as dangerous as being on a combat mission. Virtually every target of any significance in Kabul was hit by the *mujahedin*, not once, but many times. The rebels were even able to collect enough strength within cities to carry out attacks against army garrisons. Of course, several cities were never completely taken over by the régime, Kandahar and Herat being the most conspicuous examples.[23]

At night, the quality of urban security fell sharply. The streets of most cities became danger zones after dark, so Soviet and DRA forces stayed in their fortified shelters as a rule. Of course, it was at night that the *mujahedin* assembled and carried out 90 per cent of their attacks. The multi-objective raid described in Chapter 4, by no means a unique event, is a good example of the ease with which the *mujahedin* managed to penetrate the security system established by the Soviets to defend Kabul. In general, daytime was safer, the main threats being bombs, knifings, sniping, and assassination attempts.

Whenever the rebels did mount an attack, the Soviet response was primarily defensive. Very rarely did they attempt to pursue the *mujahedin* into the mountains. Occasionally, a daylight raid or rocket attack would draw an airmobile response. Airbase security overall was better than urban security for two main reasons: the area to be defended was smaller, with discrete boundaries, and personnel traffic in and out of the area could be controlled more thoroughly. Once in a while, the *mujahedin* succeeded in penetrating the perimeter of an airbase for short raids, but the main threats to airbases were sabotage from the inside and rocket or mortar fires. Some airbase security units conducted active patrolling to secure the perimeter — but only to a limited extent.

Outpost and Garrison Defence

Afghanistan was literally dotted with manned outposts throughout every province. Little Paghman Province, for example, had 40 security posts in 1986.[24] The outposts existed to protect stretches of highway, secure the entrances to and exits from cities, interfere with rebel activities, maintain continuous observation of key areas, guard border routes, and maintain a government presence in order to restrict rebel influence and control. Afghan troops manned most of the provincial security posts. However, Soviet MR troops also took part in this duty.

The size of the outposts varied considerably but, on average, they appear to have been occupied by forces between the size of two sections to perhaps a reinforced platoon. In general, the posts were established in defensible terrain, widely separated from one another (at least out of visual contact). Many of the positions were built by hand, using rudimentary construction materials, sandbags and such natural materials as were available. Some used prefabricated concrete slabs for walls.

Naturally, 360 degree defensive works were imperative. The occupying troops put out minefields and barbed wire to block possible approaches. Early warning devices, on the whole, either were not available or were not used for some other reason. The soldiers constructed individual and crew-served fighting positions with written fire plans and diagrams and cleared fields of fire where necessary. The living and sleeping quarters had to be protected in the same way. A position held by a reinforced platoon would include a mortar and/or an AGS-17 grenade launcher section for support, plus the unit's organic vehicles, of course. These crews required dug-in firing positions and sheltered areas in which the ammunition could be stored. Communications trenches connected the various components of the complex. Radio communications linked the outpost to higher headquarters and enabled the platoon leader to call for artillery support if needed.[25]

A platoon-sized outpost was described by a Soviet defector, a former tank gunner:

> We were sent to Karabakh and our mission was to guard the road. The post was small and had 24 men with 24 AK-74s, three tanks, one mortar, one heavy machine-gun, and large quantities of mines and ammo. There were also mines laid around the post. During the day, two of the tanks were assigned to guard the road, while the third stayed at the unit. At night we just stayed in our base and did guard duty.[26]

Outposts guarding highways which were open could be supplied by ground, but a great many others resembled islands in a hostile sea. They could only be supplied by helicopters or airdrops, normally on a scheduled weekly or bi-weekly run. The aircraft delivered everything necessary for basic needs — food, arms, ammunition, mail, spare parts, reinforcements or replacements, literature, even water if there was not a protected supply available. Some isolated outposts, for example on mountain tops for observation, were established with the specific intent to supply them by air.[27]

Outpost duty was dangerous and psychologically oppressive. During the day, troops could venture outside through the barbed wire and minefields, perhaps for exercise or to take up observation posts. During the night, they had to be pulled back in. The threat of a sniper's bullet was ever-present. According to General Gromov, a soldier could be assigned to this duty for as much as 18 months to two years and might find himself on a post manned only by 7–12 persons.[28] Consider the psychological tension which would mount up due to the pressure of living in a very small area under constant threat of attack by an unseen enemy.

Larger permanent garrisons were also established throughout the country and manned by units from company to regimental size (sometimes several regiments). The defensive works established to protect the garrisons followed the pattern of the outposts, but on a larger scale: larger minefields, an exterior security belt, auxiliary fighting positions, reinforcement by a full mortar or artillery battery, an AGS-17 battery, and engineer platoon, plus the unit's organic park of armoured vehicles. Normally positioned to secure provincial capitals and roads, the units in these garrisons might be called out to participate in major offensives. Road approaches to the garrisons usually were cleared of all vegetation and structures to provide unobstructed entry and exit, as well as clear fields of fire.

One such large, mixed Soviet/DRA garrison in Chaprikar District was described by the Afghanistan Information Centre:

> Now it [the garrison] has only 600 Afghan soldiers and 1,200 Russian troops. It is equipped with sophisticated arms, such as long distance rockets and missiles. The unit has a prison where suspects brought from Jalalabad are kept during six days. It has three parts: a common military centre, Russian quarters and Unit 81 headquarters. The base has about 380 tanks and APCs all under Russian control. Each night between 7:30 pm and 4:00 am flares were used. The intense light would last about 30–40 minutes. A Russian special unit is stationed there, but its headquarters are at the Jalalabad airport. Russians rarely stay at the unit headquarters during the night. Some time ago the *mujahedin* were able to launch attacks on the base. Now it is no longer possible due to several security rings around the installations.

A Soviet regimental base at Ghazni was defended in this manner:

> We had a defence perimeter of some 8 to 10 kilometres around our regiment and a minefield that was 500 to 600 metres wide. There were platoons positioned around the defence perimeter about a kilometre apart from each other. At least one battalion of the regiment was left behind for security whenever the rest of the troops were operating outside.[29]

Many such garrisons, despite their size, proved vulnerable to attacks by the *mujahedin*. They often suffered long sieges during which they were cut off from land lines of communication. The danger always existed that Afghan garrisons under siege would seek to surrender rather than fight to the death, but there are no reports of Soviet garrisons or outposts ever doing so.

Large Offensives

During the third phase of the war, the methods employed by the MR formations in the conduct of large offensives continued to follow the general pattern laid down earlier, with some improvements. The widening use of light airmobile forces on high ground put pressure on the rebels and protected the advance of the MR units into side valleys. The attachment of ground forward air controllers and artillery adjustment teams to MR elements on a regular basis led to more timely fire support. Furthermore, the introduction of new weapon systems such as the BMP-2, the Vasilek mortar, the AGS-17 automatic grenade launcher and others (see Chapter 11) helped as well.

Rather than pushing into guerrilla strongholds from one direction, the Soviet command planned two- and three-pronged offensives where possible, coupled with airmobile forces deployed to seal off all main entrances and exits to the objective area. Many of the operations of this phase of the war were intended to break sieges of large garrisons. Attacks from several directions, plus direct reinforcement of the encircled garrison by air, occasionally led to success.

The pace, number and size of Soviet military operations intensified in 1985, reaching a peak which was maintained through 1986. Co-operation between the Soviet Army and the régime forces improved; by the end of 1986, the Kabul Army was starting to show promise. KHAD and *Sarandoy* began to play a part in the offensives as well, attacking specific objectives. In addition, the rise in intensity was aided by a sharp increase in the employment of air force and CI units based in the Soviet Union. Operations to cut border infiltration put real pressure on the *mujahedin*. Soviet intelligence was better due to increased use of *spetsnaz* teams and improvements in intelligence work done by KHAD, militia and police.

Mujahedin losses increased dramatically. One thousand were killed in operations in Faryab Province in March, 1986, and another thousand at the end of the year in a large Soviet and Afghan offensive against the very strong Zhawara base in Paktia Province on the border of Pakistan. Although it had survived many attacks before, this time the base fell and all its stores were captured or destroyed.[30]

Thus, 1986 was a year of crisis for the *mujahedin*. Although they experienced high losses during that year, they managed to hang on, helped immensely by the arrival of advanced AD weapons, which led to an immediate decrease in airmobile operations in some regions. The effect of these weapons on the battlefield was dramatic.

Suddenly, the rate of Soviet aircraft losses to enemy fire increased by a factor of four or five, a level of damage which they could not sustain (see Chapter 9). For the Soviets, then, 1987 was the year of decision, the year in which they reduced air-mobile operations significantly and decided to negotiate a withdrawal from the war. Certainly other events outside Afghanistan played a part — the worsening of the economy, the unbending opposition of the Reagan Administration, the 'new thinking' of Gorbachev. However, it is equally clear that the military effect of the new AD weaponry, particularly the Stinger missile, convinced the Soviet command that the war was not winnable for them, neither then, nor later.

Operation 'Magistral' in November and December 1987 was the last very large operation by the Soviet Army. In fact, it was probably the largest operation of the war, involving 24,000 men. 'Magistral' was a sophisticated operation which incorporated advances by large MR units on multiple axes, large air assaults, direct reinforcement of the Khost garrison by air, and prescribed roles for all the elements of the DRA Armed Forces. It achieved its aim of breaking the siege of Khost, but only temporarily. The *mujahedin* were not dealt a death blow, indeed they rallied support from other areas. Despite the attention given to this operation in the Soviet press, there is no good reason to tout 'Magistral' as a great achievement of Soviet arms.

CHAPTER 8

The Soviet Counter-Insurgency Force

THE fact that the Soviet military appeared slow to implement effective changes in Afghanistan does not mean that they failed to realise the peculiarities of combat in the DRA. Analysis of the Soviet military press shows that they collected data on their operations, wrote critiques of their tactics, and assessed military requirements since the earliest days of the war.

Discussions in the military press of actual small unit operations in the DRA show a full understanding that the specific, unusual characteristics of the tactical situation required correspondingly specific and unique tactical solutions. To be more precise, the Soviets identified seven primary features of counter-insurgency warfare in the Afghan mountains which have a strong influence on the conduct of tactical operations and which elicited specific tactical responses.

Soviet Tactical Analysis

The first of these features was a new appreciation for **the influence of terrain and climate**.[1] Soviet doctrine for conventional war, even in a mountainous area, overwhelmingly stresses the destruction of the enemy as the primary goal of armed conflict. Terrain is important, yet it is only one of many factors which influence the attainment of this goal. In Afghanistan, however, the Soviets came to realise that terrain and climate occupy first place above all other factors in terms of their influence on destroying the enemy. In the DRA, terrain and climate affected everything in combat: manoeuvre, the effects of weapons, fields of fire and observation, physical readiness, logistics, communications, and the performance characteristics of weapons and equipment. In Afghanistan, the Soviet goal of destroying the enemy was dependent on the ability of the Soviet troops to cope with the severe terrain and climate.

One of the effects of mountainous terrain on military operations is the compartmentalisation of military activity which it produces. As described earlier, the Soviets found out that manoeuvreing with large forces on the valley floors accomplished little. It became evident that the only way to close with the insurgents was to pursue them through the restricted gorges and canyons, into their mountain hideouts. This activity required a high level of **decentralisation**, because the folds of the terrain naturally divide a large unit into small segments. The emphasis must necessarily be on company, platoon, and even at times, section operations. The outcome of battle in the mountains is often decided on the basis of these small, decentralised firefights, which develop in an unforeseen and unexpected fashion. The important decisions, thus, are those made by captains, lieutenants, and sergeants.

In such conditions, the Soviets discovered, small units must be able to **operate independently**, often at a significant distance from their parent battalion or regiment. In order to surprise the *mujahedin*, elements of a single unit had to be deployed miles apart in order to approach the objective from different directions. As a Soviet officer and veteran of the war noted: 'Companies, platoons, and sometimes even sections, often are forced to operate independently in separate directions.'[2]

The decentalisation of tactical operations and the independent nature of small unit actions demanded that the sub-units should be more self-supporting.[3] On a conventional battlefield, Soviet units normally enjoy continuous visual contact with the units to their flanks, front, and rear, and they can count on receiving pre-planned fire support from neighbouring and supporting units. In the DRA, a company or platoon engaged with the *mujahedin* often were not in visual or radio contact with other Soviet units nearby. In many cases, it would have been close to impossible to support those engaged units with effective fire from supporting organisations without significant delays. Accordingly, the Soviet command enhanced the capability of companies and platoons to provide their own fire support and to fight more independently through the **practice of attachments** at a very low level. These attachments consisted of sections or squads of engineers, mortarmen, grenadiers, retransmission personnel, and augmentation of radio operators and ground reconnaissance elements.[4] One interesting innovation was the attachment of artillery spotter and adjustment teams to sub-units in order to improve the use of on-call fire support (see Chapter 10). Soviet doctrine provides for the organisation of units with such combined arms attachments, but they are generally seen at a higher level or in units which have been given a special role, such as advance guard or forward detachment. What was new in Afghanistan was the attachment of these squads and sections on a regular basis to infantry platoons and companies. Their presence at such a low level permitted these small units to conduct non-standard (for them) operations — mine clearance, obstacle removal, extended reconnaissance and self-support with indirect fire — without having to depend on support from a higher level.

A fifth feature of the Afghan ground was was the realisation that decisive tactical combat must be conducted in **dismounted order**. Soviet armoured personnel carriers and fighting vehicles often could not negotiate the trails and tracks leading to *mujahedin* positions. Use of the vehicles often meant the loss of surprise as well. Furthermore, unit commanders could not rely on them for supporting fire from the main armament and machine-guns — another reason why dismounted attachments of grenadiers and mortars were necessary. The severe limitations on their mobility in the mountains also increased their vulnerability to attack. Thus, combat in the DRA demanded that Soviet personnel should 'muscle' their heavy weapons and ammunition loads into position on foot. Effective dismounted manoeuvre, the Soviets discovered from experience, depended on stealth, speed, surprise, and physical fitness. This new-found emphasis on dismounted manoeuvre constituted a fundamental change from the standard Soviet approach to an infantry attack, wherein the motorised infantrymen ride in their armoured vehicles to an attack line quite close to the final objective and dismount only for the final assault. The tactical situation in Afghanistan demanded that the approach and the attack should be conducted on foot.

Because the Soviet forces in Afghanistan possessed air superiority and overwhelming firepower, the *mujahedin* conducted many of their operations after dark, lying up during the day to avoid detection. The propensity of the guerrillas to operate at night also forced the Soviet Army to increase its stress on **night operations** since it was when the rebels were moving to attack or ambush positions or conducting resupply movements that they were most vulnerable. However, despite the very heavy emphasis in Soviet publications and training programmes on night operations, it is clear that the rebels ruled the night in Afghanistan. Soviet units seemed to be very reluctant to leave the safety of their cantonments at night. One reads only a few articles on Soviet night patrols, except in training exercises. Articles in the Soviet press attest to the fact that the great majority of Soviet operations in Afghanistan at night were carried out by specially trained light troops, about whom more will be said later.[5] Even these units, it appears, often ceased movement at night and assumed a stationary, defensive posture until morning, unless they were specifically charged with conducting a night ambush or raid. Thus, even though Soviet literature identified proficiency in night operations as a necessity, the LCSFA developed only a limited proficiency in this area.

Considering the factors described above, one cannot fail to conclude that the war in Afghanistan was a **light infantryman's war**. Decentralisation, independent operations on separate axes, overcoming difficult terrain, dismounted manoeuvre, reliance on one's organic and attached fire support, and exploitation of the night — these are all characteristics of light infantry operations. The *mujahedin*, of course, were a light infantry force (like all guerrilla units). To defeat them in close terrain, the Soviets also needed to be able to fight as light infantry. Thus, this war caused the Soviet Army to take a new interest in light infantry skills and tactics. The most important skills needed, as identified in the Soviet press, were: ability to negotiate difficult terrain rapidly and quietly; stealth; use of the terrain for protection and concealment; individual fieldcraft; tracking; expert marksmanship; skilful siting of heavy weapons; controlled expenditure of ammunition; technical skill with mountain gear; co-ordinated dismounted manoeuvre by individuals and teams; and a high level of physical fitness.

It is also clear that this kind of war requires very capable small unit commanders who can exercise initiative and who possess imagination. They must be able to make quick decisions on their own in the face of unexpected conditions, discarding textbook solutions. They must be proficient in the use of all unit attachments. Tactical flexibility, not rigidity, is a necessary prerequisite. These qualities are not routinely developed in Soviet motorised infantry commanders, especially at the junior officer and NCO level, the weakest link in the Soviet chain of command.

It is, therefore, not surprising, that the Soviet command discovered that their motorised rifle troops, units, and commanders did not possess the light infantry skills necessary to defeat the *mujahedin*. Furthermore, the Soviets were not able to develop these skills in their MR units. They accepted the fact that the complexity of the required tactical skills simply exceeded the capability of the average MR unit and commander. To put this conclusion another way, it is clear that the MR force in Afghanistan was not able to adapt to the tactical situation in which it found itself. Deficiencies in the human quality of the force and the training which they received prohibited their use tactically against the *mujahedin* in the way in which they should have been employed.

Creation of the Counter-Insurgency Force

In response to this serious deficiency, the Soviet command developed a novel approach which began to characterise their operations as early as 1983. First, MR units were withdrawn from direct operations against the *mujahedin* except in the context of the large conventional offensives. The Soviets, instead, turned to their élite units in order to develop what amounted to a direct-action, counter-insurgency (CI) force. The CI force was comprised of four kinds of units: airborne, air assault/airmobile, designated reconnaissance, and special operations units (*spetsnaz*) units. Although such units were involved in the conflict since its start (except for the air assault units), their numbers and missions changed over time, evolving into the situation, where by 1983 and continuing through to the end of Soviet involvement in the war, they bore the brunt of the fighting and suffered most of the casualties. These units numbered between 18–23,000 soldiers, or, 15–20 per cent of the total LCSFA.[6]

Of the four groups, airborne units comprised the largest part, approximately 10,000 troops, supplied from regiments from three airborne divisions, the 103rd, 104th Guards, and 105th Guards divisions, under the command of HQ 103rd Division. Next to the *spetsnaz*, there are no better troops in the Soviet army than the airborne soldiers. Airborne (VDV) troops are recruited from the cream of Soviet youth, both from volunteers and hand-picked conscripts. They undergo a rigorous, lengthy training programme which produces combat skills not matched by the ordinary MR soldier. Great emphasis is placed on physical fitness, hand-to-hand combat, marksmanship, as well as special terrain-specific skills. The capabilities of these units is well demonstrated by the testimony of a former Soviet soldier who defected and fought alongside the *mujahedin* for a while:

> This happened on 26 September 1986, in Nangarhar Province. We had taken positions close to the top of a mountain overlooking a valley and were shooting at the Soviets with BM-12s and mortars ... Then all of a sudden a VDV (airborne) company of about 90 men appeared and attacked us from behind. They had climbed straight up the mountain during the night ... Before that I had thought that the Soviet soldiers are not worth anything, but I must say that I had never seen anything like that. We had good food there and I was in good shape, but I would not have been able to climb that mountain. It was simply impossible for me. These were really tough guys.[7]

The air assault troops, which numbered from 5–7,000, came from relatively new Soviet organisations, the air assault and airmobile brigades. Also considered élite troops but slightly short of the calibre of the VDV, the air assault troops have a similar training regimen, except only half are parachute-qualified. Their normal mission under conventional conditions is to conduct *desants* (air assaults) from battalion up to brigade size into the tactical depth of the enemy in order to take some vital objective and hold it until the main force arrives. The airborne divisions, of course, have a similar mission, but they would normally conduct such operations at a great depth and as a division force. The key point is that both kinds of units are trained and conditioned to conduct independent operations in the enemy rear, albeit in greater strength than they had to do so in Afghanistan.

VDV and air assault units based in the Soviet Union often participated in operations in the northern half of the country, flying directly into combat from their secure bases.[8] However, it should be noted that the VDV force dedicated to the war performed very few parachute drops, perhaps as few as two or three.

Separate reconnaissance units also formed part of the CI force. Each MRD and regiment in the Soviet force structure includes a specially-trained reconnaissance battalion and company respectively, as do airborne divisions and air assault brigades. As a rule only the best officers and soldiers are assigned to the reconnaissance units. In conventional conditions, these units operate as mounted advance guards and as security detachments to the front, flanks, and rear. Thus, they are accustomed to the kind of decentralised, independent operations which characterised combat in the DRA. Approximately 5,000 reconnaissance troops (*razvedchiki*) were maintained in the country during the war. They probably performed the majority of the combat reconnaissance patrols and long-range patrols as well.

The Soviet press frequently referred to the operations of these three kinds of unit in the DRA. Quite a bit less is known, however, about the contribution made by *spetsnaz* troops, but it is thought that they were engaged in some limited small unit combat as well as special operations such as sabotage, deep reconnaissance, espionage, reprisals, and assassinations. One ex-Afghan Army officer and past adviser to the National Islamic Front stated that there were two special operations brigades in Afghanistan, one at Kandahar and one at Shindand, while other analysts have assumed the existence of three to five, which seems quite fanciful considering that *spetsnaz* units are a strategic asset, normally handled by the GRU, the Military Intelligence Directorate.[9] The permanent subordination of such a large number of strategic units to the 40th Army or even to the theatre command would be quite unusual.

David Isby, one of the most authoritative observers of Soviet military activity in the DRA, categorised the *spetsnaz* troops into two main groups, the *raydoviki*, i.e. raiders, perhaps similar to US Rangers, and the *vysotniki*, or high-altitude teams (author's terminology) who specialise in deep insertion (perhaps by high-altitude, low-opening parachute insertion) for sabotage, reconnaissance, and intelligence.[10] However, the *mujahedin* used the term *raydoviki* or commandos, to refer to any kind of unit using dismounted or heliborne commando tactics, as described below.

Employment of the CI Force

The various elements of the CI force were employed offensively against the resistance in typical, independent light infantry operations. Many of their early operations (1980–82) had been characterised by some of the same errors as those of the MR formations, but the CI units climbed up a sharper learning curve and learned their lessons better and faster. Previous discussions have already described in some detail how the CI force was used to support conventional operations and road convoys. The most common uses of CI units in those operations were their emplacement on high, key terrain to pre-empt ambushes and so secure the advance of the MR columns, and, as blocking forces to seal off the objective area. So many blocking operations were conducted that the Soviets resurrected the Second World War terms '*blokirovka*' and '*blokirovaniye*'. The tactical formation used to establish blocking positions most often was the enveloping detachment, described in detail below.

CI units also participated in many raids against the rebels, often in concert with MR units. Large raids almost always took place during the daytime against objectives which could be approached by light armoured vehicles. Fighter-bombers usually initiated the raid with air-strikes against the objective, followed by helicopter gunships which prepped the landing zone. The MR force maintained constant pressure with fires from their combat vehicles. The *desant* force, delivered by Mi-8/Mi-17 Hip, covered by Mi-24 Hinds, then landed and assaulted from one or more different directions, as the MR columns closed in. In large raids, the airborne/ airmobile troops would be deployed in battalion *desants*.

Desant troops also conducted small raids without motorised-rifle support against targets like a remote tea-house, a chaikhana, thought to be a rest-stop for the insurgents, or against a target of opportunity like a caravan located by air observers. Here, it was a matter of conducting a *desant* as closely to the objective as secrecy permitted and then moving in as quickly as possible for the attack, followed by an equally quick departure. These kinds of operations required good reconnaissance, detailed planning, excellent timing, and sharp execution (probably based on pre-attack rehearsals). However, the operations most characteristic of the CI force were the ones described below.

Enveloping Detachments

The use of the term '*obkhodiashchii otriad*' (OO) (flanking or enveloping detachment) by the Soviets dates back at least as far as the Great Patriotic War. Military-historical articles describe their use during the war in all of the mountain theatres of war.[11] Since the end of the Second World War, the Soviet concept of the OO has been refined and expanded slightly to the extent that its utility as a tactical formation with a prescribed form of manoeuvre is recommended in any operational zone where tactical movement is restricted due to terrain or environment. Thus, Soviet military literature promotes the use of enveloping detachments first and foremost in the mountains, but also in the desert, tundra, swamp, and jungle.

Briefly, Soviet literature describes the OO as a special tactical formation split off from the main body and sent by a separate route to the rear or flank of the enemy in order to support the advance of the main body, or, to execute a separate mission which is complementary to the mission of the main body. The missions typically assigned to an OO, according to Soviet doctrine, are: conduct of a simultaneous, supporting attack against the enemy's flank or rear as the main body attacks from the front; conduct of a diversionary attack; assumption of a blocking position; capture of an enemy headquarters or nuclear-capable unit; and, seizure and retention of a key objective in the enemy's rear until the main body arrives. Under normal conditions, a reinforced motorised rifle battalion would be designated as an enveloping detachment in a regimental or divisional attack.

Interest in this tactic in Afghanistan was sparked by the realisation that standard attacks against the *mujahedin* rarely succeeded, because the rebels were always able to withdraw through restricted passes and trails into deeper mountain bases. Attempts to pursue directly were met by ambushes, mines, and booby-traps. The Soviets turned to the OO primarily as a means of blocking the withdrawal of *mujahedin* groups which had been identified in a specific location. Secondarily, they used enveloping detachments to conduct simultaneous attacks from one or more unexpected directions. The actual practice of this tactic in Afghanistan closely conformed to the guidelines set down in doctrinal literature.

The main attack against a significant *mujahedin* base would often be given to an MR unit, let us say a reinforced battalion or a regiment, provided that a ground route to the objective suitable for tracked and wheeled vehicles existed. A separate enveloping detachment would then be formed and given the mission of moving to the rear or flank of the *mujahedin* by a separate, covered route, hopefully unguarded because of its difficulty. The route to the objective was selected on the basis of map inspection and then confirmed by personal reconnaissance if feasible.

Normally, an airborne, air assault, or reconnaissance company would be designated at the OO.[12] Platoons were usually too small to block escape routes and a battalion too large to move in secrecy. MR units were rarely given this mission; it was too difficult for them. It appears that enveloping detachments were always reinforced with engineers, grenadiers, mortars, extra reconnaissance and retrans teams, and a dedicated artillery adjustment team. The detachment began its movement before that of the main body because it had to move farther and more secretly, through more difficult terrain, quite often at night. Part of the movement to the objective could be accomplished by vehicle or helicopter, as long as surprise was not forfeited.

The dismounted tactical march could be exhausting. If mines were expected in the area, an engineer recon team would lead the way.[13] Since they were vulnerable at any time to ambush, prudent detachment commanders covered the move by dispatching forward and flank security elements and by leap-frogging observer teams on high ground. The success of the mission depended in the first place on the arrival of the detachment at the objective undiscovered, so all contact with small parties or posts of *mujahedin* were avoided. Retrans teams had to be set out in order to maintain communications with the main body. The artillery adjustment team was responsible, of course, for calling for help if the detachment got into a tough spot along the way.

If the blocking or attack position selected for occupation was close to the objective, detachment commanders endeavoured to arrive at night so as to be hidden in position by dawn. The terrain often required the company to split up to cover all the escape routes and approaches — one platoon on this hill, grenadiers above and behind them, another platoon on an adjacent hill, the mortars with a squad to protect them in a covered depression, and so on. Furthermore, care had to be taken that the detachment could provide itself with all-round observation and security, in case they were approached from the flank and rear. The commander usually worked out the final dispositions on the ground after arrival. The timing of the main attack often depended on a report from the detachment commander that he was in position

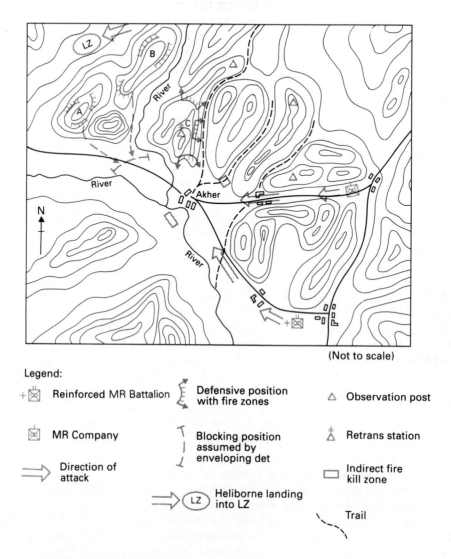

(Not to scale)

Legend:

+⊠ Reinforced MR Battalion   ⦃ Defensive position   △   Observation post
                                  with fire zones

⊠   MR Company   ⊤ Blocking position   ⊼   Retrans station
                             ⌡ assumed by
                             ⌐ enveloping det

⟹   Direction of   Indirect fire
    attack   kill zone

                   ⟹ (LZ) Heliborne landing
                           into LZ
                                                                 Trail

1. Reinforced motorised-rifle battalion attacks on two axes from East and
   Southeast to objective –*mujahedin* village Akher – using mountain roads.
2. Previously, an air assault company has landed on LZ at night
   and moved to defensive positions on hills A, B, C (NW of village).
3. Prior to attack, platoons on hills A and B move to occupy blocking
   position to the west of village. Platoon on hill C remains to
   cover escape route along trail to the north.
4. As the attack begins, pre-planned mortar and artillery fire
   block other possible escape routes.
5. Enveloping detachment is extracted by ground or air after attack.

Figure 8.1 Enveloping Detachment

and prepared. If executed properly, the enveloping detachment could squeeze the insurgents into a trap from which it would be quite hard to escape. The detachment was seldom left in position after dark; after the attack or raid was conducted, the OO moved off either to take up a new position or to be evacuated by its organic vehicles or helicopters.[14]

Clearly, this kind of manoeuvre demanded a high level of skill in planning, reconnaissance and tactical movement. It also demanded competent junior leaders capable of functioning on their own as reconnaissance and security team leaders or as commanders of supporting detachments. Each operation required every detail to be worked out in advance if possible and a whole set of standard procedures had to be established and understood by each member of the company. Training for such an operation would go on for several days before it was actually executed.[15]

When an OO failed to accomplish its mission, it was usually because they were discovered *en route*, perhaps falling prey to an ambush because of a deficiency in reconnaissance. Not infrequently, communications between the separate elements failed or insufficient co-ordination between the main body and the detachment led to unco-ordinated attacks. Some detachment commanders had trouble with land navigation and certain elements, particularly those carrying the heavy weapons, sometimes proved unable to negotiate the most difficult parts of the route. The best units, of course, expected and were able to adjust to changes in timing or march route, but such changes could adversely affect planned support from artillery or aviation. Naturally, a complicated activity like this could also be foiled by mere accident — an inadvertent noise at the wrong time, the unintended discharge of a weapon, or an unlucky contact with hidden *mujahedin* scouts. Successful execution certainly was an indication of good leadership, good planning, and good training.

Ambushes

The ambush did not become a steady feature of Soviet operations in Afghanistan until around 1983, after the CI force had been fully deployed. They were conducted most often as independent operations by reinforced platoons and companies against reliably identified targets. Probably the most common objectives of Soviet ambushes were *mujahedin* arms caravans, but Soviet *desant* units also set ambushes at water sources, river fords, in passes, and randomly along well-used trails, tracks, and roads. Some ambushes started out as combat reconnaissance patrols, which turned into fixed ambushes on the basis of information received during the course of the patrol (by radio or from the unit's own scouts). The Soviets also co-ordinated large ambushes with their major offensives in order to destroy *mujahedin* groups put to flight from the scene of battle. Day and night ambushes were employed, with no clear preference shown in Soviet commentary.

The CI force spent a good deal of time training and preparing for ambushes. The first task for all units was to study enemy operations in order to understand fully the methods and patterns of the local rebel groups. Second, commanders had to study the terrain closely in order to determine feasible, covered approaches and withdrawal routes for possible ambush sites. Frequently, Soviet ambush leaders conducted air reconnaissance of the target area, although some eschewed observation from helicopters as a certain way to attract the attention of the enemy and spoil surprise, upon the achievement of which everything depended.

According to Soviet military journals, their units spent 1–3 days preparing for an ambush. First, an experienced officer was selected as the commander of the ambush group. Next, the ambush group itself was put together with a *desant* platoon or (less often) company as the base. Care was taken not to have too many newly-arrived soldiers in the party since their inexperience might jeopardise the operation.[16] Ambush group commanders almost always received at least grenadier and engineer recon detachments in support, plus one or more extra machine-gun teams; company-sized ambush teams were augmented further with mortar crews and recon teams. In contrast, artillery adjustment teams did not routinely appear in the combat formation. It appears that the ambush group commander himself and his subordinates were charged with being prepared to call for artillery and air support if needed. Commanders then organised the ambush groups into sub-groups (attack, fire support, and recon/observation).

Some commanders used terrain mock-ups to study the ambush site and to orient group leaders on routes to be used, danger areas, tentative dispositions and so on. After a detailed attack order was issued, the ambush group passed through a standardised period of preparation (*Appendix C*). The troops exercised, had one or more meals, check-fired and re-zeroed weapons, drew ammunition, perhaps ran a rehearsal nearby, and rested. Group commanders routinely checked all the crew-served weapons and specialised equipment such as radios, night-vision devices (NVDs), silencers, mines, and rifle-grenades personally. They also spot-checked individual soldiers and their combat loads. At the appointed time, an abbreviated final order was issued and the patrol moved out.[17]

Since the Soviets assumed that they were under constant observation whenever they left their garrison, deployment of the ambush group was designed to deceive the rebels in regard to intent and destination. Several methods were used but the concept was the same. The group loaded on combat vehicles and left the garrison. At some pre-determined point, the patrol dismounted and moved off directly to the ambush site or to an initial rally point. Occasionally they were delivered directly to the ambush site. Meanwhile, the armoured vehicles (if there were any) moved to a designated location, halted, assumed a defensive position, and waited to come to the support of the ambush group if needed. Even if the patrols were deployed by helicopter (making several false insertions before and after the actual drop-off of the men), the unit's combat vehicles would deploy separately to a location in proximity to the ambush site so as to be ready to come up and support.

The group then moved in small, separate echelons to the target area, preceded by 15–30 minutes by a two-man point team of very experienced soldiers, presumably with a radio link with the patrol leader, although this point is not clear. Normally, the leader placed himself well forward in the march order with the attack group. Long approach marches were broken up by periodic rest halts. Every effort was made to avoid any contact with the insurgents *en route*, so rebel OPs were bypassed and small parties allowed to pass undisturbed. If contact could not be avoided, standard procedure was to dispatch the intruders quietly by snipers with silencers.

On arrival at the ambush site, all sub-group leaders performed a personal reconnaissance of the area and the commander made his final dispositions, making sure to provide for: mutual support between sub-groups; clear, intersecting fields

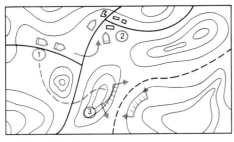

① Reinforced airborne platoon in BMDs dismounts an ambush party.
② Armoured vehicles move on to a village as a false objective and wait.
③ Ambush party moves on foot to position over-looking a trail and occupies high ground on both sides.

1. False objective

① Reconaissance platoon on BMPs simulates a breakdown, dismounts ambush party after dark.
② Ambush party moves on foot to ambush position overlooking trail and village.

2. Simulated breakdown

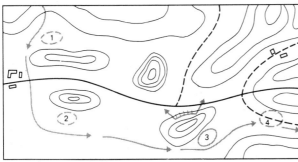

Helicopters make false insertions at ① ② ④

Ambush party dis-embarks at ③ and occupies ambush positions. Vehicles wait nearby to give help if needed.

3. False Heliborne Insertions

Figure 8.2 Methods of Disembarking Ambush Parties

of fire fully covering the kill zone; coverage of all approaches to the ambush position; early warning of the approach of the expected target; cover and concealment of all elements; visual or radio contact between the separate elements; and, unobstructed access to the designated withdrawal routes. Naturally, SOP demanded limits on moving around, talking, smoking, warming fires and use of lights.

When the target entered the killing zone (any forward security elements having been let through), the commander initiated the attack by some known signal. Fire was also lifted on signal or after a pre-designated period of time had passed. Any number of standard actions next took place. The patrol might immediately withdraw without further activity. Or, certain members of the team might be designated to comb through the kill zone quickly to get a count of the enemy dead, to search them for information, or to obtain examples of arms, and equipment. Enemy equipment left undamaged might be assembled in one spot and destroyed. In any event, the patrol did not linger too long in the area for fear that other rebel groups, having overheard the action, might initiate their own pursuit or ambush. Apparently, a common insurgent response was rapidly to mine roads and trails in the area either to catch the ambush group or to delay their link up with their combat vehicles, which would have begun to deploy immediately to a rendezvous as soon as called for by the commander. The ambush group never used the same route out as they had taken in.[18]

Naturally, the ambush groups were also trained for immediate action drills under certain conditions — crossing a danger area, falling into an ambush *en route*, being discovered while in position, or finding themselves outnumbered and pinned down by their target. These units carried smoke grenades to facilitate breaking contact if necessary.

There is some evidence that ambush patrols occasionally stayed out in position for several days and nights waiting for a particular target to pass by — perhaps a large caravan or a group led by a well-known rebel leader whose death was desired. These longer-term ambushes seem to have been based on hard intelligence on rebel movements.[19] They tested the combat discipline of a unit to the full because the soldiers were required to suppress many normal habits and remain under rigid control for so long. Food and water intake had to be regulated since they could not be resupplied in place. Except for *spetsnaz* teams, no ambush teams remained in the combat zone after an ambush took place; they always returned to garrison immediately before mounting another operation.

Overall, there was nothing remarkable in the way in which the Soviet CI force conducted its ambushes. The preparation, planning and tactics closely resembled Western practice. A notable difference in procedure, however, was the apparently infrequent use of remotely-detonated mines to trigger the ambush. In addition, the techniques used do not seem to have changed much from 1982–3, when ambushes first began to be employed, to the end of Soviet occupation in 1989.

Judging by *mujahedin* reports, many Soviet ambushes succeeded.[20] In the early years of the war, the insurgents could move with relative impunity in remote areas. However, ambush tactics forced the rebels to spend much more time and effort on their own security, especially when bringing in arms from across the border. Where Soviet ambush patrols were active, rebel groups had to move slowly and carefully, in full combat order with security patrols clearing the way. The *mujahedin* had a

FIG. 1   The Salang Pass.

FIG. 2 Main road through a high plain in Lowgar Province. Photo by J. Bruce Amstutz.

FIG. 3 Valley of the Kabul River. Photo by J. Bruce Amstutz.

Fig. 4　An Afghan 'kishlak' (village). Photo by J. Bruce Amstutz.

Fig. 5　Small band of *mujahedin* at rest on a mountain slope.

FIG. 6   A guerrilla band at rest, but on guard. Some of the men carry AK-47s, but most are armed with old model rifles.

FIG. 7   Two Soviet POWs under guard.

FIG. 8 *Mujahedin* on a narrow mountain track with a captured Soviet tank.

FIG. 9   2S3 152 mm self-propelled howitzer.

FIG. 10   2S1 122 mm self-propelled howitzer.

FIG. 11   T55 tank. This 35-year-old, Soviet-made tank formed the bulk of the
Afghan Army tank park.

FIG. 12   The BRDM-2, armed with a 14.5 mm machinegun. These
reconnaissance vehicles are the primary armoured transport for Soviet
reconnaissance units.

FIG. 13 Soviet motorized infantrymen prepare to mount three BMP-2s somewhere in the DRA.

FIG. 14 "Desantniki" on the attack during a training exercise in Afghanistan. The vehicle is a BMD-1.

FIG. 15   AN-12 Cub light transport.

FIG. 16   IL-76 Candid heavy transport.

Fig. 17 TU-16 Badger medium bomber. Several days of high-altitude bombing by Badgers normally preceded major Soviet operations.

FIG. 18 SU-25 Frogfoot, the most effective ground-attack aircraft used in Afghanistan, was fully tested during the war. This experience undoubtedly has proved most beneficial to Soviet pilots and aircraft designers.

FIG. 19 SU-24 Fencer, one of the most capable ground-attack aircraft in the Soviet inventory.

Fig. 20   MiG-21 Fishbed, an old fighter which proved to be rather ineffective in the ground-attack role in Afghanistan, although it was used widely.

Fig. 21   MiG-23 Flogger armed for air-to-air combat. MiG-23s were used exclusively for ground attack in Afghanistan.

FIG. 22 *Mujahedin* firing a Soviet 'Dushka' 12.7 mm AA gun.

Fɪɢ. 23   A Soviet Mi-8 Hip door gunner.

FIG. 24   Mi-8 Hip helicopter.

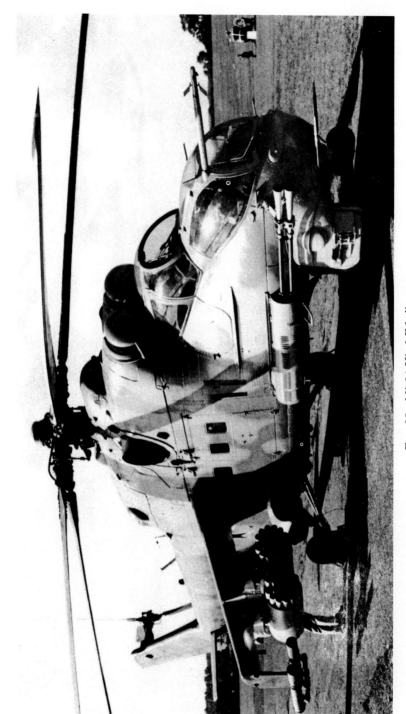

FIG. 25 Mi-24 Hind F helicopter.

healthy respect and fear for these Soviet 'commandos', and they acknowledged their vast superiority over the MR troops.

One especially daring and imaginative ambush of the insurgents took place southeast of Kabul in 1986. A rebel convoy moving into a valley was warned by the local inhabitants that Soviet forces had been in the area recently and had driven the nomads in the valley from their camp. After holding up for a day, the rebel commander moved down and fell into a damaging ambush. The Soviets had hidden out in the nomad tents and were simply waiting for a suitable target to wander into their killing zone. On the other hand, they may well have had advance notice of the imminent arrival of the rebel arms caravan and intentionally chosen this method of ambush.

On the other hand, quite a few Soviet ambush teams were themselves caught in enemy ambushes due to their own carelessness and due to the advantages held by the rebels in intelligence. Given the number of listening ears in the vicinity of Soviet garrisons and the number of unseen, watching eyes in the hills, it was not an easy task to arrive at an ambush site without having been discovered or alerting the rebels somewhere along the way. Asked how he countered the enemy's ambushes, *mujahedin* commander Abdul Haq responded:

> In order to discourage the enemy, we simply ambush the ambushers. With reliable advance information about the time and place of the ambush we took position before the arrival of the enemy. We carried out five operations of this kind, and each time we killed 10 to 15 Russians, all the élite commandos whom the Russians were not very eager to lose, and our action produced its expected results. (The ambushes ceased).[21]

Moreover, the insurgents responded to the new threat by tightening up and strengthening their forward security parties, acknowledged by the Soviets to be very good; in addition, some *mujahedin* groups conducted daily patrols in their areas to prevent surprise.[22] Naturally, as the insurgents became accustomed to Soviet practices, the success rate of the CI force fell, as noted by a Soviet military scholar.[23]

> Ambush activities of Soviet troops on the [*insurgent*] caravan supply routes did not always turn out to be effective. The movement of Soviet units and sub-units to conduct such operations and the occupation of ambush positions often could not be hidden from enemy reconnaissance. But, even if success was achieved in organising the ambush secretly, the success of the operation was still problematical. The *mujahedin* caravans were well protected by a system of march security. These forward reconnaissance patrols triggered the ambushes, and the main elements of the caravan continued forward by detour.

The ambush patrol, more than any other operation, embodied all of the features of a capable counter insurgency force. Successful execution of an ambush was an indication of good training, good leadership, and excellent combat discipline.

Reconnaissance

It would be difficult to overestimate the importance of reconnaissance and observation to the success of Soviet military operations in Afghanistan. Failure to conduct proper reconnaissance almost always led to an unpleasant event.

As a tactical function, reconnaissance in Afghanistan was much more difficult than under normal conditions. To being with, it required more manpower. Whenever a column moved out, all the entry approaches along the march route had to be investigated at depth, in addition to reconnaissance along the march route itself. Moreover, because there were no secure flanks or rear, units were forced to deploy forward, flank, and rear security. As a result, tactical formations moving to make contact with the *mujahedin* usually were augmented with additional recon assets or they detailed them from organic units, that is, a motorised rifle platoon or company was required to form a security element.[24]

Reconnaissance also took more time. The terrain dictated that reconnaissance be performed off-road in most regions since the roads and trails were considered to be unsafe until the adjacent terrain had been cleared. Soviet articles noted that reconnaissance in the DRA often took soldiers into oxygen-poor altitudes and demanded proficiency with mountain climbing gear.[25] Negotiating such terrain on foot rapidly exhausted soldiers who were not in prime physical condition, causing units to proceed slowly and with ever-decreasing vigilance. Apparently, the tasks were so exhausting at times that some Soviet commanders chose not to deploy the necessary assets. Soviet military literature is full of examples of units of all kinds which placed themselves in peril due to deficiencies in reconnaissance.[26]

Soviet units conducted three main forms of reconnaissance in Afghanistan. First, as stated earlier, any movement of a military formation into *mujahedin* territory necessitated the use of reconnaissance elements to provide all-around security. During the major offensives, wherever terrain permitted it, MR columns provided their own mounted security to flanks, front, and rear. Where the terrain became more restrictive, dismounted light elements, usually companies, deployed by helicopter on or near key terrain where they could pre-empt *mujahedin* ambushes and observe enemy movements. These separate recon elements leapfrogged forward as the main body advanced. Once the large MR units began to split up and move off into side valleys, reconnaissance became problematic and often broke down, mainly because the quality of reconnaissance provided by organic MR assets was well below that of the counter-insurgency force. Furthermore, little or no reconnaissance took place after dark.

In addition, it appears that the Soviets seldom used ground reconnaissance to identify routes or objectives prior to major offensives. They seem to have relied almost entirely on air reconnaissance, agents, or other sources to plan these operations. In short, during major ground offensives, reconnaissance was conducted primarily to provide security against ambushes and for early warning, and only secondarily to provide immediate information about the enemy and his dispositions.

The second form of recon operation in Afghanistan was the independent reconnaissance mission, performed exclusively by units of the CI force. Most often these operations took the form of a company-sized combat reconnaissance patrol of *desantniki* to an area or site thought to be occupied by the rebels. The goal was to approach the suspected enemy location secretly in order to conduct a surprise attack. In general, these operations lasted only 24 hours. The company normally moved by vehicle or helicopter to a jump-off site near the objective (but far enough away to avoid detection), after which they approached on foot. These approach marches were carried out most often by day, occasionally at night. Since the designated *desant* unit was acting on its own, it was always reinforced with engineers, mortars, grenadiers, an artillery adjustment team, and an *avianovodchik*, i.e. a ground forward air controller (FAC).

The type of movement practised by these company combat reconnaissance patrols resembled the American tactic of travelling or bounding overwatch. The commander usually divided the company into separate reinforced platoons which moved simultaneously or by sequential bounds along parallel, off-road routes, from one covered position to the next, so that continuous observation and mutual support were possible. Each leading platoon sent ahead a two-man point of its most experienced members. The point team members carried only their weapons and ammunition (no packs) in order to enhance their quick, unencumbered movement. At night, the company moved as a unit in short bounds. After a movement of 2–300 metres, the entire unit stopped, then listened and watched (using NVDs), for any signs of the enemy.[27]

If accidental contact were made *en route*, the commander manoeuvred his unit and took the necessary decisions, as dictated by the situation. Of course, any accidental contact stood a fair chance of eliminating Soviet surprise with respect to the primary objective. However, if the rebel base or objective, perhaps a guarded cache, were located without detection, the commander determined his final plan on the spot and executed the attack. Once the mission was deemed completed or aborted for some reason, the company moved off by a different route to link up with its vehicles or with a transport helicopter unit at the pre-planned point, thence back to garrison and an after-operation critique.

The third form of recon operation was the long range patrol, which differed from the combat reconnaissance patrol mainly in that the long range patrol usually avoided all contact and all combat with the enemy and was smaller in size. Since the Soviet press has not addressed these operations openly, it is probable that these patrols were conducted almost exclusively by *spetsnaz* teams. Deployed in small groups by helicopter, or perhaps sneaking into *mujahedin* territory disguised as shepherds or natives, the long-range patrol sought to identify targets for attack by air, artillery, or ground raids, targets such as *mujahedin* hideouts, caches, caravans, rest-stops, and the like. It has been reported that they also attempted to capture prisoners for intelligence and to plant mines along tracks used by the *mujahedin*. The patrols seem to have run for 2–4 days before they were extracted.[28] Naturally, they had to carry special communications equipment in order to report their information.

Reconnaissance patrols outside temporary defensive positions or from fixed installations and garrisons were not commonly practised by either Soviet CI or MR units, particularly after dark. Once the sun had set, *mujahedin* groups could venture quite close to outer defensive boundaries of such positions without fear of meeting a Soviet patrol. Occasionally, a mounted patrol would burst out during the day to conduct a quick sweep of the area or to strike against a close-in threat, but such patrols were ineffective. Rather than using ground patrols in these areas, Soviet commanders resorted to helicopter reconnaissance as a faster and safer means of keeping tabs on the area around a static position. Air reconnaissance is discussed in more detail in Chapter 9.

The tactical environment in Afghanistan also required that more observation posts (OP) be put out in both static and dynamic situations. Because of the broken nature of the terrain, observers often could not see valley or canyon floors from peaks or ridges; OPs had to be distributed down the slopes of mountains. Distribution of OPs in depth and height permitted a Soviet commander to avoid the simultaneous loss of all his OPs, as well as complete loss of observation due to fog or clouds. All Soviet blocking and ambush positions included a robust network of OPs and all troops were supposed to be trained for use as observers.

Soviet sources stress that a good deal of training was necessary to teach Soviet soldiers how to: estimate ranges in the mountains; detect artificial structures; identify danger zones; identify enemy personnel and equipment; and, use optical devices. Perhaps the most important training objective was to convince soldiers to accept the responsibility for constant observation and vigilance. This is a key standing requirement for successful operations against guerrillas, but it is not easy to inculcate the posture of constant vigilance among young troops eager for a bit of a rest. Soviet troops were not exceptions to this rule.[29]

It is interesting that Soviet military literature stresses the use of 'two-sided' training exercises as a means of developing skills in observation and reconnaissance. Apparently, *desant* units regularly ran training patrols against each other in games of hide-and-seek, or through areas specifically set up to test the ability of the units to identify enemy movement and positions. While such exercises are not unusual in the West, they may have been an innovation in Afghanistan, introduced to develop a needed tactical skill. Within the CI force, the Soviets also emphasised cross-training of the *razvedchikis*. Each trooper used in this role was supposed to be minimally qualified as a sapper (for mine-clearing), RTO, driver, and medic. It is not clear to what extent this objective was achieved.

A final assessment of Soviet reconnaissance in Afghanistan must take note of the fact that Soviet units were constantly taken by surprise while on the march and while in occupation of static positions. Many an article in the Soviet press lauding the performance of a Soviet unit or commander in the DRA begins with a description of a tactical scenario wherein a unit has been ambushed or trapped by the *mujahedin*. Numerous reports from rebel groups describe the ease with which they were able to approach Soviet field bivouacs or to avoid Soviet security elements, slipping in behind them after they had passed. One is struck by the fact that Soviet MR soldiers moving through the countryside simply took it for granted that they would be ambushed at some point in time during the tactical march. Certainly, motorised rifle units never mastered this skill and remained continuously vulnerable to surprise by the rebels. It is also clear that the *desant* units suffered through a steep learning curve in this area. Many tactical setbacks in the field took place before the CI force developed the teamwork and fieldcraft necessary to insure their security during combat operations.

Tactical Defence

The Soviets openly acknowledge that mountain terrain is better suited tactically to the defence (a conclusion also drawn by Clausewitz). In the DRA, Soviet CI units occupied the hasty defence under various conditions: during any lengthy halt in movement; when assuming a night defensive position; when occupying a blocking position; during pre-emptive occupation of dominating terrain; and, when caught in a surprise attack or ambush. These defensive positions necessarily had to be organised on a 360 degree basis, since the units normally did not have protected flanks. The defence was multi-layered with primary and supplementary firing positions located at varied heights and depths. Soviet commentary noted that intersecting fires were essential for mutual protection and all dead spaces needed to be covered by observation, indirect fires, or mines. Defensive plans for blocking positions usually also included a capability for night illumination by artillery, mortars, or airdropped flares.

Soviet units in Afghanistan also learned that they must provide for early warning in the defence, a function fulfilled by the (infrequent) use of small patrols, listening posts, dogs, signal devices, minefields, and booby traps. It has not been reported, however, that the Soviet Army used remote sensors for early warning such as were used by the United States Army in Vietnam.

In closing, let it be noted that units of the CI force were also used as quick reaction forces for: pilot rescue, immediate pursuit of guerrilla rocket and mortar parties; tracking down and elimination of rebel Stinger teams; and (rarely) dismounted patrols in the vicinity of sensitive installations to prevent surprise ground attacks by the rebels.

CHAPTER 9

The Air War

THE Soviet forces initially introduced into Afghanistan included only a small permanent air component — 20 or so helicopters and a few squadrons of fighters and fighter-bombers. Paralleling the experience of Western powers in their struggles against insurgencies since the end of the Second World War, the Soviet Army soon discovered that air power was one of the best means for carrying the war to the guerrillas in their mountain sanctuaries. By the end of the summer of 1980, the air component had been increased by several multiples and would keep increasing for several years. By 1981, practically all Soviet ground operations in Afghanistan were supported by the Air Force, which in the Soviet system includes rotary- and fixed-wing aircraft and units.

For a number of reasons, it is not easy to determine the exact number of Soviet air regiments and independent squadrons permanently maintained in Afghanistan during the war. First, a great many aircraft used in the war were actually based in the Soviet Union, including virtually all the fixed-wing transports and bombers. Second, units were frequently moved from one part of the country to another and were rotated in and out of the country every year. In addition, temporary deployments of some transports and the more advanced aircraft occurred. Thus, from year to year, it is possible to find widely varying estimates of Soviet air strength, ranging from a low of less than 300 helicopters and 150 fixed-wing to highs of 6–900 helicopters and as many as 350 fixed-wing.[1] Only the Soviets would know the exact figures, but a reasonable estimate of Soviet air strength, based on open sources, during the middle years of the war, is provided below.

Table 9.1

Soviet Air Strength in Afghanistan

Helicopters : 200–250 Mi-24 Hinds
150–200 Mi-8/Mi-17 Hips
150 Mi-2 Hoplites, Mi-4 Hounds,
Mi-6 Hooks, and Mi-26 Halos

Approximate Total : 5–600 helicopters

Fixed-Wing : 75–100 MiG-21 Fishbeds
100–125 SU-17 Fitters
30 Su-25 Frogfoots
30–50 MiG 23/27 Floggers
6–12 MiG 25 Foxbats
small number of AN-12 Cub and AN-26 Curl transports

Approximate Total: 250–300 fixed-wing

In addition to the aircraft named above, the Soviets also employed AN-22 Cock, IL–76 Candid, AN-26 Curl, AN-12 Cub transports and TU-16 Badger and SU-24 Fencer bombers which remained based in the Soviet Union at Termez, Kushka, Mary and other locations.

Soviet construction engineers, employing Afghan labourers, carried out enormous airfield construction programmes in order to accommodate these large numbers of aircraft. All the existing airports and airfields were upgraded and lengthened; several new ones were built from scratch. The most important airbases from an operational point of view were Bagram, Kabul, Shindand, Kandahar (two airfields), Farah, Jalalabad, and Mazar-i-Sharif (the main training base for the DRA Air Force).

The organisation of the air forces used during the war broadly conformed to Soviet doctrine. The air arm remained subordinate to the ground command, 40th Army Headquarters in Kabul, where a senior air force staff officer and staff section existed, but the main operational headquarters and primary logistical facilities were located in Termez. The Soviet command directed all air force operations, including those of the DRA Air Force. Fixed-wing operations remained centralised under the direction of 40th Army Headquarters, although there are some indications that regional ground commands (division headquarters) may have been delegated authority to independently plan and direct operations of the fighters and fighter-bombers in their areas. Certainly this appears to have been true for some of the smaller periodic, regional offensives employing MR units.

Helicopter operations were far more decentralised, a feature which is fully reflective of the general trend begun in the 70s to integrate helicopter units more completely into combined arms operations at low levels. In Afghanistan, decentralisation of the command and control of helicopter assets went much further than what is depicted in conventional Soviet doctrine. The key innovation here was the direct and continuing association of specific helicopter units with specific manoeuvre units, such as the independent brigades and regiments, to the extent of full operational command. The goal was to increase responsiveness, co-ordination, and integration. Of course, control of helicopter operations was often re-centralised during the large periodic offensives because these operations brought together large numbers of MR units and CI troops in one integrated plan, using hundreds of helicopters.

It would be difficult to overestimate the significance of the contribution of Soviet airpower to the prosecution of the war. The discussion below of the air war takes a compartmentalised approach which may seem artificial, but which is actually representative structurally of the manner in which the air forces were employed. Fixed-wing and rotary-wing operations, generally, were not co-ordinated closely. The fixed-wing component carried out most of the missions associated with the overall CI strategy of destruction of Afghan society and it performed general purpose, planned bombings and strikes. The helicopter arm was linked more intimately with tactical ground operations.

Fixed Wing Operations

Transport Aviation

Transport aviation functioned as an important conduit of logistical support to the

40th Army by means of regular scheduled flights from the Soviet Union into the major airbases of each region. Transport aircraft supplied isolated outposts and surrounded garrisons by airdrop. In addition, all personnel movements (replacements) into and out of the country were by air.

The Soviets also used transport aircraft for special functions. AN-12 Cubs and AN-26 Curls conducted aerial reconnaissance to identify suitable targets for airstrikes. A Rhodesian journalist reported in 1984 that small transports flew daily recon sorties out of Kabul during the morning, circled over the nearby mountains, and ceased at noon.[2] These aircraft also patrolled convoy routes and areas of expected *mujahedin* movements, alerting ground and air strike forces of suitable targets. During large operations, Cubs and IL-76 Candids also served as airborne command posts. However, the appearance of these aircraft over the battlefield constituted early warning of an impending airstrike, thus permitting the rebels time to take evasive action.

Different models providing battlefield illumination, using varying flare configurations which typically lit up an area of several square kilometres for up to 10 minutes.[3] The IL-76 airborne early warning and radar aircraft (Mainstay) is also said to have been tested in Afghanistan to monitor operations of the Pakistani Air Force along the borders.[4]

Bombers

The TU-16 Badger medium bomber and SU-24 Fencer all-weather, light bomber (an F-111 imitation in many respects) made almost daily appearances in Afghan skies from their bases in the Soviet Union. Bombers fulfilled two main roles: support of the overall CI strategy through the destruction of Afghan society, and, general-purpose, planned bombing in support of periodic offensives. In the first role, the bombers delivered hundreds of thousands of bombs from high-altitude against rural villages and agricultural targets:

> I witnessed a Soviet bombing attack on Afghan settlements in the Andarab valley, about halfway between Kabul and the Soviet border, from a nearby mountain at an elevation of 16,000 ft. above sea level. The attack continued for more than half an hour and even with clear skies and the good visibility afforded by high altitude, none of our party was able to see the attacking aircraft.
> An earlier high-altitude attack on Afghan villages in the area killed more than 700 people, the Afghans reported. They identified the aircraft as SU-24s, operating out of Termez.[5]

Bombing targets were often situated well away from the main roads and were selected on the basis of an analysis of the level of guerrilla activity in the area and the sources of food production. The Soviets also bombed suspected rebel assembly areas (for ambush) near main highways. Reprisal bombings against villages in the vicinity of rebel attacks were frequent. Such reprisal took place on a huge scale whenever the rebels crossed into Soviet territory on their raids. As a result of this indiscriminate approach, Soviet bombings produced huge numbers of civilian casualties and succeeded in causing the evacuation of entire valleys because of the destruction of the agro-economic system. The bombers carried general purpose bombs most of the time; other munitions used were fuel-air explosives, incendiary, and (infrequently) chemical bombs (by fighter-bombers). The use of bombers in the fashion described above — a brutal, indiscriminate, genocidal approach — clearly reflected Soviet frustration with their inability to identify, locate, and pin down the elusive rebels.

Chapter 2 has already noted how substantial bombing support was provided in support of the major, periodic offensives. High-altitude 'carpet' bombing saturated the objective area for days in preparation for the advance of ground forces. Once the ground columns entered the region, bombers performed barrier and denial operations to restrict the movement of the rebels. Late in the war, the Soviets even employed the modern intermediate-range Backfire bomber in the high-altitude bombing role.

Night bombing was not conducted during the war in any significant sense. Given the lack of a capability of the rebels to threaten the bombers during the day, there does not appear to have been any reason to bomb at night, unless the goal was to catch persons asleep in their village homes.

Ground Attack/Close Air Support

The fixed-wing aircraft used most often in the DRA in low-level tactical support were the MiG-21 Fishbed and the SU-17 Fitter, both quite old models ill-suited for operations in Afghanistan because of their flight performance and poor accuracy against point targets. The more accurate MiG 23/27 Flogger arrived in country in 1980, and the all-weather, variable geometry SU-24 made its appearance in 1982. (The SU-24, a versatile aircraft, conducted independent bombing operations with the TU-16, it also was used in a ground strike role in close support of manoeuvre units.) Both these models increased the lethality of Soviet air attacks. However, the most lethal attack aircraft in the DRA was the SU-25 Frogfoot.

The Frogfoot was designed in the mid 1970s; it seems to be a copy of the Northrop A-9, an American attack jet not purchased by the US Air Force. The SU-25 can carry from 8–10,000 pounds of ordnance on 8–10 external pylons. It is protected by titanium alloy armour and is specially strengthened around the cockpit against ground fire.[6]

Two SU-25s (Frogfeet?) were sent to Afghanistan in 1980 for testing, followed by six more in early 1981. The first 12-aircraft squadron deployed to Bagram Airbase by the end of the year, with a second squadron moving to Shindand in 1982.[7] In Afghanistan, the aircraft was nicknamed 'gratch', i.e. the rook. The *mujahedin* greatly feared the 'rook'. It repeatedly proved itself to be very accurate, even at considerable ranges from its targets.

Munitions employed by Soviet attack aircraft included 30-mm cannon, 57- and 80-mm unguided rockets, general-purpose bombs up to 500 kg, fuel-air explosives, cluster bombs (deployed on drogue chutes for dispersal, which sometimes failed to operate), as well as white phosphorus, incendiary, AP mines, and chemical bombs.

Attack aircraft were used most often for planned strikes against clearly identified targets, while helicopters performed the majority of on-call strikes. Jets also prepared the objective area for large, raiding helicopter *desants*.

Against defended positions, the jets operated in pairs, coming in on slightly different approaches, with the lead jet making two runs. As the lead jet conducted the initial strike, the second airplane conducted distracting manoeuvres at higher altitude to draw attention of any AA weapons in the area and/or it dropped protective flares. If the enemy AA positions were well located, the second jet might attack them directly. The leading jet completed the attack with a second run, generally with unguided missiles, then both aircraft departed, dispensing flares as they climbed away.[8] The size and durability of the target and the nature of the terrain determined how many sorties were flown on any given mission. An airborne forward air controller (FAC) in an Mi-4 Hound helo often directed the attack. The FAC was also able to advise the attack aircraft on the best approaches and munitions to use. Still, a fly-through was sometimes required to get properly lined up. Of course, fly-bys forfeited surprise and gave the rebels the chance to take cover.[9]

Analysis of Soviet military literature reveals that sortie leaders were most concerned about four basic difficulties in their ground attack missions, all connected with complications introduced mainly by terrain: navigation to the target area, selection of the best approach for the attack, accurate location of the target, and selection of the most suitable munitions. Pilots attempted to work out all these questions in the map-room before taking off, but, of course, it was not always possible. Post-sortie critiques were held to improve individual and unit performances. Fluctuating weather conditions and the absence of a radio-beacon-grid (for ground control and vectoring) also complicated their operations.

Non-Soviet observers have commented that in the early years of the war, jet pilots seemed unduly cautious. One oft-quoted source noted how fighter-bombers released their bombs from 5,000 feet and fired their rockets from too great a distance.[10] Moreover, many bombs failed to detonate. By 1983–84 however, these errors were less evident. Soviet pilots overcame their fears and inexperience; they developed effective evasive and deceptive techniques which increased their confidence in their ability to close in and strike targets without damage. It took the appearance of the Stinger in 1986 to throw them back on their heels and force a re-evaluation of their attack tactics. (See below)

Helicopter Operations

The employment of helicopters was the most dynamic and effective feature of Soviet tactical operations in Afghanistan. Given the decentralisation of operations and the great expanse of largely inaccessible territory, it would have been impossible for the Soviets to maintain pressure on the *mujahedin* and to defend and supply their dispersed garrisons without the helicopter. Helicopters provided mobility of combat power (which the insurgents in no way could match), enhanced surprise, reduced rebel reaction time, enabled Soviet forces to respond to rebel threats very quickly, and provided the Soviets with their most effective means of exercising initiative through direct action. Moreover, the low air defence threat enabled the Soviet command to test its pilots and machines thoroughly and it allowed them to engage in a great deal of (relatively) danger-free tactical trial and error. In short, the experience and knowledge of helicopter performance and tactical employment gained in Afghanistan were undoubtedly the most significant military benefits achieved by the Soviets during the war.

Soviet helicopter operations fell into six main categories: logistical support, reconnaissance, convoy security, evacuation, tactical lift, and fire support. The majority of sorties flown in the DRA, according to the Soviets, was for logistical support, i.e. the transport of fuel, food, ammunition, personnel, mail and supplies to fixed garrisons and outposts. Soviet press accounts put great stock in the number of sorties flown to deliver needed supplies of food, medicine, clothing, fuel, and building materials to the suffering villagers. It is quite clear that many outposts were supported for months at a time solely via the '*vozdushnyi most*', or air bridge. In 1983, the garrisons at Bamiyan, Ghazni, Gardez, and Khost — all quite large — were cut off by the *mujahedin* and supported solely by helicopter and airdrops. Some remote outposts were, in fact, established with no other link to the outside world other than their radio and fortnightly supply run.

The Soviet Air Force used helicopters widely in reconnaissance operations: to keep the areas surrounding fixed garrisons and facilities clear of *mujahedin*; to drop flares at night for illumination; to patrol along the border and identify infiltrations and caravans for attack; to identify targets for other means of attack; and to reconnoitre routes used by manoeuvre forces and Soviet convoys. In the latter role, the air reconnaissance operated well in advance of the ground convoy. In some cases, route reconnaissance was conducted by attack; in others, light helicopters performed the mission but were accompanied by attack helicopters or called for support from attack helicopters standing by at readiness. Mi-4 and Mi-8 models were probably used most widely for reconnaissance.

Many of the missions in the roles of direct fire support and tactical lift have already been cited earlier: insertion and evacuation of ground units (including elements mounted in light armoured vehicles); conduct of air-strikes, sometimes in co-ordination with fixed-wing aircraft; insertion and re-positioning of ambush groups; conduct of planned fires in support of air assaults and raids; on-call fires in support of threatened Soviet and DRA forces; transport of enveloping detachments; reinforcement of units in contact; and adjustment of artillery and mortar fires. One interesting tactical innovation here was the use of helicopters to reinforce garrisons and outposts besieged by the *mujahedin*. Instead of breaking the siege from the outside, helicopters often lifted reinforcements directly into the garrison. These reinforcements then attacked and broke the siege from the inside out.[11] Khost was reinforced in such a way with 3,000 troops in 1983 and again in 1987 with 6,000 Soviet and 2,000 DRA troops.[12]

The Mi-24 Hind and the Mi-8 Hip were the workhorses of the rotary-wing force. All models of the Hind were observed in the DRA: Afghan pilots flew the older, more vulnerable A and B models, while the Soviets retained the D, E, and (new) F models. The Hind's heavy titanium armour and bullet-proof glass made it almost impervious to machine-gun fire and its heavy armament (12.7-mm four-barrel machine-gun or 23- or 30-mm cannon, 32- or 57-mm rockets, and two pylons for AT missiles or bombs) presented a formidable threat to point and area targets. In the early years of the war, the sighting of a Hind was enough to throw many *mujahedin* groups into sheer panic. The Hind can also carry 8–10 troops in the rear cabin. Some Hinds carried a high-powered searchlight mounted on a pylon for night operations.

The large, unarmoured Hip was yet more heavily armed than the Hind. Capable of carrying 28 troops or almost 9,000 pounds of cargo, the Hip packs 192 57-mm rockets or four 250-kg bombs, four AT missiles, and has a 12.7-mm, four-barrel nose gun. The ability of the Hip to provide its own fire support meant that it could operate without Hinds if necessary.[13] In Afghanistan, Hips were also fitted with door light machine-guns for flank protection and self-defence while on the ground. On the other hand, defecting Afghan pilots have criticised the Hip's non-crash-worthy exposed fuel system and its poor performance at hot, high altitudes, especially with respect to trim control. Moreover, the 1,500-hour rotor life and the lack of a capability for quick engine changes meant that the aircraft was too frequently out of service for maintenance. The main complaints about the Hip's flying characteristics were that it was not designed for nap-of-the-earth flying, which it often had to perform to elude missiles, leading to the occasional crash, and that it was underpowered for some of the missions and manoeuvres which it had to perform.[14]

The Hinds (and SU-25s) functioned much like the *shturmovik* attack aircraft of the Second World War. Operating in pairs, Hind pilots used several techniques to attack point targets (identified to them by FACs or by independent search). Depending on the terrain, the helicopter might make a steep, diving attack, or, use a long, low run-in (7–8 kilometres), popping up to engage the target at the maximum range of its weapons systems. If several aircraft attacked the target, each Hind would make its pass, breaking away sharply while the next charged in, repeating this circular or wagon-wheel pattern for as long as necessary. Of course, if a missile threat was suspected, the Hinds would dispense flares as would, perhaps, the air FAC directing the attack.[15]

Attack helicopters and jet aircraft sometimes worked together against large, hardened targets (a major *mujahedin* base, for example) and in major *desant* raids. In these instances, the SU-25, MiG 23/27 Floggers, and SU-24 Fencers conducted the initial strike. Up to eight aircraft in four sorties of two aircraft each were known to have been used in this manner. The helicopter assault followed next, supported throughout by Hind gunships or the gunship version of the Hip.[16]

Helicopter and Desant Tactics

Desant tactics loosely resembled US practice in Vietnam. One helicopter group, composed of Hinds or Hips or both, prepared the LZ and surrounding area, then provided continuous coverage while the second group, the assault echelon, landed the *desant* force. A third helicopter circled high overhead as the command and control ship. Sometimes the LZs were so small that only one aircraft could land at a time, or, every so often the aircraft could not even touch down; troops had to leap down carefully.

Some Soviet reports indicate that air assaults sometimes suffered from inadequate co-ordination. Too often, misunderstandings arose because the details of the mission were insufficiently planned beforehand. One pilot described how, on several missions, the details of the assault operation were not worked out until the *desant* force was being picked up.[17] Other sources simply noted that the aviation-infantry co-ordinating link needed to be strengthened. There is no evidence in the literature on the war that helicopter units conducted air mission briefings for the *desant* force commander and his subordinates as a matter of routine, as is done in the United States Army. If no such formal mechanism exists in the Soviet Army, one should be developed.

During the Second World War, *shturmovik* pilots sometimes operated as 'free hunters', i.e. single and paired aircraft sent into the enemy rear to discover and attack targets of opportunity.[18] A similar practice was observed in Afghanistan, but on a small scale and always with pairs of helicopters. The pairs varied. A pair might be Hind-Hind, Hind-Hound, or Hind-Hip. One aircraft would perform reconnaissance, attempting also to draw fire, while the Hind loitered and followed from a covered flight path, ready to attack the exposed rebel gunners. The tactic is reminiscent of the American 'pink team' combination (a Cobra attack helicopter with a light observation helicopter), which had the same purpose. Rebel caravans commonly fell victim to these hunter teams.

Forward Air Controllers (FAC)

One area in which the Soviet Air Force obtained a tremendous amount of valuable experience was the use of airborne and ground FACs (*avianovodchiki*) through which manoeuvre units received on-call close support. Soviet Army units used FACs far more often than the frequency envisioned in their conventional doctrine (except by forward detachments and mobile groups). Ground FACs accompanied convoys and MR units and occasionally flew in with the CI force on their deep (mounted) raids. However, they rarely accompanied DRA forces.

Ground FACs often functioned as low as battalion level for the MR forces and occasionally down to company level for the independent operations of the CI force. But all ground FACs remained mounted, apparently because the communications equipment required a vehicle for transport and power. No reports of dismounted FACs have surfaced.

Their mission, obviously, was to call for close air support either from helicopters or fixed-wing aircraft against unplanned targets and rebel threats to the unit which they were supporting. Soviet literature on the subject stresses that FACs should be experienced pilots (either helicopter or fixed-wing), although it is clear that some non-flyers, perhaps ex-pilots (or medically grounded pilots) performed this function.[19] It was vital that the FAC should know several different methods of directing aircraft on to targets and be proficient in describing the best approaches to be used as well as munitions. FACs were also charged with keeping supporting aircraft informed about weather conditions and the the enemy AA situation.

Other skills cited as necessary to the ground FAC were:

▶ The ability to direct strikes simultaneously against more than one target.
▶ The ability to pick the best position in the march column where he could see probable targets and observe supporting aircraft.
▶ Proficiency in map reading, navigation, and terrain recognition.
▶ Proficiency in operating the radios and maintaining uninterrupted communications.
▶ Proficiency in the use of many different weapons for self-defence.
▶ The ability to use pyrotechnics and rockets.

FACs were strongly encouraged to get deeply involved in the planning stage of all operations. Having FACs alongside them more or less permanently was a new experience for manoeuvre commanders. They grew to value them highly. Supposedly, ground commanders tried to 'adopt' the FACs with whom they liked to operate and in whom they had confidence.[20] The *avianovodchiki* acquired the nickname '*mayak*', meaning beacon, ostensibly because they were the 'beacon' used to call in air support, or perhaps they actually employed some kind of homing beacon. Ground commanders are said to have adopted a new rule of combat — 'never take your eye off your '*mayak*'!'[21] Overall, the performance of ground FACs and their integration into the manoeuvre system seem to have been one of the major successes of the war.

In contrast, it appears that very few MR commanders developed the know-how to obtain close air support from either helicopter or jet units on their own, without the aid of a FAC. FACs were even used to call in medevac helicopters. Even the officer component of the CI force did not acquire this skill widely. It may well be that the strict compartmentalisation of Soviet combat activity and responsibility worked against crossing such functional boundaries. In any event, obtaining on-call support was very much dependent on the presence of a FAC.

Airborne FACs supported assault landings; directed planned air strikes by helicopters and attack jets; participated in on-call missions to assist units trapped in ambushes; and played the role of the reconnaissance helicopter in the free hunter team. The Mi-4 Hound, fitted with marking rockets, most often carried the airborne FAC, whether he was directing fixed-wing or rotary wing strikes, but FACs also utilised Hinds and Hips. Overall, airborne FACs and attack pilots worked quite well together in the DRA, developing good timing and teamwork in the conduct of air strikes.

Medical Evacuation and Rescue

The Soviet Air Force in Afghanistan expended extraordinary efforts to rescue Soviet wounded and dead, particularly downed pilots. Several Soviet articles recount how such operations might go on for long hours, even days.[22] The Soviets were even known to negotiate with the rebels for the return of the bodies of Soviet troops killed in action. One reason for this intense interest in recovering the dead was that the rebels often mutilated the bodies of their enemies, particularly pilots and crewmen.

A typical rescue team into a hostile zone comprised four aircraft in some combination of Hinds and Hips, with at least two Hips present. The Hinds were charged with suppression of the enemy, the Hips with the actual pick-up once the persons in danger had been located. (This was the time when the door gun was manned for use — during loading.) When the situation demanded it, MR units and *desant* groups participated in the search and rescue.[23] Response times seem to have been reasonably good.

Rescue teams like this were also dispatched to pick up enveloping detachments, ambush units, and recon groups which had got into a tight spot or were on the run. In a pinch, of course, any helicopter might be used for medevac or rescue. It seems that evacuation missions into non-danger zones were performed by single helicopters. The Soviets also responded to Afghan calls for help, but the response times here could be much longer. In general, the Soviet command took care not to sacrifice too many of its machines and pilots in the rescue of DRA troops.

All pilots in Afghanistan carried homing beacons and survival kits to facilitate their discovery by search parties. The rebels opposed such rescues vigorously. They were known to use captured radio beacons to confuse the search helicopters and lure them into ambushes. Soviet pilots clearly took heart from the assurance that if they were shot down, their comrades would mount immediate rescue operations to save them. However, the likelihood of their recovery dipped sharply in the last year of the war when helicopter units were withdrawn at such a rate that few were available to do medevac.

Mujahedin Air Defences

During the first six to seven years of the war, the *mujahedin* remained extremely vulnerable to Soviet airpower because of their poor capability for air defence. Through 1983, their primary means of defence were the various models of heavy machine-guns captured from the occupation forces and obtained from China. The Hinds proved almost invulnerable to these weapons owing to their heavy armour, while the fleet jets were quite difficult to hit.

In 1983, the insurgents began to receive SA-7 missiles from various sources (see Chapter 4). Although many of these missiles malfunctioned or were mishandled by their users, their effects were felt immediately.[24] For a while, Soviet pilots responded by flying much more defensively, to include the release of their ordnance at excessive distances from the target. After a few months, the Soviets responded more efficiently to the new threat by fitting most aircraft with flare-emitting devices to confuse the heat-seeking head of the missile. Thereafter, air attacks were accompanied by the discharge of these flares on attack runs and *desants*.

Transport aircraft taking off and landing at airbases were protected in the same fashion. Quite often a separate aircraft dispensed flares in order to protect the slow-moving transports. Whenever a VIP flew in or out of Kabul, the sky resembled a veritable display of fireworks from the defensive flares fired to divert any SA-7 launches. The tactic generally proved effective, although heavy personnel losses occurred from time to time when a missile got through and destroyed a troop-laden Mi-8, IL-76, or AN model transport. An AN-22 Cock, for example, was shot down by an SA-7 missile in October, 1984, possibly with over 200 Soviet troops on board.

The Soviets also mounted infra-red beacons on some helicopters above the hot parts of the aircraft to induce the missile to pass over the aircraft. A third response was the installation of protective boxes to shield the exhaust of helicopter engines. The boxes contained an air intake which mixed cool air with the hot exhaust gases and so reduced the thermal signature.[25]

The *mujahedin* learned to set up air ambushes near airbases, along known flying routes, and in the path of obvious approaches to their bases. These 'helo hunters' moved rapidly by truck or motorcycle to and from their ambush site. Several techniques were used to draw in the victim. For example, the insurgents organised ground ambushes for the express purpose of eliciting a response from Soviet air forces. The hunter team was set up on carefully selected ground and engaged the aircraft as they appeared.

Another technique was to set up several different AA positions, with one as a decoy. When the aircraft appeared, the decoy position, normally a heavy machine gun, began to fire, causing the helicopter to move away from it or to bear in for an attack. At that time, a hidden missile team or perhaps another machine-gun team would engage the enemy aircraft from close range from its hidden position.

Soviet pilots reacted to missile fire by flying very low to the ground (nap-of-the-earth). Since the missiles would not operate properly if fired at a target below their launch position, the insurgents responded by using RPGs against the low-flying aircraft. It is not known how effective this technique was, but several different sources report that at least a few helicopters were destroyed in this fashion.[26]

The anti-aircraft threat from the rebels changed abruptly in 1986. In the summer of that year, the *mujahedin* started to receive Oerlikon 20-mm AA automatic cannons. British model Blowpipe missiles made their appearance in August, 1986. The Blowpipe is a command-guidance missile which depends on the operator manipulating a control board/joystick to guide the missile on to the target. Thus, it was not susceptible to the use of flares. On the other hand, it required a high level of training by the operator in order for it to be effective. Many guerrilla gunners failed to achieve the necessary proficiency.

The Turning Point

The real breakthrough in rebel air defence came with the arrival of US-made Stinger missiles. For years, the United States authorities resisted suggestions to send Stingers to the *mujahedin* for fear that they might be sold or diverted to Middle East terrorists. Moreover, missiles captured by the Soviets would undoubtedly be exploited technologically and tactically. However, in view of the Soviet escalation of the war during 1985–86 and what seemed to be a serious decline in rebel resilience, the United States Department of Defence approved the missile's release.

The *mujahedin* preferred the Stinger above all other AA mans for several reasons. In the first place, it is easy to operate; an apt student can be trained in under one month, whereas the Blowpipe takes twice as long. Second, it is a fire-and-forget weapon, allowing the gunner to seek cover after its launch. Third, it is much faster and has a greater range than the SA-7. Fourth, unlike the tail-chasing SA-7, the Stinger can attack an aircraft from any direction. Finally, the Stinger acquires its targets by two means: an infra-red heat seeker and an ultra-violet lock-on, the combination of which enables the missile to defeat counter-measures like flares.

The appearance of the missile jolted the Soviets severely and created unprecedentedly high losses, estimated to be as high as one aircraft a day during the initial 90 days of its use.[27] Similar loss rates were also noted during the summer of 1987.[28] A US Army report in 1989 noted that the rebel gunners achieved hits in 79 per cent of their launches (the anticipated rate based on testing was 77 per cent).[29] There are good reasons to be sceptical of this figure, but the fact remains that Soviet aircraft suddenly began falling out of the sky more often than ever before. The relatively friendly skies of Afghanistan turned overnight into a major danger zone.

When the new missile proved to be immune to flares and evasive manoeuvres, the Soviet helicopter pilots responded tactically by taking to the protection of the ground while jet pilots moved up to higher, safer altitudes. They also began to conduct air operations at irregular hours. They increased the use of artillery and rockets to provide support previously provided in large measure by aircraft. Another response may have been the installation of unspecified jamming and blast-protection devices.[30] Finally, the Soviet Army intensified its efforts to track missile supplies and it launched special anti-SAM operations against single gunner teams, caravans, and storage sites.[31] Regions in which the missiles were being used were subjected to intensified high-altitude bombing as a deterrent reprisal. These measures failed to have any appreciable effect upon the impact of this new weapon.

Ultimately, the Soviets were forced to cut back on their air operations, particularly by helicopters. Routine sorties dropped dramatically. Commanders refused to approve missions into regions known to be furnished with Stingers. Many Afghan pilots just refused to fly any more sorties into 'Stinger country': the Soviets had to increase incentive pay greatly in order to keep the DRA Air Force in operation.[32] Overall, Soviet pilots became much more defensive-minded, giving up a good deal of their previous advantages in initiative. An experienced Western journalist reported in October 1987 that 'Helicopters have disappeared from the Afghan sky except to escort convoys and attack Massoud (Panjshir Valley commander), who doesn't have Stingers'.[33]

The *mujahedin*, in contrast, grew bolder. The threat to their caravans reduced, they were able to move more freely about the countryside. Moreover, their sanctuaries could now be defended from air attack. The boost to rebel morale was also an important result.

The effects of the Stinger would have been greater if there had not been serious problems with its distribution. The United States authorities placed quite restrictive controls on weapons supplies. Each gunner received only the launcher and one or two missiles. He had to return to Pakistan for additional reloads (where he was debriefed by US intelligence on his use of the weapon). The round trip, obviously, represented a long period of time when the launcher was not in use. Distribution was also uneven; the Americans followed a strange policy in regard to which insurgent groups were to receive the missiles. Hezb-i-Islami, the least co-operative group of all (with ties to Iran as well), received more weapons than the others, while Ahmad Shah Massoud, perhaps the most effective rebel leader of all, received none.

Thirdly, many of the weapons disappeared before they were ever used. The Pakistanis stripped off a significant number as a 'missile tax' on their transit. Others were probably sold. Then, Soviet and DRA troops captured some as well. Perhaps a third of the missiles were lost from use by these means.[34]

Soviet Air Losses

Estimates of Soviet air losses vary a great deal, depending on the point of view of the observer. A number of different sources are in general agreement that the Soviets lost approximately 600 aircraft of all types by the summer of 1986, i.e. prior to the introduction of Blowpipe and Stinger missiles.[35] An extreme estimate was made by a defecting Afghan pilot in 1989, who said that in 10 years of war, the DRA Air Force lost 975 aircraft and the Soviets 1,700.[36] After 1986, aircraft losses skyrocketed to an annual rate of 438–547 annually.[37]

Disagreement exists with regard to how many aircraft were lost due to enemy fire and how many failed due to mechanical malfunctions and/or pilot error. In Vietnam, the United States Army lost about 20 per cent of its helicopter park to operational attrition every year. It seems reasonable that Soviet losses would be yet higher, considering that the flying conditions in Afghanistan are more severe than Vietnam. The thin air of high altitude starves gas turbine engines and negatively reinforces existing problems caused by the low power-to-weight ratio of Soviet aircraft. Obviously, vigorous evasive manoeuvring in restricted terrain, nap-of-the-earth, or at high altitude is also going to produce mechanical losses and crashes.

Certainly, during the first two years of the war, the great majority of Soviet aircraft losses (75–80 per cent) must be attributed to non-combat causes, plus losses suffered on the ground due to raids, rocket attacks, and sabotage. During the middle years of the war, the share of losses to rebel fire undoubtedly rose slightly, given the growing experience of the insurgents and the increase in the number of AA systems in their hands. However, there can be no doubt at all that the Stinger turned the ratio on its head, so that from late 1986 to 1989, the greatest danger to Soviet pilots was rebel fire, not operational attrition. A conservative estimate of all Soviet aircraft losses during the entire war might be put at 1,300–1,500.

Incidentally, the sharp increase in aircraft losses due to the Stinger came at an awkward time for the Soviets. During the three years prior to the introduction of the Stinger, the Soviets had cut back fighter and helicopter production, so that there were fewer machines on hand to replace their new losses. In addition, Gorbachev and his advisers were beginning their first tentative discussions on the idea of withdrawing forces from Afghanistan in early 1987. The impact of the Stinger on these discussions must have been quite great.

Other Observations on the Air War

It should be noted that helicopters (Mi-4s, Mi-17s) were also used as aerial retransmission stations, orbiting over a mission area for hours at a time.[38] Their extended use in this role during major operations seems to have been routine practice. The artillery also employed helicopter pilots as aerial observers, particularly to adjust its lengthy bombardments for full and proper coverage of the target area.

The Soviet Air Force performed all major maintenance (overhauls, major component replacements) within the safety of its own borders at Termez, the main Air Force logistics centre. Minor and routine maintenance was performed at each airbase by Soviet technicians who, it seems, were largely commissioned and warrant officers. Soviet technicians also maintained Afghan aircraft and kept control of all spare parts in order to prevent sabotage.

One feature of helicopter operations which clearly emerged from this war is that all Soviet crew-members are officers. Even the door-gunners of Mi-8/Mi-17 aircraft are officers. Each aircraft also appears to have been checked out before each mission by a Soviet officer-technician. The omnipresence of officers and warrant officers at such low levels for such tasks is an indicator of the serious shortfall in the quality of Soviet airmen and NCOs.

What about night flying? There is little evidence of substantial night operations by the fixed-wing component. On the other hand, helicopter units spent an appreciable amount of time aloft at night. For example, medevac missions could not wait for daybreak to launch — help had to be sent right away. Night-flying posed some serious problems. Soviet articles make no references to the use of night-vision devices (NVDs) by pilots, although some helicopters were fitted with searchlights. Naturally, the darkness increased the possibility of getting lost or crashing in the already difficult flying conditions. One Soviet pilot on a medevac mission reported how he had to circle a wide area to contact his objective on the ground; he had no radio contact with the unit, so had to hover with his running lights off until they recognised the sound of the helicopter, after which they set out ground flares to guide him in.[39] Another pilot claimed that flying at night was just as dangerous as flying in the face of rebel fire.[40]

Finally, Soviet fighters and fighter-bombers frequently crossed into Pakistani air-space in order to bomb rebel caravans, and in some cases, the refugee camps themselves. The frequency of the air-space violations varied from year to year, but it may have averaged in the neighbourhood of 1–200 violations a year during the first half of the war. The Pakistanis routinely scrambled their border units to confront the Soviet intruders. The Soviets committed air-space violations against Iran as well, but the response there was different; in general, the cross-border ground and air strikes by the Soviets tempered Iranian willingness to supply the rebels.

Pilot Training, Readiness, and Combat Performance

Soviet military literature quite clearly admits that the majority of pilots and units sent to Afghanistan were insufficiently prepared for the combat tasks which they faced. To begin with, it appears that few pilots received specialty training after being identified for assignment to the DRA.[41] For example, one Afghan veteran, a helicopter pilot, stated that neither he nor his comrades had any significant experience in mountain flying before their arrival in the country.[42] Other sources reveal that helicopter pilots needed more training in standard flying techniques and in ground support operations after they arrived.[43]

The main problem, voiced by many veterans of the war, lay with the general VVS pilot training and exercise programmes. Afghan veterans have complained often, and sometimes bitterly, that current flight training is too rigid, unimaginative, and oversimplified. So much care is taken to avoid accidents, that training exercises lack realism and challenge. As a result, the system produces poorly trained aviators who do not possess the necessary qualities of initiative, decisiveness, boldness, and independence of mind. Consider the judgements of two Afghan veterans on the effects of this kind of training on combat performance in Afghanistan:

> Restrictions and oversimplification [of flight training] gave rise to a low level of preparedness of both aviation commanders and their subordinates, which became the reason for many unpleasant events, among which were tragedies.[44]
>
> 'The fact is', said the squadron commander, 'that in normal training we are used to acting *shablonno* [*by rote, textbook procedure*], not moving away from the standard solution. But when the situation becomes complicated as in battle, we are not able to cope with the task before us. That is the cost of oversimplification and the lack of initiative'.[45]

Oversimplification is a term which appears often in pilot complaints about Soviet training programmes. One example should suffice to clarify the criticism. In training for the conduct of air assaults, Soviet pilots are normally given the opportunity to make several passes over the landing area in order to pick the best approach, judge the wind, and select the best points for touch-down. Soviet articles on combat in the DRA warn their fellow aviators that they will not be able to make such multiple passes; it will be necessary to approach, land, dismount the *desant* party, and depart all in one quick pass.

The results of this kind of training programme were indecisiveness, excessive caution, an institutionalised fear of taking on responsibility, uncertainty in the face of unexpected situations, and a fixed tendency always to play by the rules, never deviating from standard procedures, even when it was clear that standard procedures were dangerous.

The urge to return to these methods was even present in Afghanistan. Should an accident occur and an aircraft be lost, higher authorities invariably clamped down, restricting the activities of aviation units and imposing timidity in the taking of risks. A good example, cited in 1989, concerned a recon group which was surrounded and pinned down. The group commander requested air support and evacuation. However, since weather conditions were marginal, although flyable in the opinions of pilots who were ready to complete the mission, permission was refused. Two days went by. Casualties mounted. Only when the trapped unit was almost out of ammunition did the senior commander grant permission to conduct the mission.[46]

Complicating the situation even further was the fact that getting ready for service in Afghanistan was essentially a 'self-help' exercise. Incredibly, the VVS made no attempt to capture the lessons of Afghan Air War, nor to transfer them to units based in other regions, nor even to regiments designated for rotation into Afghanistan![47] Several ex-squadron and regimental commanders have described in print how, in the absence of official guidance, they sought out pilot veterans for advice and assistance. These commanders set up their own pre-deployment training programmes based on what they were able to glean from the experience of others.[48] Not surprisingly, the most important lesson stressed by the '*Afgantsii*' was to learn how to think tactically and not be bound by a textbook approach. Attaining this objective was obviously not easy, since it required a radical change in attitude and mental process.

These significant deficiencies frequently revealed themselves in the combat performance of Soviet pilots in the war. In the early years, pilots sometimes failed to take evasive action in the presence of an air defence threat and they flew straight into air ambushes rather than deviate from the flight path which had been planned and ordered. Facing an unexpected situation, pilots showed hesitation; sometimes the mission was aborted because it did not conform to the situation, which had been briefed. Perhaps the most common error in judgement was the tendency of the pilots to strike only the targets designated for them, even if these targets had been abandoned by the *mujahedin* or if other, obvious, better targets were visible.[49] Journalist Paul Moorcraft made an observation typical of this shortcoming.

> In July 1984, I witnessed an example of the Soviet failure to go for the jugular. Our crew was caught in the open on a hill in Jigdalek, not far from the capital, Kabul, by two Mi-24 gunships. As the deadly flying tanks dropped down on us, we threw ourselves into a small ditch, and the cameramen used my back as a tripod. We thought we were about to film our own demise.
> The two helicopters then circled as four MiG-21s wheeled gracefully in the sky and bombed the valley below us. Despite obviously sighting our group of 50 exposed guerrillas, and the chatter of a Dasheka machine-gun, the choppers ignored the lush target ... the rigidity of Soviet planning often forbids initiative or the ability to snap up a target of opportunity.[50]

Another significant deficiency was the apparent difficulty pilots experienced in solving a tactical problem while airborne. In particular, fighter and fighter-bomber pilots sometimes were unable to select an approach and/or ordnance suitable to the target.

Certainly, shortcomings of this kind were corrected by individual pilots and units as they gained experience, but the learning curve seems to have been quite lengthy. Moreover, possibly because of the policy of rotating in entire units, each air unit had to go through its own learning curve, committing many of the errors of the units which they had replaced. It would be interesting to know whether or not departing units passed down their field SOPs to arriving units and whether training and operations circulars were used in Afghanistan to advise units of lessons learned and new developments.

It is inappropriate to focus only on the weaknesses displayed by Soviet pilots when there is some evidence of innovation and imagination, and many examples of courage and heroism under fire. One of the best examples of Soviet innovation was reported by the *mujahedin*. Soviet aircraft operating near the Pakistan border were experiencing some difficulty in attacking rebel positions set up to protect passage to and from the refugee camps. The positions were sited in such a way that they were invulnerable to aircraft approaching them from Afghan airspace. The Soviet pilots solved the problem by crossing into Pakistani airspace and attacking the *mujahedin* from the rear.[51]

Soviet helicopter units also used false insertions to good advantage, usually to deceive the enemy as to intent. On other occasions, false *desants* into LZs known to be covered by strong rebel forces were intentionally made in order to induce the rebels to open fire, revealing their dispositions and the locations of heavy weapons. The assault helicopters then pulled up and away while an airborne FAC guided in the jets to pound the now exposed insurgent defences.[52]

The standard tour for a pilot was one year. Air regiments and independent squadrons rotated in and out of country on a yearly basis. The average pilot, rotary and fixed-wing, flew from 200 to 300 combat missions during the course of the tour, sometimes flying three or four missions a day. All pilots performing acceptable service routinely received two or three decorations.[53] Many received early promotions as a standard reward for combat duty.

It has often been claimed in the Western press that the combat experience obtained by the Soviet Air Force in Afghanistan will serve to strengthen the entire Air Force for some time to come, making it a formidable opponent. While this is undeniably true at a certain level, the level of individual pilot expertise and with respect to the testing of equipment, it is equally false at a higher level. Strong evidence exists that the VVS has continued to ignore the experiences of the Afghan War in its obsession with the big war in Europe. Articles in the military press concerning air operations in the DRA are today more open and honest than before, but they are not any more frequent and they do not appear to exercise much influence on the VVS training programme.

For the past several years, a multitude of articles and letters to Soviet military publications (particularly *Red Star* and *Aviation and Cosmonautics*) reveals that Soviet pilot veterans have generally been unable to put their combat experience to use in the units which they have joined after leaving Afghanistan.[54] In many instances, their comments and suggestions are resented. Independent attempts to introduce innovative training or to increase the level of realism are rebuffed. The level of frustration felt by the *Afgantsii* is quite high, as is their resentment that their combat experience apparently does not count for much:

> There is an order, for example, which states that pilots returning to the unit following duty in the Republic of Afghanistan shall occupy the positions they held prior to their tour duty in Afghanistan. It is hard to say what reasoning was being used up the chain of command, but the consequences are paradoxical. Those who by virtue of their sweat and sometimes blood as well earned the right to command flights and serve as a detachment deputy commanders returned to their units as senior pilots. And considerable time would pass before their names would be entered into that next-higher box. The result was that the right to command, which had been earned in battle, had to be defended by performance in the landing pattern.[55]

At the very end of 1989, the Soviet military press published an article which stands as a damning indictment of the VVS training and exercise programmes, as viewed by Soviet pilots. In an 'expert' survey conducted from 1987–89 (i.e. during the last years of the war when pilot-veterans were well spread throughout the Air Force), pilots of fighters, fighter-bombers, and bombers were asked the question, 'Are you satisfied with current methods of tactical training?' The results of the survey were astonishing: 87 per cent of the fighter pilots, 98 per cent of the fighter-bomber pilots (most Afghan veterans fall into this category), and 50 per cent of the bomber pilots answered negatively. The primary criticism was that they do not train to accomplish the tasks nor to acquire the skills which will be necessary in combat. The pilots in this survey repeated much of the criticism cited above. Training programmes, they said, are formalistic, deadening, unimaginative, simplistic, and devoid of creativity or risk-taking.[56]

With regard to the inability of the VVS to reform itself, taking into consideration its combat experience in Afghanistan, the words of the General Major of Aviation N Posrednikov are appropriate:

> There has recently been more discussion on developing the creative possibilities of every pilot. But appeals and demands to develop independent tactical thinking in every warrior and the ability to calculate, work out and implement new, original combat techniques very often collide with all kinds of limitations and constraints. For example, is it really possible 'to create, to think up new things, to try things out' when the layout of training targets stays the same for years on end, and when the target approach course is always the same? Moreover, even the altitudes of target approach are limited both above and below. There is little room for creativity when a pilot flies many years in succession along the same standard route.[57]

How long can air combat experience of the war remain fresh and important under these numbing, stultifying conditions? And, how long can the veteran pilots keep demanding innovative, realistic training before they are crushed by the weight of the system? It is far more likely that any favourable influence of air force experience during the war will quickly and quietly dissipate like the waters of a spring rain flowing into the sands of the Afghan desert.

CHAPTER 10

Combat Support

Neither the motorised rifle nor the counter-insurgency force conducted operations in Afghanistan without the important combat support provided by artillery, communications, engineers, and — vital to CI operations — intelligence organisations. To a lesser extent, the Soviets also employed chemical munitions in support of both kinds of operations. The sections below describe the use of these elements in the LCSFA.

Artillery

The Soviet 40th Army deployed a fairly standard artillery establishment to Afghanistan. In addition to the artillery complements of each MR division, airborne division/regiment, and separate MR brigade/regiment, the 40th Artillery Brigade (the army artillery) was stationed at Khair Khana camp on the outskirts of Kabul.[1] Thus, the types of artillery and rocket launchers deployed to the DRA included the following systems:

    M43   120-mm mortars
    new   type 120-mm SP mortar
    D30   122-mm howitzers
    2S1   122-mm SP howitzers
    2S3   152-mm SP howitzers
    M46   130-mm field guns*
    2S5   152-mm SP guns*
    240-mm mortars*

    BM-13 132-mm MRLs (16 round)
    BM-14,-16 140-mm MRLs (16 round)
    BM-14,-17 140-mm MRLs (17 round)
    BM-21 140-mm MRLs (40 round)
    MB-27 220-mm MRLs (16 round)*

*Army-level systems. The rest are regimental or divisional systems.

It seems likely that some separate large calibre battalions were deployed on a regional basis, but this hunch has not been confirmed openly.

97

The 2S5 and BM-27 are relatively new systems which undoubtedly were sent to Afghanistan in part for testing under combat conditions. The Soviet Union tested three new mortars during the war: the 2S9 240-mm SP mortar, a new 120-mm SP mortar, and the new 82-mm *Vasilek* automatic mortar, which is said to be capable of firing 120 rounds per minute. It was seen in Afghanistan in its towed version and in a (possibly improvised) turreted mount on the BTR-60 and BTR-70 APCs. Organic to the MR battalion, the *Vasilek* mortar provides a tremendous amount of immediate firepower. It was probably used widely as well by the CI force and added to their force structure as a field improvisation since there are many references to the use of mortar systems in support of dismounted operations.

During the last year of the occupation, the Soviets introduced SCUD-B tactical missiles to provide a very-long-range area suppression system to compensate for the withdrawal of artillery units. Thirteen launchers were positioned in the vicinity of Kabul and Mazar-i-Sharif, and possibly a few more in Shindand. Most of the missiles have been launched since the Soviets departed — at least 900 between February and October 1989 — but under the direction of Soviet advisers left behind. Using SCUD missiles (300 kilometres range, 2,000 pound warhead) against guerrillas can be compared to using a sledge hammer against flies. It made a loud noise and a big hole, but its inherent inaccuracy kept it from doing much damage except by luck. The exceptions were the 20 or so missiles which hit Afghan refugee camps.[2]

Artillery units were assembled into battalion groupings, sometimes sharing a garrison with MR units. The guns and supporting vehicles occupied a doctrinally standard layout within the confines of the garrison. The guns normally were not dug in, since the rebels did not possess significant long-range attack means to threaten them. In later years, the Soviets mixed different calibre weapons and MRLs on the same base. Where possible, firing units supported operations from normal garrison locations.[3]

Soviet use of artillery conformed to doctrinal patterns and previous historical practice. It has been noted earlier how Soviet offensives were preceded by lengthy air and artillery preparations against all likely and suspected enemy positions. Pre-planned attacks then continued during the course of the operations as ground columns advanced. Barrier fires were used, often effectively, to block the movement of insurgent groups. Moreover, on some occasions, short artillery preparations preceded heliborne *desants* into LZs. During the last year of the war, when many helicopter units began to be withdrawn to the Soviet Union, the Soviets turned more and more to artillery to replace the fires previously provided by the 'flying artillery'. However, Soviet and Afghan sources alike tend to show that the majority of artillery and rocket attacks were unobserved, planned fires against targets obtained from map spots and/or aerial reconnaissance, not on-call concentrations against targets of opportunity. Artillery units also fired many illumination missions on a routine basis.

On the other hand, the Soviets recognised that the decentralised nature of operations and the frequency of surprise attacks against Soviet units sharply increased the demand for on-call fire. As a result, they modified their fire control system to be able to provide more timely, responsive fire against unplanned targets. The most important innovation was the attachment of artillery adjustment teams to low tactical echelons, sometimes as low as platoon level for the *desant* forces.[4] The presence of artillery adjustment teams at sub-regimental level meant that, if the unit needed immediate fire support, it now had access not only to its own organic mortars but also to regimental and divisional artillery, without going through one or more layers for approval. These teams were occasionally attached to DRA units as well. Some improvement was noted in the responsiveness of MRL firing units to on-call requests and in the co-ordination of artillery fire and close air support against the same target. However, *mujahedin* commanders concurred that Soviet on-call artillery fire remained relatively slow and inaccurate.[5]

It appears that the team included a combat vehicle crew, artillery officer, and RTO when a mounted operation was in progress and just the artillery officer and RTO when they accompanied a dismounted unit. Incidentally, there is some evidence that line officers were encouraged to develop expertise in obtaining on-call fire support independently, that is, without the aid of an artillery adjustment team, but this objective was not achieved widely, particularly not in MR units.

Another innovation was the mounting of the BM-21 MRL on ZIL-131 trucks instead of their standard carrier, the Ural 375D truck. It is likely that the smaller and lighter ZIL truck was used because it gave the system better mobility in the rugged terrain.

The effectiveness of field artillery fire in the mountains was rather low. Many *mujahedin* positions were located in 'dead space' which could not be reached because of the low trajectory of the rounds: once a round crested a ridge or mountain peak it simply sailed past the far side (the reverse slope) for a long distance before falling to ground. In addition, adjusting indirect fire on a steep mountain slope is far more prone to error and erratic fall-of-shot than targets on even ground. The character of the rock further protected the rebels from everything but a direct hit. Moreover, the *mujahedin* normally could move out of the areas selected for pre-planned bombardment. The use of mechanical time and variable time fuzes against rebel bases might have produced better results, but the Soviets seem to have stuck to standard high-explosive, quick-fuzed ammunition. The *mujahedin* suffered few casualties from artillery fire.

Actually, mortars (as opposed to howitzers) were far better suited to attack the rebels because of their high trajectories, high rates of fire, and lighter weight, which meant that they could be transported deep into the mountainous terrain. In general, the CI force relied heavily on mortars for immediate fire support while the MR units relied more on gunfire. This is not to say, however, that the CI force seldom used artillery. Indeed, the CI force used artillery widely and seldom ventured beyond artillery range on their raids and ambushes.

Artillery and rockets were also used widely in reprisal attacks and in the economic war against the countryside, to devastating effect. Hundreds of villages laid waste and the villagers driven off by massive, indiscriminate artillery and rocket fires. Fields and irrigation systems were destroyed in this process by means of HE, incendiary, and, in some cases, chemical munitions. The artillery distributed thousands of AP mines for the same purpose. Finally, indirect fire was used to destroy entire sections of cities held by the *mujahedin*, particularly in Herat, Kandehar, and Farah. The cost in civilian lives of this tactic was shockingly high, but it failed completely to achieve its aim, the destruction of urban rebel strongholds.

The Soviet military press has not devoted a great deal of attention to artillery operations in Afghanistan, although there are a few noteworthy images which emerge. First, Soviet artillerymen acknowledge that delivering accurate fire in the mountains is more difficult than in the plains. Some problems occurred in regard to accurately identifying battery locations because of the lack of a geodesic net and the difficulty of the terrain. The new position-locating device used by artillery units to provide instantaneous readouts of altitude, direction, and location worked poorly. The frequent twists, turns, climbs, and drops put the machine off its stride and few survey points existed where it could be calibrated.[6]

When batteries moved out of garrison on operations, they often could not be positioned on one site because of the nature of the terrain, so they were split into separate platoons, an adjustment which complicated the computation of firing data, since more than one 'base piece' had to be employed; sometimes individual corrections for each piece were necessary. To a typical US firing battery, such adjustments are routine, although they require good training and standard procedures. To the Soviets, these complications seem to have been somewhat daunting. Unless a unit was exceptionally well-trained, operations by firing platoon sharply reduced timeliness for on-call fires.[7] Moreover, firing units were strictly limited to movement by road.

Unpredictable weather and lack of survey data for the target area further complicated computation of firing data. Judging by Soviet comments on this problem, the average firing unit did not routinely update its corrections to firing data for weather several times a day, as is done in the West. The positioning of the weather station too far from the scene of action was also a problem.[8] Registrations had to be carried out more frequently to maintain accuracy. Problems occurred, for example, when there was a significant difference between the altitudes of the firing units and the altitude of the registration point and target area. Such tactical and technical requirements necessitated special training.

Artillery units also needed special training in driving in mountains, in immediate action drills (e.g. actions during ambushes in movement), and in individual and unit self-defence. Battery and platoon commanders quickly learned to establish an all-around defence including the use of local observers to avoid being surprised. Artillery units must have been well-protected since there are few reports of batteries being surprised and destroyed by the guerrillas. (Of course, their positions several kilometres from the main scene of action would have reduced their vulnerability to rebel attacks.)

The weapons themselves apparently proved to be quite reliable in the extreme climatic conditions, another testimony to the excellence of Russian artillery construction. There are no reports of ammunition shortages, despite the loss of several huge ammunition depots to rebel rocket attacks. However, the Soviets and the *mujahedin* alike have reported a substantial number of dud rounds (artillery, mortar, and rocket rounds) which should have prompted the Soviet authorities to look into ammunition manufacturing and handling procedures for flaws. Communication breakdowns between artillery adjustment teams and firing units also occurred too frequently, largely because of blockages by the terrain, failure to deploy retrans stations, and failure to plan for and establish contingency communications.

Notably absent from Soviet artillery operations was the 76-mm mountain gun, an old weapon for sure, but one which is still used in mountainous military districts in the Soviet Union. This weapon, seemingly, could have been of some use in the mountains of Afghanistan, since it is far less tied to a road network than all the other pieces. The proliferation of mortars of various calibres undoubtedly compensated for its absence.

In conclusion, the main contribution of indirect fire to the Soviet war effort occurred in the area of economic destruction and area suppression and denial. The Soviet Army could employ its artillery on such a massive scale without fear of reprisal because the rebels had no counter-battery capability and, except for rockets, no long-range means of striking back. As long as the ammunition supply held firm, the guns could keep firing, and so they did. Pin-point accuracy was seldom achieved, but seldom needed except when units became pinned down under heavy attack. Soviet artillerymen spent most of their time pumping round after round into the countryside, not against confirmed enemy positions. More casualties probably occurred in the ranks of the *mujahedin* due to AP mines sown by the guns than by the fire itself.

Although a United States Army report in 1989 claimed that the Soviets used their artillery imaginatively in Afghanistan, their own commentary in the military press does not make a similar claim and the observations made above would seem to refute the claim.[9] It is true that a limited number of innovations were introduced, as noted above. On the other hand, no radical changes took place. No heliborne artillery raids, for example, are known to have been conducted, although mortar units often moved by helicopter to positions where they could support dismounted operations. The Soviets have not indicated that they experimented with fundamentally new methods of tactical fire control, such as the use of dedicated batteries. On the whole, the artillery component of the 40th Army appears to have stuck with its tried and true methods, the best indicator of which was the continued prevalence of preplanned fires versus on-call fires. In short, Soviet artillery did not distinguish itself during the Afghan War, but it did not deeply embarrass itself either.

Incidentally, there is at least one report of a Soviet command post calling for artillery fire directly on to its location. The information on this event is limited, but quite interesting, because the officer who called for the fire support was the last commander of the 40th Army, General Lieutenant B V Gromov. He did so in order to prevent his CP from being overrun by *mujahedin*. It appears that this heroic action may have won him the Order of the Red Star.[10]

Tactical Communications

Weakness in tactical communication endured as one of the most glaring deficiencies in Soviet military performance during the entire course of the war. Judging from the Soviet military press, all types of units in Afghanistan, MR troops and CI forces alike, experienced frequent breakdowns in radio communications, which was, of course, the primary means of tactical communications. Naturally, maintaining radio contact in mountainous terrain is quite difficult, given that most tactical radios are limited-range and line-of-sight. A separate column only had to move around two or three bends in the road before it lost contact with the command post because of the intervening land mass. The results of such outages could be disastrous, for example, as when an MR column lost contact with its security elements and stumbled into an ambush or when an artillery adjustment team could not raise its firing batteries for support.[11] Ample evidence exists to show that communications breakdowns often paralysed a unit into inactivity until contact was restored. Still, such problems are not insurmountable. They can be solved through systematic training and improvisation, but the Soviets never seemed to get a firm grip on the problem.

The first adjustment which the Soviet Army had to make to maintain tactical communications was to increase widely its use of retransmission stations. Not only did more retrans stations have to be deployed, they had to be moved frequently. In practice, this meant the deployment and orderly displacement of many small, decentralised retrans teams from one point to the next, exposing them on high ground in dangerous territory. If the teams were not cautious in their movement and careful about their security, they were sure to become casualties.

There were several other reasons why Soviet units found it difficult to keep radio nets functioning. In the first place, Soviet communications troops simply lacked the training to perform these functions reliably. The tasks demanded skills which they did not possess, such as map reading, terrain recognition and negotiation, and stealth. They also lacked the physical and psychological conditioning necessary. Establishing a retrans station or a communications centre on a mountain peak usually meant multiple hard climbs on foot in harsh weather, carrying heavy equipment, extra batteries, while encumbered with flak vest, weapon, and combat gear. Moreover, sitting on such an isolated post for long periods of time could induce severe stress. There also appears to have been a shortage of qualified NCOs and warrant officers to lead these teams and to take well-considered decisions in unexpected circumstances. Failure to plan ahead was a fourth reason. Quite often, commanders of units did not deploy retrans stations until after communications failed.[12] Even then, it appears that immediate action to restore communications was not taken until a unit found itself in trouble; one party was always waiting for the other party to take the necessary action.

Wire communications seem to have been used only during large offensives to link command posts which occupied temporarily fixed positions in cleared areas. Thus, in a ten-day operation in the Panjshir Valley, for example, regimental or battalion command posts might be linked by wire, or battalion OPs linked to the main fire control centre. The problems experienced here are common to any army: delays in laying the wire, its vulnerability to disruption by traffic, exhausted wiremen, shortages of cable, and problems with choosing the paths over which the wire was to be strung.

Another deficiency in the communications elements was the lack of tactical training received by Signal troops. Ostensibly, communications training schools in the Soviet Union focus heavily on technical skills at the expense of common tactical skills. As a result, many of the communications troops in Afghanistan had not learned how to choose and build an individual fighting position using natural cover, how to conduct basic fire and movement, or how to camouflage. Some did not even know how to destroy their equipment and codes if forced to abandon them. Afghan veterans who returned to the Soviet Union to training institutes and units have issued numerous, urgent calls to raise training standards in this area and they have expressed chagrin at being discouraged from doing so through their own efforts.[13]

Deficiencies in technical skills also prevailed. Soviet articles addressing communications in Afghanistan have stressed the need for additional expertise in making minor equipment repairs in the field, working through atmospheric interference, tuning the equipment for better reception and transmission, and taking simple, but non-standard actions to restore radio contact, such as breaking into another net for assistance, moving a retrans site (without orders to do so) to a more suitable location, or noting down the locations, frequencies, and call-signs of units in the same area in case they are needed.

Several other observations are appropriate. First, there is little or no evidence in the Soviet military press of training in the use of field-expedients such as long-wire or directional antennae to maintain or restore communications. Second, there are frequent references to the use of manual retrans in combat operations as opposed to automatic retrans. In fact, it is possible to surmise that most of the lower level retrans stations were manual, which is to say that the retrans operators received a message from one station, copied it out by hand, and then retransmitted it to the intended receiver. This is a long, tedious process subject to error. One can understand the use of manual retrans in emergencies, but not as a routine procedure, which it seems to have been, unless the equipment was not available. Some use of airborne retrans also occurred, particularly during airmobile operations, but there is insufficient open information on this issue to reach any conclusions on the frequency or conditions of its use. There are also no references to the use of secure devices during tactical operations. It may well be that all messages containing sensitive information had to be manually encoded for transmission.

One cannot help but conclude that the widespread deficiencies in tactical communications are fully reflective of endemic Soviet inflexibility, lack of imagination, compartmentalisation of even basic technical skills to specialists, and reluctance to depart from rote, textbook procedures, even when they don't work.

Mine Warfare and Tactical Engineer Operations

Mine warfare occupied a central place in the Soviet-Afghan War, primarily as an independent form of violence against Afghan society, but also as an integral part of offensive and defensive operations against the *mujahedin*. Literally millions of mines were emplaced by the Soviets (and thousands by the rebels), so many in fact that several decades will pass before they have all been cleared or rendered harmless by time.

Mine warfare fulfilled several functions in the overall Soviet CI strategy, particularly in regard to the destruction of the rural economy and the displacement of the population. For example, the Soviets dispensed thousands of mines in farmers' fields and pastures for no other reason than to kill off the livestock and make the field untillable. They saturated villages suspected of harbouring rebels with mines in order to trap the residents or to make the villages inhabitable. Mine attacks of this nature were also carried out as reprisals for *mujahedin* attacks.[14]

Anti-personnel mines were also used simply to terrorise the civilian population. The most commonly used mine in this role was the PFM-1 'butterfly' mine, so called because its size and shape permitted it to flutter to the ground from its airborne dispensers.[15] This mine usually did not kill its victims, but only caused severe wounds. Many of the AP mines were designed to resemble toys, pens, watches, or the like in order to entice their victims to pick them up. The Soviets designed booby traps for a similar purpose. Thousands of militarily meaningless casualties occurred as a result, as witnessed by the alarming number of Afghan citizens with only one eye, one leg, or one arm.

The goal of maiming rather than killing was intentional because the wounded citizens then became an economic burden to the community. Causing these kinds of casualties among the insurgents accomplished a triple purpose: it reduced the number of effective rebel fighters, while forcing others to care for the wounded, slowing down the movement of rebel groups. It also had a depressing effect on the healthy members of the group.

Mines in vast quantities were widely used as part of the periodic Soviet programmes to close off the Afghan borders to rebel traffic and to restrict movement in heavily trafficked areas where Soviet and DRA forces were not operating. Although the rebels learned to distinguish the mines used in this manner, they were difficult to detect because they possessed a shape and colour which allowed them to blend into the rocky countryside. Discovery of mines along a trail would immediately bring a rebel group or caravan to a halt.

AP mines were dispensed by several means, but most commonly by air using Mi-8 and Mi-17 helicopters. One Mi-8 helicopter could carry two mine dispersal units, each with 72 mines. The mines are scattered at random by airflow once released.[16] Reports indicate that mines were also dispensed by artillery, MRL, large-calibre mortar, jet aircraft (in canisters), and by missiles at long range.[17]

The indiscriminate use of mines in remote areas sometimes backfired. Unmarked minefields emplaced by one unit every so often claimed victims among another Soviet unit operating in the same area, particularly when one unit replaced another.[18] Soviet writings on the war stress the danger of incurring friendly casualties because of the failure to mark minefields.[19]

Offensively, the Soviets used mines in their large operations to block passes, either to prevent the withdrawal of the *mujahedin* or to prevent the approach of supporting groups from other areas. Mines were also dispensed directly on to suspected *mujahedin* positions in order to pin them or to force them to move through the hasty minefield in order to avoid a Soviet attack. In one case, hearing of the meeting of a large number of *mujahedin* commanders in a certain area, the Soviets dispensed 20,000 mines among the nearby villages.[20] The *mujahedin* cleared the mines in the usual way, by throwing stones at them.

Mine warfare figured less prominently in the small, independent operations run by the CI force. Ambush parties sometimes emplaced remotely-detonated mines to trigger their ambushes. They occasionally used mines to cover an open flank or rear once they were in position. If a Soviet unit on reconnaissance or on a search-and-destroy mission were forced to flee, it might also call for mines to be sown to block pursuit by the *mujahedin*. However, such examples are rare.

For the most part, Soviet ground forces were more concerned with protection against enemy mines than with using them against the rebels. In the early years of the war, the rebels used many home-made devices, often gathering explosive material from unexploded Soviet bombs. By 1983, however, the rebels obtained a steady supply of quite modern mines, including plastic models, which are much harder to detect, from foreign sources. The Soviet press seemed to take a perverse delight in identifying the manufacture and make of the foreign-made mines which they were able to capture or neutralise.[21]

The insurgents used mines every bit as widely as the Soviets but on a much smaller scale. No Soviet or DRA vehicle moved anywhere in the country without the expectation that it would at some time run into a section of road mined by the rebels. Under normal conditions, the *mujahedin* could not mine large sections of road, so they always chose the narrowest, most twisting parts where a damaged vehicle would bring the entire column to a halt. The most likely places were sharp turns and areas where the road was bounded on either side by ditches, cliffs, or drop-offs. If an ambush was planned, command-detonated mines might well be used in order to break a column up into several parts blocked front, rear, and middle. The rebels also used mines in fills, cuts, tunnels, and on bridges simply to destroy the road system and so disturb the logistical lifeline. In such areas, detours around and approaches to the destroyed section would also be mined, including, for example shallow or dry river beds. The rebels generally covered their mine obstacles with fire, making the clearing of them more difficult.

The rebels changed their methods and used imaginative techniques to deceive their enemies. For example, mines would be placed at various depths; the shallow ones would be detected but the deeper ones would be missed. They placed mines in wheel or track ruts and even under hard pavement, carefully replacing the damaged roadway. On an off-road track, the mines might be placed quite deep so that several vehicles could pass over them without harm. Eventually, the protective layers of soil would be disturbed and thinned to the point that the mine detonated.[22] In addition, many mines were rigged so that they could not be extracted. If discovered, they had to be neutralised by destruction. The rebels also worked fast. Roads which had been clear one day, would be mined during the night if the *mujahedin* heard that a convoy would be using it the next day. The Soviets state that most roads were mined at night, making the morning the most dangerous time for travel.

In addition, the *mujahedin* used mines in defence of their bases and storage sites. If they held a town or government post under siege, very heavy use of mines was made in order to prevent reinforcement of the post by ground. In this case, long stretches of road would be mined and held under observation and fire. In 1988, the rebels put 70 kilometres of the Kabul-Jalalabad road out of action. General Lieutenant Gromov has described how his engineers had to remove thousands of mines under fire along the Gardez-Khost road in order to break the siege of Khost during the brutal Magistral operation of November, 1987. Gromov also noted that during the course of the entire year, Soviet engineers disarmed or destroyed 4,882 AT mines, 3,800 AP mines, and 1,162 fougasse.[23]

The Soviet army made many adjustments to its combat methods in order to deal with the mine threat. In the first place, they employed larger than normal engineer mobility detachments (OOD), varying the organisation according to the terrain or situation. These OODs included tracked engineer vehicles, tanks with mine rollers, mine-detection sections, and dogs. Elements of the OODs often led a combat column, although the order of march was frequently changed. Over relatively even ground, a tracked vehicle with mine roller would lead the column, detonating the mines in its path. Over very rough ground, where a tank roller or blade might lift up and skip over a section of ground, engineers proceeded on foot with dogs and mine-detectors. This was hard, nerve-wracking work. Soviet studies show that the effectiveness of dismounted engineers performing this function in the heat dropped to 50 per cent after 1½ to 2 hours and to 20–25 per cent after three hours.[24] The dogs do not seem to have been especially effective, although this is hard to judge. One Soviet source, lauding the performance of a dog, reported that in two years the dog discovered 10 mines and two fougasses, a small number it would seem for two years.[25]

By 1988, the Soviets fielded two new mine-clearing vehicles to assist their operations. The first to appear used the T55 tank hull fitted with a new type of roller. The turret was removed and an armoured superstructure added, with a 12.7-mm machine gun for protection. The second model appears to have been based on the M1977 armoured recovery vehicle (also a T55 derivative). It uses the KMT-5 combined mine roller and plough system and includes a 14.5-mm machine gun turret. The mine roller is mounted on the front and detonates mines in front of the vehicle. The plough is designed for rear mounting; it digs the mine up rather than exploding it. The roller and plough cannot be used at the same time. The complete system, weighing about two tons, has a quick-release feature which enables the driver to disconnect them if necessary.[26]

The CI force too had to be concerned about mines in their attacks against rebel bases protected by minefields. The *mujahedin* also mined trails which they suspected the *desantniks* of using, as well as water sources and probable LZs.[27] As a result, *desant* companies routinely deployed with engineer detachments which they needed for de-mining and reconnaissance. Often, the first flight into an LZ carried an engineer squad to check and clear it of mines before the rest of the force landed.[28] If mines were suspected en route, the engineers moved to the front once again. (Allegedly, soldiers took special care to step directly in the footsteps of the person in front of them when mines were suspected.)

The Soviets themselves deployed mines for purely defensive purposes. All fixed installations and remote outposts were surrounded by dense minefields covered by fire. In the field, units invariably laid hasty minefields to cover flanks and to provide early warning.

The level of attention in the Soviet military press devoted to the issue of mine warfare indicates that the use of mines by the *mujahedin* posed a continuous, major threat to Soviet units. Apparently, engineers conducted critiques after operations as a matter of routine and attempted to pass on what they had learned to sister units. Real concern existed about the constant introduction of new methods by the rebels; Soviet engineers recognised that techniques which they had used on one operation might fail them on the next because the rebels continuously tried to adjust their use of mines to their observations of Soviet defensive actions.

It appears that the Soviets relied almost exclusively on their engineers to lay mines and to locate and neutralise the enemy. Cross-training of infantry soldiers and leaders in this role, to share the burden, was limited. (In contrast, United States use of mines in Vietnam during American patrols and ambushes was strictly an infantry affair; all infantry officers and NCOs learned, for example, how to emplace

Claymore mines and how to recognise and neutralise enemy booby traps.)

Finally, the use of mines in such vast qualities by the Soviets represents their attempt to use superior technology to overcome some of the advantages of the primitive insurgency in concealment, dispersion, and tactical mobility. It was also a means of striking back without having to locate the guerrillas firmly or to close with them in the field. Certainly, mines hampered the ability of the *mujahedin* to move about the country freely and helped keep the rebels away from the door. But they can hardly be considered to have had a decisive influence on the course and outcome of most tactical operations, much less the war. In essence, the mine was a cheap weapon delivered at long-range in huge quantities against a faceless enemy, at least to the person operating the dispensers, who did not have to be especially concerned about who might step on it. Soviet mine warfare against the *mujahedin* represents one more failed attempt to solve the difficult problems of counter-insurgency warfare with a simple, technological solution.

Soviet Intelligence

In counter-insurgency war, as in all military operations, effective intelligence is one of the most important contributors to success. The converse is also true. Without good intelligence, CI operations almost invariably come to naught. The Soviet Army employed a wide variety of measures to obtain information and produce intelligence in the DRA, but they were hampered by the fact that they had to rely overmuch on Afghan institutions. The Soviets had no pre-war, colonial structure through which they could work. Because of the immediately apparent differences in physical appearance and language between Soviet and Afghan citizens, they could not use very many of their own people as agents in covert operations. That left the KHAD (Afghan Secret Police), the police ministry, and the DRA armed forces as the primary collectors. These institutions were riddled with informers and sympathisers who were able to neutralise a great many intelligence operations by means of warnings and tip-offs. In addition, vast areas of the State's territory fell beyond the control of these institutions.

The KHAD used the typically brutal methods of secret police forces all over the world. Villagers, captured and wounded *mujahedin*, and suspected sympathisers were tortured to reveal information. Unprotected family members were seized and used as leverage. The KHAD also recruited informers in the villages. They sent secret agents into Peshawar and other refugee camps to gather information, sow discord and to carry out terrorism and assassinations. Three *mujahedin* commanders, for example, fell victim to such attacks in January, 1986.[29]

The refugee camp informers and agents provided valuable information on the movement of caravans, delivery of arms and ammunition from foreign sources, activities of rebel training centres, etc.

The KHAD also infiltrated the fighting organisations, their agents posing as deserters or angry citizens victimised by the régime. The *mujahedin*, after discovering thirty such agents by tip-off in Ningarhar in September, 1986, executed them all.[30]

The police ministry employed similar methods, while their military units in the provinces sought to capture Army deserters and individual rebel fighters. Militia units and the border brigades reported on rebel movements in the border regions. Fixed outposts, naturally, provided reports on rebel activity in their area.

In the grim economic conditions of war-torn Afghanistan, bribery and monetary rewards proved to be a suitable means for obtaining information. Tribal chiefs were paid handsomely to restrict rebel operations in their territory and to provide information on the strength and activities of the guerrillas. Unable to resist the financial rewards offered, a number of resistance leaders changed sides during the war. The régime also placed bounties on the heads of many *mujahedin* commanders.

The Soviet Army also obtained intelligence through its own resources. Fixed-wing transports and helicopters flew air reconnaissance missions on a regular basis. Soviet CI units conducted long-range patrols to locate the enemy for immediate attack by artillery or air strikes. In addition, Soviet *spetsnaz* units are said to have disguised themselves as shepherds, nomads, and itinerant traders in order to circulate in rebel-held territory for the purpose of gathering information. On the other hand, there is no evidence that the Soviets used such means as unattended ground sensors, passive listening devices, or very long-term, hidden listening posts/observation posts (LP/OP) in rebel territory.

Certainly, Soviet and régime intelligence gathering were a source of concern to the *mujahedin*, particularly the activity of KHAD agents. However, the intelligence effort as a whole fell short of providing what was needed to keep constant, paralysing pressure on the resistance. The intelligence leaks within the régime organisations with which the Soviets had to work were too pervasive to be plugged. It is true that the Soviets tried to use those leaks to their advantage at times — letting information slip, for example, of a future offensive in a certain area, only to conduct the offensive in a different one — but such attempts bore little fruit. The fact that the rebels controlled so much of the Afghan landscape meant that the reach of Soviet and régime intelligence organisations was quite short. Lack of intelligence and vulnerability to *mujahedin* intelligence gathering were two major weaknesses of the Soviet military effort.

Chemical Warfare

Early reports of the use of chemical weapons by the LCSFA in Afghanistan were initially received with scepticism in the West. At this point in time, however, no objective observer challenges the credibility of those claims.

Soviet employment of chemical weapons against the *mujahedin* began as early as March 1979, when Soviet helicopters fired rockets filled with toxic smoke and harassing agents at rioters and insurgents during the Herat uprising.[31] According to the US Department of State, chemical agents continued in use during the remainder of 1979 with seven reported uses.[32] Soviet units employed the illegal substances within the first two weeks of their deployment into the country.[33] By the summer of 1980, all major resistance areas were reporting incidents of chemical attack.[34]

The use of chemical weapons by the Soviet Army has been confirmed by several means:[35]

▶ Eyewitness testimony of *mujahedin*, refugees, and journalists.
▶ Testimony by medical technicians and doctors who have treated the victims.

▶ Testimony by Soviet defectors.

▶ Testimony by defecting KHAD agents and DRA Army personnel.

▶ Analysis of physical samples containing chemical residues.

▶ Photographic evidence of both the conduct of a chemical attack and its physical effects.

▶ Satellite photographs of Soviet decontamination equipment in Afghanistan.

In the face of such evidence, Soviet use of chemical weapons cannot be doubted. Table 10.1 describes the types of agents used, their means of delivery, and the regions in which they are known to have been used.

Table 10.1

Soviet Use of Chemical Weapons in Afghanistan

Types of Agent	*Means of Delivery*	*Localities Where Used*
Harassing agents	Helicopters	Wardak
Incapacitating agents	Fixed-wing aircraft	Ghazni
Blister agents	Artillery	Herat
Blood agents	Rockets	Badakhshan
Napalm	Chemical mines	Paktia
Nerve agents:	Hand-placed in wells,	Kandahar
VX	irrigation canals,	Paghman
Tabun	caves, rivers, etc.	Farah
Picric acid/picrine		Nangarhar
Liquid fire		Paktika
Phosgene oxime		Laghman
Trichothecene micotoxins		Jozjan
		Konduz
		Kunar Valley
		Panjshir Valley
		Termez–Salang route
		Kabul
		Baghlan

Note: The Soviets employed non-persistent agents as far as is known. Other localities undoubtedly suffered chemical attacks in addition to those cited above.

Employment of chemical agents in the DRA was uneven. After fairly consistent use from 1979–82 (hundreds of reported incidents), the Soviets used chemical weapons sparingly in 1983, probably due to sensitivity to international outrage, but then intensified their use in 1984 and again in 1986. However, chemical weapons did not form an integral part of Soviet military operations. It is true that they were employed in tactical operations, but not in any major, systematic fashion. Had the Soviets wanted to, it is clear that they could have used chemical weapons to neutralise many of the tactical advantages of the insurgents. Poison gas is heavier than air; it flows downward and is wafted into nooks, crannies, caves, and ditches where shells and shrapnel cannot penetrate. As such, it is a perfect weapon for the destruction of bodies of men holed up in conventionally impregnable positions, particularly when the victims have no means of chemical defence.

Thus, the Soviets could have used chemical and biological agents in most of their raids, attacks, and offensives to destroy the *mujahedin* in their assembly areas and strongholds. However, they chose not to, ostensibly because their use on that kind of scale could not have been kept secret and would have provoked the most severe international consequences. In addition, such widespread use would have also produced many collateral civilian and friendly casualties.

The primary motivation behind the use of chemical weapons in Afghanistan was the desire to exploit the battlefield there as a testing ground, from both a tactical and technical point of view. Tactically, the Soviets experimented with different methods of employment, they varied the timing of chemical attacks, they studied their influence on tactical success, and they tried the agents out in independent operations, such as blocking infiltration routes. Technically, they studied the physical means of employment, the quantities required, safety measures, and the effects of various agents, including new agents fresh from Soviet chemical warfare laboratories. According to a soldier of the Soviet Chemical Troops captured by the guerrillas, he was directed 'to examine villages after a chemical attack to determine whether or not they were safe to enter or required decontamination.' He also had to 'visit the contaminated areas to collect soil, vegetation, and water samples after Soviet chemical attacks.'[36]

Brigadier Watay, an Afghan defector and former Chief of the Chemical Department, 99th MRL Regiment, reported in 1984 that his department was charged with the protection of troops from the effects of chemical weapons (his unit would have fired chemical rockets) and with the analysis of their effects on the battlefield.[37]

Two new, unusual chemical weapons are worthy of notice. The first, a kind of spongy powder, was reported to have been used in Jozjan Province. Spread over the fields there, the powder started 'to smoke and burn as soon as it was hit by the sun.' The chemical set the vegetation on fire and produced fumes which caused nausea, vomiting, and unconsciousness. When the sun set, the agent returned to dormancy, but became active again the next morning. The process repeated itself four to five times before the active ingredient was exhausted.[38] Only one report of this agent is known, so it may be misleading.

The second agent, termed 'liquid fire' in the Western press, has also not been documented and confirmed in detail, but it bears a certain resemblance to the substance described above. (In fact, it could be a derivative or a later version of the first agent). Supposedly, the Soviet Air Force distributed a black tar-like substance in the eastern provinces of Afghanistan. Dropped in containers which burst open in mid-air, this substance fell to the ground in droplets which can lie on the ground for months. However, when stepped on, the droplets burst into flames, which produce nauseating fumes. Trucks which drive over the 'liquid fire', even on dirt roads, are said to have been completely consumed by fire as a result.[39]

The Soviets also confirmed in Afghanistan that the helicopter was an outstanding platform for the dispersal of chemical spray. The Mi-8 and the Mi-24 performed this mission, particularly the latter. Operations demonstrated that the NBC protection systems of the Hind-D and E models were capable of giving full protection to the crews of the aircraft from the effects of the spray which they dispensed.[40]

Overall, the military effects of Soviet chemical weapons on the course of the war were negligible. They certainly had a certain 'terror' effect on villagers and *mujahedin* wherever they were used. They also played a part in the eco-war, being used to burn fields, poison water sources and food supplies (livestock destruction), and to drive villagers away. They were not used, on the other hand, to the extent that they could have been used to block infiltration routes (with persistent agents, for example). In terms of casualties, in 1982 the US State Department estimated that Soviet chemical weapons had caused the deaths of 3,000 persons — mostly civilians. This is an appalling number, to be sure, but a number which represents only a small percentage of war casualties overall.

Undoubtedly, the greatest benefit achieved through the inhuman use of these outlawed weapons is the empirical evidence which the Soviets obtained, evidence which can be applied to chemical operations in a future war. In fact, some analysts believe that the experience gained in the DRA has already played an important role in the design of a new generation of chemical and biological weapons by the Soviet Army.[41]

CHAPTER 11

Troop Support

LYING behind every successful military operation are the elements of logistics, quality and suitability of equipment, preparatory training and quality of leadership. The war in Afghanistan was no exception. Some of these elements have already been touched on; this chapter deals with them in more detail.

Logistics

As in so many other areas, the LCSFA was unprepared logistically for the occupation of Afghanistan. Western analysts of Soviet military affairs have long speculated that logistical sustainment of combat operations would be a problem for Soviet forces in any future war. The record of the Soviet-Afghan War certainly fully supports this assessment.

On the surface, the logistical requirements of maintaining a force of 120,000 men in a country sharing a border may not seem daunting, especially when one remembers that the United States fielded a force almost five times as large in Vietnam across an ocean lifeline which stretched thousands of miles. Distance was not the main obstacle for the Soviet Command, although Afghanistan is a large country. The primary obstacles to logistic support were the inhospitability of the terrain and climate, the grossly underdeveloped road network, the absence of railroads, and the primitive Afghan infrastructure of depots, supply nodes, and repair facilities. It should also be remembered that the Soviets had to arm and maintain the Afghan Armed Forces as well as their own (although, incredibly, they required the Afghan régime to pay them $2 billion a year for this military aid).[1]

It is clear that Soviet planners underestimated the severity of the logistical problems facing them. Prior to the Soviet invasion, few resources were devoted to building up the maintenance, repair, and supply facilities which would become vital to sustainment of the force in country.[2] Certainly, the expectation that the invasion force would accomplish its mission quickly and with minimal combat operations influenced this absence of preparation.

Soviet forces moved into Afghanistan supported by their organic maintenance and supply units, which functioned out of tents and rough shelters for several years, in many cases. Once the command recognised that the LCSFA would be staying indefinitely, a comprehensive building programme was undertaken to strengthen the logistical infrastructure. Soviet engineers and construction battalions (*stroibat*) widened, improved, and extended highways; expanded existing airfields and built new ones; built fixed structures for repair facilities; established and hardened depots and storage facilities for ammunition and fuel; and laid Afghanistan's first railroad line in the north (to facilitate the export of Afghan natural resources to river ports, then to the Soviet Union). In some locations, the Soviets employed Afghan labour, in others military units and thousands of Soviet civilian workers performed the work.[3] Major logistic centres were established at Pol-i-Khomri, Kabul, Shindand, and Jalalabad. In addition, traffic along the main highway arc was supported by a new system of smaller bases which provided traffic control, repair facilities, refuelling, as well as security for rest stops and overnight stays.

Keeping the flow of supplies moving in Afghanistan was a major problem, and not just because of rebel attacks. Judged by Western standards, Soviet driver-mechanics are notoriously inexpert. When faced with the harsh driving conditions of Afghanistan — poor roads, sharp turns, steep climbs and descents, extreme weather, dust — Soviet drivers experienced an unexpectedly high rate of breakdowns. Wheeled and tracked vehicles designed for the flat terrain and good highways of Europe could not stand up to the demands of movement in the DRA. It was soon realised, as noted above, that driver-mechanics desperately needed to pass through a long training course specifically developed to teach them how to operate and maintain vehicles in mountainous and desert terrain. These courses led to an improvement in operator skills, but the Soviet and Afghan armies still lost so many trucks to breakdowns and combat damage that several repair plants were built new or were modernised in the country.

In addition, SOPs were instituted to handle routine situations. For example, march columns were put together at certain major assembly areas along the highway arc. Convoys were dispatched only after they had attained the requisite size and received the necessary command, security, and maintenance elements to accompany them. Tow bars and chains were distributed liberally throughout the columns. When a vehicle broke down, the convoy would halt for no more than 10–30 minutes. If the repair could not be accomplished in that time, the vehicle was towed to the nearest repair facility.

The extreme conditions of weather and terrain affected all military equipment, not just vehicles. Aviation maintenance units struggled under the burdens of primitive field working conditions and the increased servicing requirements which arose from the heavy daily use of airpower in both combat and routine logistical operations. Naturally, the more that aircraft were used, the more often did periodic services have to be performed.[4]

Owing to the regional dispersion of airpower, particularly helicopters, the Soviets introduced some innovations in maintenance procedures to provide decentralised support. Mobile repair trailers were devised to carry the materials necessary to do minor repairs to aircraft at remote sites (skin-patching, for example). Portable argon arc-welders were also developed for field repairs.[5] Some repairs normally done at special workshops in peacetime were carried out at field locations. The clear intent of these workshops was to repair aircraft as quickly and as far forward in the maintenance hierarchy as possible. Overall, they seem to have succeeded. On the other hand, limitations in repair facilities meant that Soviet aircraft had to be ferried back to the Soviet Union for major overhaul and repairs.

Maintenance of communications equipment was a third area highlighted in the

Soviet press as a significant problem. The sources of the problem are familiar: low levels of competence of operators and repairmen, deficiencies in design, and the toll exacted by the harsh, non-standard operating conditions. The 40th Army never solved these problems; communications breakdowns plagued the forces in the field throughout the war.

Soviet soldiers in Afghanistan also lacked the personal equipment necessary for combat, at least initially. Before his departure in 1980, General Tukarinov attempted to obtain a remedy.[6]

> We organised an exhibition of the equipment, arms, and gear that our soldiers had altered and adapted for military actions in the mountains and desert. Marshall Sokolov summoned weapon designers and rear service workers to look and learn. And soon, BTRs, helicopters, and certain types of weapons and gear underwent changes.

However, later reports dispute the idea that all the problems with equipment were resolved quickly. Several years into the war, participants still complained that they needed better uniforms with more pockets and subdued, not shiny, buttons. Rucksacks also needed more outside pockets and reinforced stitching.

Deficiencies in the Soviet logistical base created serious operational consequences. To begin with, because of the toll exacted by rebel attacks, stocks of materials were constantly being depleted. Each major Soviet offensive was always preceded by a logistical build-up of ammunition, fuel, food, and spare parts. Most Soviet operations were terminated after 4–6 weeks because they reached a logistical (as opposed to operational) 'culminating point'. The command simply could not sustain a large force out of garrison beyond that time. Moreover, a lengthy recovery period followed each operation.

Water was one of the primary limiting factors. An extensive, reliable system of water supply, consisting of wells, cisterns, ditches, and underground channels had existed in Afghanistan for many years prior to the Soviet invasion, but it was largely destroyed in the Soviet eco-war bombings. As a result, Soviet forces had to carry water with them on their operations, replenishing them only rarely from local supplies. Water shortages, in fact, also caused the Soviets to abandon some bases in the countryside.[7]

Two other facets of logistical support bear mention. The first concerns the food supply and the second, health services. If the quantity of food provided for Soviet soldiers in Afghanistan was sufficient, the quality varied widely from unit to unit. Apparently, the CI force enjoyed rations much superior in taste and variety to those of the MR force. Where the CI force at times received fresh meat, fruit, and vegetables, motorised rifle personnel received only canned food.[8] Food shortages sometimes occurred on a spot basis. The fact that Soviet soldiers frequently sold military equipment and supplies or exchanged it for fresh food in Afghan bazaars indicates dissatisfaction with the usual diet. In addition, there are many reports of Soviet soldiers confiscating food from Afghan villagers and travellers under threat of violence.

The quality of health services presents a much darker picture. Providing adequate medical support to troops in combat has been a major problem for the Russian and Soviet Armies in every conflict since at least the Crimean War. Despite its much more limited extent, the Soviet-Afghan War is no exception to this rule. The problem has its primary source in the fact that Soviet peacetime, medical support to soldiers is abysmally poor. Recent articles in the Soviet military press attest to a long list of fundamental deficiencies including:[9]

▶ inadequate diet
▶ insufficient medical facilities
▶ poorly trained medical personnel in insufficient numbers
▶ lack of systematic, preventive health care
▶ low standards of hygiene in food preparation, sewage and water supply
▶ shortcomings in laundry and bath facilities
▶ inadequate measures to prevent the spread of infectious diseases
▶ widespread disregard for safety in many specialities

Under such conditions, it is not surprising that many Soviet soldiers suffer sickness or injury. A former Soviet military doctor who worked as the Chief of the Dysentery Ward in the Trans-Baikal Military District in the 1970s claimed that about half of all Soviet conscripts are treated for dysentery at least once during their two years of service.[10] In one test, 20 per cent of the men in a regimental sized unit were found with skin infections.[11] A third Soviet report estimated that perhaps as many as 15,000 Soviet soldiers died in service from 1985–89 as a result of accidents, disease, or malice.[12]

Alarming though these figures are, conditions were even worse in Afghanistan. An official television series on life in the Soviet Army (*Sluzhu Sovetskomu Soyuzu* — 'I Serve the Soviet Union') described in 1988 how the medical service in Afghanistan lacked the means to deal with the epidemic, infectious diseases encountered in the country and implied that more soldiers died from disease during the war than from combat.[13] In 1987, it was reported that the largest Soviet military hospital in the country (Kabul) was operating with only half of the required nursing staff and less than one-third of the laboratory technicians needed.

The shortage of water mentioned earlier also played its part. According to Soviet veterans of the war, most units had no running water and hot water was seldom available. Soldiers often went a month without a bath or shower, dinner plates and utensils were scrubbed, but not washed, laundry seldom got cleaned nor bedsheets changed, and drinking water was often impure. Diseases like jaundice, dysentery, hepatitis, malaria, typhus, intestinal parasites, and skin infections approached epidemic proportions.

> All the hospitals in Afghanistan were packed. One time, 20 per cent of my unit were in the hospital with hepatitis. Also there were many cases of dysentery, malaria and typhus, and everybody had boils and skin infections. Those who were very sick would be sent to the hospital in Termez.[14]
>
> Medical care in our regiment was very poor... There was not enough medicine. They would keep you two days (in the aid tent), give you pills of some kind and let you go, and that was it. Jaundice was a real epidemic in our unit; you know how your eyes and skin turn yellow and you feel nauseous all the time. About a third of the soldiers got it while I was there.[15]

Heat stroke and dehydration created many casualties as well during the summer and frostbite during the winter. Such casualties often surpassed the capability of medical detachments to treat them during actual operations. According to one sergeant, nine soldiers in his regiment died of heat stroke during a four-month period.[16] Casualties from heat stroke, dehydration and frostbite are easily avoided with good training and simple precautions. In most armies, a high rate of such casualties is considered to be a sure sign of sub-par leadership, inadequate training and the absence of combat discipline. The prevalence of these casualties among the LCSFA, especially amongst those whose contact with the enemy, and therefore exposure to the elements, was sporadic, is symptomatic of third-rate military performance. One is reminded of the performance of Argentine forces in the Falklands War.

Being sent to a hospital was no guarantee of recovery from illness or injury. In the first place, serious wounds and injuries could be treated only in Kabul or in the Soviet Union. The lengthy time required for evacuation sometimes meant death. The testimony of a nurse who served in an infectious diseases ward in Afghanistan creates images of criminal neglect. She claimed that medical supplies and medicines were so deficient that the nurses often used one syringe over and over again. Wounds were treated with petrol. Naturally they healed poorly. Many patients did not even have pyjamas or blankets; such things were sold on the black market for money to buy drugs and food. The hospital in which she worked had beds for 300 persons, but it regularly harboured 1,000 lice-infested patients who lay on the floor on their greatcoats. Facilities were so badly needed that a stable was converted into a hospital. She laments further that:[17]

> I could have saved more, but there wasn't the medicine that was needed. Also, the wounded were brought in too late ... I could have saved them but I could not rouse the drunken surgeon ... There were many [soldiers] who had gone out of their minds.

Continuing health problems constitute one area about which Soviet veterans of the war frequently complain in letters to newspapers and journals. Apparently, many have been unable to obtain adequate follow-up care since their discharge. In a Soviet survey carried out in 1989, 31 per cent of the respondents (7–8,000 Afghan veterans) stated that the restoration of their health was the most troublesome post-war problem they had had to face. Another 35 per cent cited the restoration of mental equilibrium. One of the respondents claimed that, 'The main thing for us is to restore our health. One half of us lost our health and so how are we to live?'[18] Perhaps, the latter claim is an exaggeration. On the other hand, it is likely that non-combat health hazards and improper medical care accounted for far more deaths in Afghanistan than official Soviet statistics allow.[19]

Equipment Testing

If the war ended unpleasantly for the Soviet Armed Forces, it at least proved to be a boon with respect to tactical and technical testing of equipment and weapon systems. Aircraft and air operations occupy first place in this field, particularly with regard to the SU-25 Frogfoot ground attack air jet and the Mi-24 Hind helicopter and the aircraft which accompanied them. Table 11.1 enumerates the other important systems tested during the war, most of which have been discussed earlier. However, several of these items deserve closer investigation because of their adaptability to counter-insurgency warfare.

First, the AGS-17 automatic grenade launcher proved itself to be one of the most versatile and effective Soviet weapons employed during the war. Known as the *Plamya* (flame), the AGS-17 dates from 1975.[20] It is a tripod-mounted indirect fire weapon which fires a 30-mm grenade from a 29-round drum magazine to a maximum range of 1,500–1,700 metres (effective range about 1,000 m). Several kind of ammunition are available, although the LCSFA used simple high-explosive most of the time. With a rate of fire of 65 rounds a minute and a bursting radius of 3–5 metres, the weapon can deliver a tremendous amount of immediate firepower against targets which are inaccessible to direct fire weapons either because of range or of defilade cover.

One drawback is weight. Fully assembled and loaded, the *Plamya* weighs 45 kilogrammes (99 lbs). Magazine reloads weigh 14.7 kg (32 lbs). Man-packing such heavy loads is an exhausting business, forcing the gun sections to practice careful ammunition conservation when dismounted at a distance from an armoured carrier.[21] The experience of Afghanistan has led Soviet designers to look into the manufacture of a skid or trolley in order to reduce the burden of dismounted movement.

The AGS-17 is normally found at company level of both BTR- and BMP-equipped motorised rifle units. Each gun section is made up of a sergeant section leader, who directs the fire, and two three-man gun teams: the gunner, who carries the sight and barrel; the assistant gunner, who carries the tripod and ammunition; and, the ammunition bearer, an infantryman detailed from the company, who carries additional drums. Under conventional tactical doctrine, the gun teams dismount and deploy slightly to the rear of the company, the two launchers on line, 10–20 metres apart. From here they provide a base of fire against pre-planned targets to cover the advance of the company.[22]

In the DRA, the tactical organisation of the section often varied. MR units were often up-gunned, i.e. equipped with additional gun teams to increase support. In addition, the CI force employed the weapons in single-gun teams, attaching them to individual platoons, recon parties and ambush groups. The weapon was also observed mounted on BTRs. No special mount was noted. Apparently, the gunners simply placed the tripod on the deck plates and fired from there. Soviet satisfaction with this weapon is well-documented in their military press.

A second weapon used sparingly, but effectively, in small unit operations is the RPO-50 flame rocket launcher. Externally, the weapon resembles a recoilless rifle. It fires incendiary rockets to a maximum range of 400 m (effective range approximately 200–250 m). The Soviets used the launcher against rebel fortifications and cave positions.[23]

A third weapon tested in the war was a new light anti-tank rocket, the RPG-22. Like the RPO-50 flame rocket launcher and the AGS-17, the Soviets employed the RPG-22 against fortified positions and rebel vehicles. Larger than the older RPG-18, the new AT rocket fires an 80-mm rocket with a potent HE warhead. Effective range is 250–300 m. Like the American LAW, the RPG-22 is a throw-away weapon. Once the rocket is launched, the tube is discarded.[24] The simplicity and light weight of the weapon permitted a useful number to be carried as auxiliary weapons on small, dismounted, independent operations where larger vehicular systems could not be used. Naturally, the Soviets had to be careful about letting the weapon fall into *mujahedin* hands since it could easily knock out Soviet light armoured vehicles.

Table 11.1

Soviet Military Equipment Field-Tested in Combat in the DRA

SU-25 ground attack jet
Mi-24 Hind armoured attack helicopter
BM-27 16-round, 220-mm multiple rocket launcher (also known as
    the BM-22)
BMP-2 armoured combat vehicle (tracked)
BTR-70 and -80 armoured combat vehicle (wheeled)
2S9 240-mm mortar
AGS-17 automatic grenade launcher
Vasilek 82-mm automatic mortar
PKPE-1 multiple grenade launcher
RPG-22 AT rocket
RPO-50 flame rocket launcher
KMT-5 mine roller system
AK-74 automatic rifle
Various AP mines and mine dispensers
Liquid pressure-sensitive mines
Fuel-air explosives
Various types of chemical weapons and dispensers

It is noteworthy that the Soviets did not deploy two new model helicopters, the Havoc (attack) and the Hokum (multiple role), to Afghanistan for testing. It is likely that the decision not to combat test them was based on a fear that foreign intelligence services might be able to exploit any helicopters brought down by rebel fire or accident.

It bears repeating that the Soviets showed a moderate degree of imagination and improvisation in the manner in which they adapted tactics and weapons to the Afghan environment, such as the use of anti-aircraft guns mounted on trucks for convoy protection and the modification of armoured vehicles to carry light mortars and grenade launchers. They also responded rapidly to changes in rebel methods of capabilities, the best examples being modifications introduced on helicopters for defence against hand-held SAM missiles.

Training

Several earlier sections of this book have discussed some aspects of the subject of training. In Chapter 1, it became clear how the reserve Central Asian divisions initially deployed to Afghanistan were too poorly trained even in conventional operations to be of much use. The replacements introduced in the first half of 1980 were better trained as individuals, but did not function much better as units, especially when faced with the unconventional requirements of counter-insurgency operations.

The casual observer may not appreciate the fact that a company of trained men does not mean that you have a fully trained company. Once soldiers have acquired the necessary individual skills, then they must be trained to operate successively as members of a team, squad, platoon, company and battalion. Because of the decision to employ reserve divisions in the occupation force, the Soviet Command saddled itself with a severe training problem.

The nature of the standardised Soviet training programme contributed to the perpetuation of the unreadiness of the LCSFA. The Soviet Army is a conscript army. Draft call-ups are carried out twice a year; the men are called for two years service. Conscripts receive only three weeks basic training and are then sent to their units where there training is completed. Thus, every six months, a typical unit discharges 25 per cent of its enlisted component — the best trained segment since they are at the end of their service — and receives in replacement a cohort of men with a mere three weeks of rudimentary training.[25]

The training of NCOs is somewhat better. Conscripts selected for service as NCOs go to special training divisions where they pass through a six-month programme before being posted to a unit. Unlike NCOs in Western armies, who attain NCO rank only after multiple enlistments, Soviet NCOs are no older and only slightly more experienced than the soldiers they lead.[26] Naturally, neither NCOs nor soldiers normally receive any special training for climactic regions or special forms of combat.

The readiness of the 40th Army was adversely affected as a result of this approach to training. The requirement to train the soldiers assigned to the LCSFA interfered with the demand to conduct combat operations against the rebels. Since it would have been unwise to reduce the number of units committed to local security and criminal to send not yet fully-trained soldiers out on operations, the command often faced a shortfall in ready manpower. Nevertheless, many soldiers were assigned to combat duties before they completed an in-country training programme. The competing, simultaneous demands of conducting operations and training the force were difficult to manage and guaranteed to produce unsatisfactory results in both areas.

It was plain to the Soviet command that its occupation forces were unsuitably trained, both for basic combat operations and CI war. The generals made some effort as early as 1980 to assess the tactical requirements of combat in Afghanistan and to apply remedies.[27] Such efforts were hampered by lack of time and resources. In addition, the rapid growth in the size of the LCSFA during the first several years meant that the leadership had to spend much of its energy on reorganisation, establishing garrisons, and constructing logistical bases. More than two years passed before the command introduced necessary changes to training programme.

Beginning in mid-1982, the Turkestan Military District became the training base for soldiers bound for the DRA. The major training centre was Ashkhabad where the 280th Training Division made its home. Other training posts were established at Termez, Iolotan, Chardzou, Tedzhen, and possibly Kushka.[28] Here, soldiers experienced climatic and topographic conditions similar to what they would meet in Afghanistan. [*The mountain warfare centres which existed prior to the war in the Caucasus and Tajikistan may also have been used to prepare soldiers for Afghanistan, but there is no strong evidence of this.*]

Infantrymen, driver-mechanics, and most other specialists (engineers, artilllery-men and communications personnel) received pre-deployment mountain and desert training at these sites, with a clear emphasis on the special requirements of combat in Afghanistan. Mock Afghan villages were built by the troops then 'razed to the ground' in live-fire exercises.[29] Recon sappers received extra training in mine-clearance techniques and bomb-disposal in Chardzou. An artillery sergeant reported that he had been trained thoroughly in the use of 122-mm howitzers in mountains in Turkestan.[30] Night training and hand-to-hand fighting were also emphasised. Apparently, Afghan veterans were used widely as cadres throughout the training base.

Drivers were singled out for special emphasis, since Soviet drivers in the first years of the war had been noted as exceptionally poor. The training programme lasted from three to six months. Recruits were taught how to operate vehicles on different kinds of mountain roads under all weather conditions, and how to perform the repairs and maintenance necessary to keep a vehicle running. They also learned basic defensive skills and immediate action procedures for ambushes.

> Before I went to Afghanistan, I spent two and a half months at a training centre in the town of Elatane in the Turkmen SSR. There I improved my skill as an armoured personnel carrier driver and learned other military skills, from firing in mountainous conditions to hand-to-hand combat.[31]

Some drivers bound for Afghanistan may have been trained in this manner in Bulgaria.[32]

Apparently, once this training programme went into effect, the requirement to conduct training by the LCSFA diminished significantly. Testimony from Afghan veterans indicates that relatively little formal training took place in their Afghan garrisons and it seems that the training which was conducted was designed more to test readiness than to develop or sharpen skills.[33] Once assigned to a unit, an individual soldier simply had to fit in best he could and try to catch up to the level of experience of his comrades. Failure to conduct systematic unit training in Afghanistan undoubtedly kept MR units from achieving a high degree of coherence and integration, given the relative infrequency of manoeuvre operations. Any unit held in garrison performing security functions for months at a time will inevitably experience a diminishment of its combat readiness before it embarks on its next manoeuvre operation. The combat edge of a unit must be kept sharp, either through actual operations or through training exercises. In Afghanistan, MR units always had to pass through a learning curve each time they were ordered out on an offensive because of their inactivity between offensives.

The training picture for the CI force was much brighter. In the first place, these élite forces consisted of a higher quality of manpower hand-picked from volunteers and the draft cohort. Second, they passed through a much longer, varied, and more rigorous training programme. Officers and men in these units are required to participate in such activities as hand-to-hand combat, martial arts, survival training, long forced marches in harsh weather, strength and confidence drills, extra marksmanship, and, of course, extended tactical drills in varied terrain, mounted and dismounted. Standards of performance are quite high.[34]

Third, some companies of recruits were apparently formed, trained, and deployed as units to Afghanistan, a significant departure from standard practice since the Soviets employed an individual replacement system for Afghanistan, except for Air Force units.[35]

Once in Afghanistan, the CI force trained much more often than the MR force, despite the fact that it also maintained a much higher frequency of direct action against the *mujahedin*. Tough, daily, physical fitness and weapons training programmes maintained individual skills. Many small unit operations were rehears-ed before execution. In addition, it is clear that the airborne and air assault units occasionally conducted training patrols under combat conditions with a real chance of contact in order to 'bloody' a unit, to expose the men to combat before full im-mersion in a major long-term operation. Many times, only those units which had demonstrated the highest level of combat readiness would be selected for the most important missions. The CI force managed to maintain a high level of combat readiness through these means.

Determining how well the Soviet army in Afghanistan studied its experience and updated its training and tactical operations based on lessons learned is not easy. General Tukharinov has referred to a circular which his staff disseminated in March 1980, to describe how the *mujahedin* operated.[36] Other veterans have mentioned post-operation, debriefing sessions at which they discussed new enemy techniques and tactics and appropriate responses and counters. On the whole, however, there does not appear to have been a systematic comprehensive, command-wide effort to use training circulars, briefings, SOPs, operational notes, or manuals to keep the LCSFA continuously informed about new tactical developments. It was up to in-dividual units, more or less, to update their own procedures based on their own experiences. There are few indications of lateral flow of this kind of information between similar units. Many tactical lessons probably had to be re-learned over and over again, especially in view of the frequent change-over in personnel.

Some operational problems were never solved on the training field. Throughout the war, Soviet units consistently failed to achieve the standards of performance re-quired in the areas of vehicle operation and maintenance, communications, quick defence, dismounted manoeuvre, reconnaissance, and night operations. Surprising-ly, physical fitness was another area where the MR force fell short.[37] It is surpris-ing because, given any group of reasonably healthy young men, physical fitness can be raised rapidly and sustained through a steady, demanding training programme requiring less than one hour a day. The fact that physical fitness remained a problem simply means that the Soviet leadership in Afghanistan made little effort to correct it.

On the other hand, as we have already seen, a great deal of very useful information about Soviet combat operations in Afghanistan has appeared in military journals. Undoubtedly, officers bound for Afghanistan made good use of this material as preparation. Some Air Force units (see Chapter 9) depended on journal articles and the aid of Afghan veterans as the only pre-deployment training resource available to them. However, it is quite difficult to tell how well the 40th Army staff and its constituent sub-commands exploited this resource in country. Certainly, the intro-duction of a separate CI force into Afghanistan and the almost full reliance on it as a direct-action force against the rebels strongly indicates that the Soviet Command drew the conclusion that it could never train the motorised infantry arm to carry out the kinds of decentralised, independent, dismounted operations necessary to destroy the *mujahedin*.

Leadership

At this point, it seems superfluous to dwell overlong on the question of Soviet military leadership. Clearly, a substantial differential existed between the tactical skill and leadership of the MR force and that of the CI force. Although the tactical leadership of the MR force improved significantly from 1980 to 1983, it never surpassed a rather crude level of bare adequacy. The great majority of Western and Afghan observers of the war present a uniformly bleak picture of MR leaders, characterising them as unimaginative, predictable, inflexible, textbook-bound auto-matons applying rigid 'school solutions' and Soviet templates to tactical situations, no matter how poorly they applied.[38] A myriad of examples exists to support these evaluations. In contrast, for reasons which have been described previously — higher quality manpower, better training, a hand-picked officer corps — the leadership of the CI force achieved much higher standards of tactical skill. Rather than rehash these now familiar themes, a more valuable exercise would be to investigate how the Soviet Armed Forces evaluated the quality of its officers and NCOs during the war.

Internally, the Soviet High Command recognised that its officers and NCOs were not well prepared for the tactical requirements of the war in Afghanistan, which were spelled out in detail in the Soviet military press (Chapter 7). Many other companion articles further identified the tactical and technical skills needed by the officer corps in Afghanistan. Not surprisingly, these confirm the weaknesses observed by Western and Afghan observers and the prescriptions they provide for improvement are predictable.

At the tactical level, these writers cited the need for junior officers capable of acting with initiative and creativity. More precisely, Soviet critics insisted that officers must be capable of making decisions without guidance from higher headquarters in situations of great stress. Furthermore, such decisions needed to go beyond the rote responses learned in military schools; they had to demonstrate imagination and flexibility to fit the non-standard combat conditions. Some authors, particularly aviators, encouraged unorthodox tactical techniques and risk-taking. One expression in particular, *'Boyevat' ne chislom, a umeniyem'* (Fight with skilful art, not strictly by the book), a well-known maxim of Russia's most famous and able Marshal A V Suvorov, is repeated over and over in these articles.[39] By the end of the war, some authors were advising officers virtually to throw the book out the window.

On the other hand, some of the actual combat activities cited by these authors as examples are really quite trivial from the Western perspective. In one example, a simple out-flanking manoeuvre is cited as an imaginative, unusual approach.[40] In another, several rather petty departures from standard procedures are mentioned with pride: the use of single-shot fire in limited visibility, the use of visual and sound signals together for redundancy and reliability, and frequent changes in co-ordination signals (ostensibly to prevent their compromise by the insurgents).[41] A third example, often cited in different settings, was the bold officer or NCO who, communications cut with higher command, acted on his own using his best judgement until communications were re-established. In contrast, any Western officer or NCO who sat on his hands in the absence of guidance from above would likely be relieved from duty.

The fact that such actions are described as unorthodox, non-standard, even bold decisions worthy of emulation, demonstrates just how tight and binding are the controls on Soviet initiative. Fear of responsibility and risk-taking and rigid adherence to standard procedures are so deeply ingrained in the Soviet mentality that any movement toward independent thinking and action represents a breaking of the mould. Furthermore, the fact that calls for the exercise of creativity and imagination on the part of officers were repeated constantly throughout the war, constitutes strong evidence that little widespread progress occurred in remoulding Soviet officers, especially within the MR force. Moreover, it is clear that, even in Afghanistan, there were sharp limits on the exercise of initiative. All but minor deviations from the given plan required approval from supervising headquarters.

With respect to technical, personal skills, Soviet military literature points out a number of areas where improvement is recommended. The strict compartmentalisation of duties in the Soviet Army where every officer, specialist, or technician, has his own established set of duties and no cross-over is permitted did not serve the army well in the DRA. In standard Soviet operations, only artillery officers plan or call for artillery fire support. Only engineers set out mines and only radio operators handle the radios. This system is too rigid to support small units operating independently as they so often did in Afghanistan. Consequently, the most successful officers in Afghanistan endeavoured to acquire skills which formerly only specialists performed. Among those mentioned (and recommended) in the Soviet military press were direction of indirect fire and air support, defence against booby traps, the offensive use of mines, arranging air medevac support, attaining a higher level of physical fitness, and wider expertise with weapon systems, radios, and vehicles. In general, these articles attempted to instill the attitude within the leadership that officers were responsible for every aspect of combat, not just those for which they had personal responsibility. The attitude that one could avoid responsibility by claiming that a function performed unsatisfactorily was 'not my job' was censured sharply.[42] Thus, an ambush leader who failed to put out mines because he had no engineer detachment present with him did not meet the new standard called for in these articles. However, once again it is clear that only a small percentage of Soviet officer veterans of Afghanistan responded to these new demands.

A third aspect of leadership addressed in the Soviet military press is the role and position of the sergeant. In peacetime, Soviet sergeants have little responsibility or authority. Most of the quite important duties performed by sergeants in Western armies are undertaken by officers in the Soviet Armed Forces (helicopter crew chiefs and door gunners are enlisted positions in the West and officer slots in the Soviet Union, for example). This system had an adverse effect on operations in Afghanistan because teams and squads of soldiers led only by sergeants very often had to carry out independent missions. The unfitness of the Soviet NCO Corps for such a role became painfully evident in the DRA.

Afghan veterans have stressed that the officer corps must make special efforts to train NCOs more fully and to strengthen their authority. The tendency of troops to bypass their sergeants and go directly to officers for problem-solving must be discouraged.[43] One officer implemented a periodic 'sergeants' day' during which the unit NCOs occupied all the positions of authority and carried out the day's activities. He identified several areas where airborne sergeants need additional training: teaching methods, tactics, firing techniques, physical fitness, and drills.[44]

Another common theme was the need for improving relations between officers and NCOs with the goal of placing more trust in NCOs. Given the youth and limited experience of Soviet NCOs and the lack of an institutional base for a real NCO corps, it is not surprising that few significant improvements in this area occurred, except perhaps within the CI force.

If the authors cited above were mostly young officers willing to speak candidly about the flaws in military leadership revealed in Afghanistan, the Soviet Army's senior commanders have shown much less openness and an unwillingness to recognise widespread deficiencies in the training and performance of the officer corps. Their public pronouncements on the war consistently praised the high qualities of the officer corps and the warm relations which existed between officers, NCOs, and the men. General Gromov, for example, categorically denied that Soviet officers in the DRA were untalented, callous, or narrow-minded. If there were such officers, he says, they were exceptions.[45] Such statements have no credibility when compared against the testimony of the Soviet military press in general and the testimony of individual soldiers in a variety of forums.

There are two other non-combat areas which permit an assessment of Soviet military leadership in Afghanistan: troop support is one area and the other is the question of the illegal conduct of Soviet soldiers. Even if one concedes a significant divergence in military culture between East and West regarding the quality of life due to a soldier in wartime, one cannot dispute the fact that the Soviet command failed to provide an adequate level of troop support. As noted above, medical care was abysmally poor and living conditions (for an occupation force) were primitive. In addition, the command made little effort to relieve the boredom and sense of isolation felt by the troops.

Physical beatings of soldiers by officers, apparently, were common.[46] Officers often used soldiers virtually as personal servants. *Dedovshchina*, the unofficial but tolerated system of privileges demanded by senior conscripts at the expense of new recruits, a system which has long disrupted unit cohesion and morale in the peacetime Army, flourished in Afghanistan as well. Occasionally, frustration and despair over the sadistic and cruel treatment meted out by the '*stariki*' (older soldiers) led the newer men into acts of desperation: fragging, desertion and suicide.[47] Responsibility for this state of affairs must be laid at the door of the officer corps. It is noteworthy, however, that *dedovshchina* and abuse of soldiers by officers were not as common in the more professional CI force as within the occupation force.

Under the conditions just described, many Soviet soldiers turned to the use of drugs and alcohol to suppress their troubles. Interviews with Afghan veterans and the more explicit articles appearing in the Soviet press in the late 1980s give good reason to believe that the majority of Soviet soldiers in the DRA, including many officers, used drugs — hashish, opium and marijuana — on a regular basis. Theft and sale of military supplies, which was also widespread, is another example of serious indiscipline within the LCSFA.

> Our soldiers would try to sell anything they could in order to get extra money and drugs. They would steal and sell to the Afghans spare parts, tyres, cooking pots, even cartridges.

> My friend and I were heavily involved in the sale of ammunition to the Afghans ... We even sold them some single-shot RPGs. We had several soldiers and officers in our unit who were caught selling weapons and ammunition.

> We smoked *chars* (opium) every day and got it from the Afghans in exchange for gasoline and ammunition. We sold diesel fuel from the tank almost every day. Sometimes we would exchange also for money and food such as melons and grapes.[48]

Perhaps the most alarming illegal conduct tolerated, and even instigated, by the officer corps was the wide-scale, commonplace looting and massacre of Afghan non-combatants and prisoners. The scope of this activity is not well-known in the West, having been largely ignored by the major media, but the Afghan people will long remember the thousands of times they endured the plunder of their homes, the stripping of their belongings at search points, the rape of their women, the mutilation of bodies, the torture of their men, and the callous, indiscriminate slaughter of villagers. It is no exaggeration to say that every Soviet soldier assigned to Afghanistan witnessed or participated in atrocities of this nature at some time in their service.[49]

All guerrilla wars are characterised by atrocities, most often committed by the insurgents who use such activities to terrorise the population and demonstrate the impotence of the governing powers. Indeed, the hands of the *mujahedin* were not innocent in this regard. However, a disciplined, professional army will not tolerate atrocities. This is not to say that atrocities will not be committed by such an army. The point is that the command structure will punish offenders and strive to eliminate atrocities as illegal, uncivilised acts of barbarism. Professional soldiers view such criminal acts with repugnance, seeing in them the seeds of destruction of their own forces. In Afghanistan, although a few soldiers were punished for indiscriminate brutality, rape, and murder, the Soviet command in fact directed the carrying out of some atrocities and looked the other way in most other cases. The enormous scale of atrocities in Afghanistan is perhaps the best indicator of the failure of the Soviet leadership and the evidence of an Army without a soul.

CHAPTER 12

Conclusions

IN contrast with the expertly planned and executed coup, the Soviet Army which occupied Afghanistan in December 1979 was handicapped by five severe deficiencies:

▶ a false expectation that a show of force and brief occupation would be sufficient to accomplish its objectives
▶ a flawed assessment of the strength and resilience of the *mujahedin*
▶ the burden of a force structure and tactical doctrine unsuited to military operations in Afghanistan
▶ logistical unpreparedness
▶ an ideological blindness to the requirements of counter-insurgency war

Overall, the Soviet Army adapted quite slowly to the unexpected conditions that confronted it. Some necessary adjustments were recognised quickly, e.g. the need to reorganise the occupation force, sending home unnecessary elements and de-centralising the remainder. Other lessons took longer to register: several years passed before the Soviets established a training base in the Turkestan Military District and no training base was ever established for the VVS.

Eventually, the Soviet command developed a CI strategy that included a military component tailored to the particular conditions of anti-guerrilla warfare in a large, underdeveloped mountainous country. But, neither the CI strategy as a whole nor the military response produced decisive results. Although this book is not intended to be a critique of the Soviet CI strategy, it is impossible not to note that the strategy was fundamentally flawed. It lacked the essential ingredients of wide popular support, understanding and respect for local culture, legitimate authority of governing bodies, integrated civil-military intelligence, strong regional military presence, and continuous military pressure against the insurgents. The Soviets made no efforts to win the hearts and minds of the people except through crude propaganda and forced measures. Indeed, the strategy ultimately took a genocidal form through the failed, but tragically costly, attempt to crush resistance by destroying Afghan society and the rural economy.

The principal form of military operations against the *mujahedin* was the periodic conventional offensive. The conduct of these operations improved year by year as the Soviets perfected co-ordination between the MR force, the CI force, and the arms which supported them — artillery, bombers, ground attack aircraft, and

126

helicopters. Improvements in this area included the development of new tactics, such as *blokirovaniye* (blocking tactics), isolation of objective areas, the creation of fire traps, and the broader use of enveloping detachments and ambushes. The Soviets learned to create an effective balance of heavy, ground forces and light, airmobile forces in these operations and demonstrated increasing sophistication in command and control. In addition, the LCSFA adapted, again slowly, to the *mujahedin* threat and changes in rebel capabilities. Significantly, it appears that most of these gradual Soviet changes were instituted from above, i.e. by the regional and 40th Army headquarters and not by the forces in contact. This approach was entirely in keeping with the historical Soviet approach to change on the battlefield.[1]

Due to logistical shortcomings and manpower constraints, the Soviets could not sustain these offensives for more than a few weeks. Moreover, despite the changes cited above, the offensives retained too much of a conventional character and Soviet unit commanders continued to be bound by unimaginative, stale, inappropriate tactics. As a result, they did not prove decisive, although they were sufficient to maintain a stalemate.

Some relatively minor technical and tactical innovations characterised other aspects of Soviet operations, such as: the use of AA guns and AT missiles in a ground attack role during convoy escort; double or triple employment of retrans stations in the mountains to improve the reliability of communications; modifications to fixed-wing aircraft and helicopters for protection against missiles; use of heliborne mortars to support isolated, small-scale operations; attachment of FACs and artillery adjustment teams to units below normal doctrinal level.

Throughout the course of the war, the Soviets relied overmuch on technological solutions to the problem of Afghan resistance. Ignoring the lessons of history, that guerrillas must be defeated man-to-man at close range on the ground, the Soviets persisted in attempts to use superior technology to grind the *mujahedin* into submission from long range. The ubiquitous use of AP mines, the constant artillery shield during operations, and the extensive high-altitude bombing campaigns are the best examples of this failed approach. Dependence on technology also revealed a reluctance on the part of the Soviets to close with the rebels in isolated small-scale combat, probably because of their sensitivity to high casualties (and poor casualty exchange ratios) and the realisation that they seldom achieved success at that level.

Tactically, the Soviet command properly analysed the requirements of combat operations against the *mujahedin* only to discover that Soviet motorised rifle troops were entirely unsuited for this role. Although Soviet tactical doctrine describes the (light infantry) functions needed for the Afghan War as legitimate functions for mechanised troops, the conventional orientation, tactical rigidity, and generally poor quality of MR units and their commanders prevented them from acquiring the necessary skills. The continuing poor tactical performance of the MR force throughout the course of the war severely limited the tactical utility of the force, as demonstrated in the words of rebel leader Abdul Haq, who noted in 1988 that, 'The Soviets have conscript soldiers, a frontier force, heliborne forces, and *spetsnaz*. They can only change tactics when they change troops'.[2] The Soviets simply accepted the fact that they were unable to raise the level of proficiency of the motorised-rifle force above a certain basic level.

Some individual arms within the larger MR force performed more creditably than the infantry. In particular, the artillery and engineers lived up to a higher standard, as described in Chapter 10 above, although it should be reiterated that the influence of the artillery on the outcome of battle rarely was significant.

In response to the pressing need to field a force capable of meeting the *mujahedin* in combat on their terms — on foot in the mountains — and in recognition that the MR force could not be trained up to the necessary level, the Soviets developed and deployed a separate counter-insurgency force. The employment of this force, composed of airborne, air assault/airmobile, reconnaissance, and *spetsnaz* troops, in small, independent operations on a regular basis constituted a significant departure from standard Soviet practice. These better-trained, higher quality units performed much more ably than the MR force, adapting their small-unit operations to the military environment and winning the grudging respect of *mujahedin* leaders. Still, the record shows that the CI force also had to struggle in the first few years to master the terrain and insurgent threat. Although these units practised a tactical style similar to that of the insurgents, they failed to match the *mujahedin* in many light infantry skills, relying too much on technical advantages and not enough on tactical superiority and fieldcraft. The employment of the CI force increased pressure on the *mujahedin*, restricted their activities, and raised the number of rebel casualties, but it did not cripple the resistance. It must be admitted, on the other hand, that the limited numbers of these units and their inability for security reasons (hostility of the populace above all) to disperse and base themselves in the countryside precluded them from having a decisive effect against the resistance. Even at its best, the combined forces of the LCSFA remained unable to shut down *mujahedin* resupply, eliminate urban centres of resistance, protect garrisons and outposts, or pacify a single province.

The Soviet experience in Afghanistan demonstrated beyond doubt that there is a wide gap between what is prescribed in Soviet tactical writings and what their units can actually perform, including the élite units. All military units, of course, lack proficiency in certain areas; it is impossible for any unit to be constantly ready for every potential mission. That is, indeed, why units train. What is surprising about Soviet combat experience in the DRA is the *breadth* and *time span* of the gap between tactical doctrine and tactical proficiency. Even after years of fighting the *mujahedin*, Soviet units continued to fall short of the standards demanded for tactical success.

General Gromov himself acknowledged this deficiency:

> The war in Afghanistan demonstrated the large rupture between theory and practice. It revealed a row of problems ... I repeat the most important weakness — that was the gap between theory and practice. But that is unavoidable.[3]

The last statement by Gromov is one with which few professional officers would agree. It is obviously an attempt to play down the significance of the tactical failures of the MR force and the Soviet leadership. The fact is that such a gap between theory and practice is inevitable only at the outbreak of war. Good training and good leadership will close that gap rapidly. The LCSFA was unable to close that gap appreciably, precisely because it lacked good unit training and good leadership.

There is no reason to believe that the deficiencies identified in the MR infantry, which forms the vast bulk of the Soviet Army, is peculiar only to those units deployed to Afghanistan. The same systemic flaws which hindered the adaptation and employment of the LCSFA in non-standard battle conditions will hinder the Soviet Army as a whole in any future conflict. It is safe to say, in fact, that were the Soviet Army to become involved again in a similar conflict, its MR troops might well perform even less ably today, given the trying conditions in which the Army now finds itself. In addition, many of the obvious deficiencies in the MR force, particularly tactical rigidity and unimaginative leadership, would seriously degrade the performance of the Army in conventional operations as well.

Transfer of Soviet Combat Experience

> Today [*Afghan War*] veterans are the bearers of priceless combat experience. Unfortunately, up to recent times, this experience has not been applied, neither in studies nor in exercises.[4]
> (*Military Herald*, May 1990)

Despite the tragic results of the Vietnam War, the tactical experience of that war has proved valuable to the United States Armed Services in terms of the personal combat experienced by a generation of leaders and in terms of the tactical and technical lessons of the war, particularly in regard to small-unit operations, air-mobile operations, army-air force co-ordination, and low-intensity, counter-insurgency operations. (In the latter category, many of the lessons learned were negative in essence, i.e. how not to pursue long-term CI operations.) Many Western analysts have assumed that the Soviet Armed Forces will benefit from their combat experience in Afghanistan in a similar fashion. This study suggests that this conclusion is ill-founded and premature. Most of the open evidence indicates to the contrary that the Soviets *have not* translated their Afghan combat experience in a way which will be generally beneficial to the force as a whole, nor *will* they do so in the future.

Chapter 9 has already shown how the Soviet Air Force has ignored the applicable lessons of the war. Training programmes have not changed appreciably. Initiative and independent action are not being encouraged or rewarded. Afghan veterans, so far, have not exercised any appreciable influence on the manner in which pilots are trained and conditioned. In fact, the hierarchy appears somewhat hostile to the concrete suggestions of the *Afgantsii*, while paying lip service to the need to develop creativity and raise the quality of the force. It is possible, of course, but by no means inevitable, that as the Afghan veterans rise in seniority, this institutional indifference to the Afghan War may dissipate.

The record of the Ground Forces in this area is better, but mixed. During the course of the war, the Soviet Army did try, in a modest way, to transfer the lessons learned in Afghanistan to other units, particularly to units training in or expected to operate in mountainous regions. Articles in the Soviet military press in the 1980s discussing training activities in the Soviet Union often cited DRA experiences in support of the points being made. A great deal of emphasis was placed on heliborne *desants*, employment of mounted enveloping detachments, wide-ranging reconnaissance, physical fitness, terrain negotiation, pre-emptive occupation of dominating heights and so on. A lively appreciation for the utility of grenadiers, mortars, and gunship support was shown. Nevertheless, a close reading of this literature reveals that the conventional context prevailed. Dismounted manoeuvre, a feature of CI war, was seldom practised by motorised troops in the Soviet Union. Guerrilla groups like the *mujahedin* were never simulated. The enemy in training exercises was always conventionally armed and disposed. Major air and air defence operations by both sides, as well as NBC conditions, characterised Soviet training exercises during the period of the Soviet-Afghan War.

The *Kavkaz* (Caucasus) *85* exercise is a perfect example of this pattern. Conducted by 25,000 troops in the Caucasus Mountains, the exercise stressed the co-ordinated, but separated movement of small mounted units through mountain passes, emerging into areas of major engagements. Heavier forces, including tanks, moved along valleys, while lighter forces approached the objective area indirectly through more restricted terrain. Continuous pressure was maintained on the enemy so that the main attack force could remain in march order as long as possible. Both opposing forces remained under constant threat of air attack by the other side. A major highlight of the exercise was a bold raid against the forward command post of the defending headquarters prior to the main attack by a heliborne 'commando' team with special attachments. One can see here clear evidence of the influence of DRA tactics superimposed upon a conventional scenario in mountainous terrain.[5]

One 'conventional' area in which Soviet combat experience has translated directly is that of airbase defence. Soviet airbases in Afghanistan came under frequent attack by the *mujahedin* using multiple means — direct ground attack, sabotage from the inside, and stand-off rocket or mortar bombardments of short duration. Although the Soviets suffered significant losses from these attacks, they never lost control of an airbase, owing to the effectiveness of the security measures introduced (and the inability of the *mujahedin* to mass significant combat power against large defended installations).

Recognising that their airbases in Europe might be subject to attack in a future war by special forces, deep airborne or airmobile raids, or even partisans, the Soviets applied lessons learned in Afghanistan to airbase security in Europe. The new approach integrates dedicated MR defence units with self-defence measures undertaken by the Air Force units occupying the base. Responsibility for defence is assigned to an Air Force officer since he can better assess priorities in the organisation of the defence. Under his command, a dedicated MR company (or larger unit, depending on the size of the airbase) physically located on the base, provides the first reaction to any attack against the installation. Should this force fail to repel the enemy, trained VVS ground crews would implement a last-ditch defence from pre-designated defensive positions within the base. In addition, anti-aircraft weapons such as the ZSU-23-4 SP automatic cannon would be used against enemy equipment and personnel. These procedures, which follow the Afghan pattern, were tested in exercises in Europe in the late 1980s.[6]

In addition, what the Soviets call special troops have benefited importantly from combat experience in the DRA. A deliberate effort to pass lessons learned by engineer, communications, and reconnaissance troops in Afghanistan to similar units in the Soviet Union took place during the 80s. Unquestionably, Soviet capabilities in mine and anti-mine warfare and communications in mountains have improved as a result of the war. However, the aim was not always achieved: many Afghan veterans in these arms have complained that they face strong resistance whenever they try to depart from established training programmes in order to introduce innovations sparked by their combat experience.

Like the Air Force *Afgantsii*, Ground Forces officers have complained that their senior commanders refuse to accept any deviations from official procedures. Training inspectors quickly note and condemn violations of approved training plans. Few commanders are willing to take the responsibility for the risk of trying something new. Innovators are curbed by censure and official reprimands.

In a few instances, innovative commanders at low levels have succeeded in pushing through needed changes.[7] By and large, however, these examples are presented as rare exceptions to the standard training regimen. As a group, Afghan veterans have displayed a strong desire to put their combat experience to good use in their assignments subsequent to duty in Afghanistan, but they are disheartened by a deep sense of frustration in their inability to exercise the same level of initiative and creativity which some achieved there.

Here exists an interesting paradox. Soviet difficulties in Afghanistan found their sources, above all, in the lack of creative, innovative leadership. Accordingly, during the war, few issues were covered in more detail and as repetitively as the issue of leadership. Soviet military writers and analysts stressed the need and repeated the call for the development of initiative, imagination, and creativity among the leadership of the Armed Forces. If limited progress was achieved in this area in the LCSFA, the average officer and sergeant back in the Soviet Union seems hardly to have been influenced at all. Outside Afghanistan, it was much safer and easier to conduct oneself strictly by the book. The Armed Forces as a whole proved resistant, indeed, virtually immune, to the introduction of these essentially alien concepts. Still, the Soviet press has continued without abatement in the 1990s to cry out for improvements.[8]

Quality of leadership and quality of training are inextricably intertwined. It is not surprising, therefore, that Afghan veterans have severely criticised Soviet military training, emphasising firmly that current training programmes fail to prepare soldiers and units for war. In particular, veteran officers express dissatisfaction with: lack of realism and excessive simplicity in training exercises; excessive controls on scenarios; spending too much time on parade drill and administrative activities; and, the predictable, repetitive pattern of training. These officers say that training is too easy, too simple, and far removed from actual combat requirements, and too much under the unbending control of unimaginative plans written in stone and forced down from above. As improvements they suggest:

▶ incorporating several related training objectives in a single exercise (e.g. conducting dismounted tactical movement, rather than a simple march, to a rifle range, or, combining engineer mine clearance operations with reconnaissance, complicated by an ambush)
▶ more use of non-standard task organisations
▶ more cross-training of personnel within units
▶ use of sister units as aggressors on a regular basis
▶ incorporation of unplanned changes to a scenario
▶ full blending of tactical and technical training
▶ more reliance on junior leaders
▶ less interference and direction from higher headquarters

Obviously, these suggestions are designed to introduce more realism into training and to develop creativity and imagination within cadres. Individual officers and commanders have succeeded in making such changes on a limited scale. Only time will tell whether such reforms will spread more deeply.

However, it does appear that the failure of Soviet arms in Afghanistan and the vehement complaints of veterans have influenced the initiation in the Soviet Army of a re-evaluation of its tactical doctrine. On 7 January 1989, the editors of *Red Star* (*Krasnaya Zvezda*), the newspaper of the Soviet Armed Forces, opened a debate on the question of the military readiness of the forces. They invited their readership to correspond with the newspaper in order to identify deficiencies in training programmes and tactics and to share ideas on the solutions to these problems. The introductory article for this dialogue, 'Revival [*of Tactics*] as Art', was written by General Lieutenant B Khazikov, Deputy Chief of the Main Administration of Combat Training of the Ground Forces. This article was quite pointed in its criticism of unimaginative training, slavish adherence to textbook tactics, and incompetent commanders. Complementary articles on 2 February and 5 April by senior officers extended the dialogue further.

In January 1990, a distinguished Soviet senior officer, General Major I N Vorobyev, Doctor of Military Sciences and contributing author to many Soviet military texts such as *Taktika* (Tactics), weighed in on this issue with vigour, in the most prestigious Soviet military journal, *Military Thought*. Echoing the comments of Afghan veterans, Vorobyev tied the stagnation in Soviet tactics directly to unsatisfactory training methods.[9]

> The deep-seated roots of the lag in the development of tactics must be sought above all in routine tactical thinking, in administrative pressure, voluntaristic methods of directing combat training, in ostentation, in subjectivism, and in the parochialism of a certain portion of the military cadres.
>
> ...the fact that young officers formed a light impression of battle and the opinion predominated that it could be won without special exertion and without the most thorough preparation ... was facilitated by the archaic, stereotyped methodology of conducting exercises, especially field-fire exercises, by a run-through of tactical episodes in which everything was written out and rehearsed in advance. This attempt to present one's activities in a 'rosy light' led to a predominance of 'show' tactics, where no room was left for a display of creative quests either on the part of training activity leaders or the trainees.
>
> The training of personnel took place in the channel of a monotonous tactical orientation. Regulation, over-organisation, and the fear of retreating from regulations continued to stifle live, innovative thought.

Warning that 'this heavy legacy of stagnation will drag tactics backward for a long time yet if not fought decisively', Vorobyev suggested that 'a quality research work on the development of tactics in local wars generalising the experience of combat operations, in Afghanistan above all, is also very necessary for officers and generals'.[10]

Thus, if Vorobyev and others are heeded, the legacy of the Soviet-Afghan War may yet influence the implementation of significant reforms in Soviet tactical doctrine and training. However, this task will not be easy since it goes against the very grain of Soviet military mentality. Undoubtedly, the most important obstacle to be overcome is continued resistance at high levels to the idea that major change is necessary. For example, General Gromov, who speaks with great authority in the Soviet Army, while acknowledging the need to dedicate more time and resources to training, which must also be better integrated, has also argued that he 'would not change anything fundamental in the Army as a result of the war'.[11]

Throughout the course of the war, the Soviet High Command viewed counter-insurgency operations as an anomaly not likely to be repeated. There were no attempts in the 1980s to develop and maintain a separate CI force, outside of the élite units. However, since the war ended, there is some slight evidence that the Soviet leadership is beginning to take a deeper interest in CI operations as a form of combat for which their forces must be prepared in the future.[12] This interest is directly connected with the projected, unavoidable use of regular forces as peace-keeping and stabilisation forces in regions of ethnic unrest in the Soviet Union. Already, Soviet Army troops (primarily, but not exclusively, airborne units) have been committed to such operations in the Caucasus, Central Asia, and the Baltics. Pressure is growing for the General Staff to give more attention to CI operations since it is clear that the Internal Troops of the Ministry of Internal Affairs will not be able to handle future flare-ups alone. The conflicts between Armenia and Azerbaijan and in parts of Georgia have already taken on the character of civil war. The experience of the Soviet Army in Afghanistan should acquire new significance and urgency in this situation.[13]

In conclusion, the Soviet High Command cannot but be alarmed about the military performance of its forces during the Soviet-Afghan War. The Soviet command in Afghanistan failed to achieve even one of its primary objectives. Despite overwhelming advantages in material and technology, the LCSFA could do no better than to achieve a stalemate. Ultimately, Soviet forces were compelled to withdraw. The motorised-rifle arm of the Soviet Army never adapted to counter-insurgency war in a satisfactory manner. Furthermore, the Soviet military has not done a good job of exploiting the combat experience of the war, turning a deaf ear to the sometimes bitter pleas of Afghan veterans for change.

Beyond doubt, with regard to the lessons of the Soviet-Afghan War, two contradictory impulses are at work today in the Soviet Army, one demanding deep reform, the other resisting change in tactical doctrine and training. The sheer weight and volume of the voices demanding change, unprecedented in scale and level of open support, certainly comprise an important advantage. On the other hand, the difficult circumstances in which the Soviet military now finds itself may well work to drown out the voices of reform. At the present time, the Soviet High Command is hard pressed to deal with the concrete consequences of Gorbachev's new military thinking. Preoccupied with the questions of substantial force reductions, withdrawal from Eastern Europe and Mongolia, a shrinking budget, very serious housing shortages, draft resistance, diminished prestige, an adversarial civilian press, rising competing influence of civilian analysts, and general loss of authority in government and Party circles, the Soviet military leadership may not have the resources to reform itself simultaneously from a tactical and training viewpoint, even it was clear that it wanted to. And yet, if the High Command does not address itself promptly to the concerns noted above, firmly facing the problems revealed through the refining fires of war in Afghanistan, the opportunity may slip away.

Chapter Notes

(For abbreviations used in these notes see Glossary, page vii.)

Chapter 1. The Invasion

1. J Bruce Amstutz, *Afghanistan: The First Five Years of Soviet Occupation* (Washington, DC: National Defense University Press, 1986), p. 59; Mark Urban, *War in Afghanistan* (London: Macmillan Press, 1988), p. 40.
2. 'Kak prinimalos' resheniye' (How the Decision Was Made), *KZ*, 18 Nov. 1989, p. 3.
3. *Afghanistan: A Country Study* (Washington, DC: The American University, Foreign Area Studies, 1986; produced for the US Government), p. 303.
4. 'Afghanistan: One Year On', *IA*, Mar. 1980, p. 88 (no author). An excellent, perceptive discussion on the issue of the decision to invade Afghanistan can be found in: Cynthia Roberts, 'Glasnost' in Soviet Foreign Policy: Setting the Record Straight?', RFE/RL *Report on the USSR*, Vol. 1, No. 50, 15 Dec. 1989, pp. 4–8. See also General Major K M Tsagalov, 'Ne Vse Tak Prosto' (Not Everything is so Simple), *SShA*, No. 6, 1989, pp. 62–68.
5. 'Kak prinimalos' resheniye', p. 3.
6. Ibid.; see also, 'Lieutenant General Varennikov Interviewed on Entry into Afghanistan', *Soviet Patriot*, 27 Dec. 1989, pp. 1–2 (FBIS translation, JPRS-UMA-90-007, 23 Mar. 1990, p. 123).
7. 'Kak prinimalos' resheniye', p. 3.
8. Both of these commanders, like many other general officers associated with the war, rose to the pinnacle of their profession during the 80s. Lushev was appointed C-in-C Warsaw Pact Forces in 1989; in 1990 Maksimov was C-in-C, Strategic Rocket Forces.
9. John Erickson, '*Afghanistan. A Review of Current Developments*', unpublished manuscript, 1980, p. 4.
10. 'Former 1st Deputy Commander, Turkestan MD on Invasion', *SR*, 20 Dec. 1989, p. 6 (FBIS translation JPRS-UMA-90-007, 23 Mar. 1990, p. 125). See also Urban, *War in Afghanistan*, p. 41.
11. Ibid.
12. *Afghanistan: A Country Study*, pp. 302–303.
13. Edward Girardet, *Afghanistan: The Soviet War* (London: Croom Helm, 1985), p. 13.

14. *Afghanistan: A Country Study*, p. 305.
15. Ibid.
16. Girardet, p. 15.
17. Ibid., p. 14.
18. David C Isby, 'Soviet Tactics in the War in Afghanistan', *Jane's Defence Review*, Vol. 4, No. 7, 1983, p. 685.

Chapter 2. The Second Phase of Soviet Occupation, 1980–82

1. 'Lieutenant General Varennikov Interviewed on Entry Into Afghanistan', p. 123.
2. General Lieutenant B V Gromov, 'Pravda Vyshe Sensatsii' (Truth is Higher Than Sensation), *SR*, 15 Nov. 1989, p. 4.
3. S Enders Wimbush and Alex Alexiev, 'Soviet Central Asian Soldiers in Afghanistan', RAND Note N-1634/1, Jan. 1981, p. 4.
4. The question of the introduction and withdrawal of Central Asian soldiers and their military utility is not especially germane to the main themes of this book, so the issue will not be discussed here. Readers are advised to refer to two RAND reports for excellent discussions of this issue: Alexander Alexiev, 'Inside the Soviet Army in Afghanistan', RAND Report R-3627-A, May 1988, and Wimbush and Alexiev, N-1634/1, cited above.
5. Erickson, p. 5.
6. Joseph Newman, Jr., 'The Future of Northern Afghanistan', *AS*, July 1988, p. 730.
7. Urban, *War in Afghanistan*, pp. 66–68.
8. Ibid., pp. 63, 68.
9. AIC 20, Dec. 1982, p. 3; AIC 28, July 1983, p. 10; Louis Dupree, 'Afghanistan in 1982: Still No Solution', *AS* Feb. 1983, pp. 133–142.
10. Colonel Ali Jalali, 'The Soviet Military Operation in Afghanistan and the Role of Light and Heavy Forces at Tactical and Operational Level', *Report of Proceedings: Light Infantry Conference, 1985* (Seattle: Boeing Corporation, 1985), p. 174.
11. A *mujahedin* commander quoted in Amstutz, p. 149, derisively remarked that, 'Most of the time they [Soviet troops] meet us in their armoured vehicles. They seldom go into battle as infantry.'
12. Joseph J Collins, *The Soviet Invasion of Afghanistan* (Lexington, MA: Lexington Books, 1986), p. 151.
13. Isby, p. 689.
14. Jalali, p. 175.

Chapter 4. The *Mujahedin*

1. See for example, A Rasul Amin, 'Unity is the Remedy', *WUFA*, Vol. 1, No. 1, 1985, pp. 9–15.
2. AIC 21, Dec. 1982, p. 14; AIC 24, March 1983, p. 8.
3. Zalmay Khalilzad, 'Moscow's Afghan War', *Problems of Communism*, Jan.-Feb. 1986, p. 12.

4. AIC 27, June 1983, p. 6.
5. AIC 28, July 1983, p. 9.
6. Girardet, p. 61.
7. Amstutz, p. 189.
8. AIC 43, Oct. 1984, p. 18.
9. AIC 70, Jan. 1987, p. 18.
10. AIC 58, Jan. 1986, p. 20.
11. AIC 41, Aug. 1984, p. 13.
12. AIC 30, Sep. 1983, p. 9.
13. AIC 73, Apr. 1987, p. 13.
14. AIC 28, July 1983, p. 9.
15. Amstutz, pp. 217–222.
16. Ibid., p. 193.
17. D Meschaninov, 'A Powerful Blow by the Afghan Army: A Major Insurgent Base Destroyed', *Izvestiya*, 26 Nov. 1986 (FBIS translation JPRS-UMA-87-006, 30 Jan. 1987).
18. AIC 41, Aug. 1984, p. 14.
19. AIC 49, Apr. 1985, p. 8.
20. Captain V Lavremyuk and Senior Lieutenant A Kutz, 'Chemu Nauchila Voina?' (What Did the War Teach?), *VV* No. 1, 1989, p. 60.
21. Senior Lieutenant A Shmatko, 'Bez Nastroya Net Pobedy' (Without the Right Attitude There is no Victory), *VV* No. 6, 1989, p. 47.
22. AIC 23, Feb. 1983, p. 12.
23. Leo O Coldren, 'Afghanistan in 1984: The Fifth Year of the War', *AS*, Feb. 1985, p. 172.
24. AIC 20, Dec. 1982, p. 5.
25. Amstutz, pp. 194–195.
26. Richard Mackenzie, 'Afghan Rebels Never Say Die', *Insight*, 25 Jan. 1988, pp. 8–16.
27. AIC 77, Aug. 1987, p. 11.

Chapter 5. The Doctrinal Dilemma

1. See for example, Colonel N Nikitin, 'Nekotoryye Operativno-takticheskiye Uroki Lokal'nykh Voin Imperializma' (Several Operational-Tactical Lessons of the Local Wars of Imperialism), *Voyenno-Istoricheskii Zhurnal* (Military History Journal) (hereafter cited as *ViZh*), No. 12, 1978, pp. 60–66; General Major V Matsulenko, 'O Vnezapnosti v Lokal'nykh Voinakh' (On Surprise in Local Wars), *ViZh*, No. 4, 1979, pp. 54–65.
2. The best known of Tukhachevskii's writings on the subject is a very short article, 'Voina Klopov' (War of the Bedbugs) in M N Tukhachevskii, *Izbrannyye Proizvedeniya* (*Selected Works*), Moscow: Voyenizdat, 1964, pp. 106–108. However, another of his articles — 'Bor'ba s Kontrrevolyutsionnymi Vosstaniyami. Iskoreneniye Tipichnogo Banditizma' (The Struggle Against Counter-revolutionary Uprisings. Rooting Out a Typical Case of Banditism), *Voina i Revolyutsiya* (*War and Revolution*), August, 1926, pp. 4–15 — is a fine example of counter-insurgency analysis. Describing his handling of the Tambov

Uprising, Tukhachevskii laid out an excellent framework for putting down a regional insurrection. Tukhachevskii clearly identifies the primary features of a successful counter-insurgency strategy. He lays down the necessary organisational structure and he shows how the tasks of the various component elements — the army, the police, the intelligence services, and the administration — must be integrated under the authority of one commander. (He also very openly describes harsh measures which should be taken against the insurgents and their supporters such as the confiscation of property and the seizing and evacuation of family members as hostages.) In short, the article is a masterpiece of coherent thought which could have formed part of the base for the full development of a CI doctrine.

3. For example, Colonel V Andrianov, 'Partizanskaya Voina i Voyennaya Strategiya' (Partisan War and Military Strategy), ViZh, No. 7, 1975, p. 30. In addition, the official Soviet definition of the military term, counter-insurgency war, specifically describes it as an imperialist concept.

4. L V Sosnovskii, 'The Concept of Counter-guerrilla Operations', *USA: Economics, Politics, Ideology*, No. 5, May 1971, pp. 118–123, as translated in JPRS 53268, 2/6/71, pp. 146–155.

5. *Lokal'nyye Voiny: Istoriya i Sovremennost'* (*Local Wars: History and Modern Times*), edited by Army General I Ye Shavrov, Moscow: Voyenizdat, 1981.

6. Ibid., pp. 116–128.

7. Sosnovskii, pp. 146–155.

8. *Military Thought. 1937–1973. Chronological, Author, and Title Index*. Edition 4, Defense Intelligence College, Washington, DC, 1981.

9. For example: F Shesterin, 'Protivo-Vozdushnaya Oborona v Lokal'nykh Voinakh' (Air Defense in Local Wars), *ViZh*, No. 10, 1977, pp. 70–77; General Major V Larionov, 'Nekotoryye Voprosy Voyennogo Iskusstva po Opytu Lokal'nykh Voin' (Several Questions of Military Art From the Experience of Local Wars), *ViZh*, No. 4, 1984, pp. 46–52; General Major V Matsulenko, 'O Nekotorykh Voprosakh Upravleniya Voiskami v Lokal'nykh Voinakh' (On Several Questions of Troop Control in Local Wars), *ViZh*, No. 3, 1980, pp. 52–63; many more articles of this nature could be cited.

10. See, for example, A Sinitskii, 'Nekotoryye Takticheskiye Vyvody iz Opyta Agressivnoi Voiny SShA protiv V'etnama' (Several Tactical Observations from the Experience of the Aggressive War of the US Against Vietnam), *ViZh*, No. 6, 1979, pp. 53–57.

11. For example, General Lieutenant V Kozhbakhteyev, 'Razvitiye Taktiki Deistvii Voisk v Gorno-Lesistoi Mestnosti' (Development of Tactics in Mountain-Forested Terrain), *ViZh*, No. 2, 1981, pp. 36–43; Army General I Tretiak, 'Organizatsiya i Vedeniye Nastupatel'nogo Boya v Gorno-Tayezhnoi Mestnosti' (The Organisation and Conduct of Offensive Combat in Mountain-Taiga Terrain), *ViZh*, No. 7, 1980, pp. 42–49; Colonel V T Yeliseyev, 'Iz Opyta Armeiskikh Nastupatel'nikh Operatsii Pri Gornym Usloviyam' (From the Experience of Army Offensive Operations in Mountainous Conditions), *ViZh*, No. 1, pp. 16–23.

12. Colonel V G Safronov, 'Kak Eto Bylo' (How it Was), *ViZh*, May 1990, p. 68.

Chapter 6. Armed Forces of the DRA

1. Louis Dupree, 'Afghanistan in 1982: Still No Solution', *AS*, Feb. 1983, p. 134. See also AIC 23, Feb. 1983, p. 5; AIC 42, Sep. 1984, p. 4.
2. AIC 42, Sep. 1984, p. 18; AIC 76, July 1987, p. 8. In May 1987, a 1,200-man garrison attempted to surrender to the *mujahedin*. To prevent their dispersal, Soviet aircraft dropped AP mines on them and in the immediate area.
3. AIC 52, July 1985, p. 6. The sabotage of these aircraft was confirmed by many other sources.
4. AIC 20, Dec. 1982, p. 17. In response to the execution of twelve pilots suspected of sabotage in the autumn of 1983 in Shindand, a large number of DRA security troops and frontier military units changed sides, forcing the Soviets to assign more of their own troops to security duties: AIC 31, Oct. 1983, p. 11.
5. For example, see AIC 63, June 1986, p. 3.
6. AIC 24, Mar. 1983, p. 13.
7. AIC 90, Sep. 1988, p. 9; AIC 63, June 1986, pp. 9–11.
8. AIC 63, June 1986, p. 8.
9. Mark Urban, 'A More Competent Afghan Army?', *JDW*, 23 Nov. 1985, p. 1147.
10. Louis Dupree, 'Afghanistan in 1983: And Still no Solution' *AS*, Feb. 1984, p. 232.
11. AIC 42, Sep. 1984, p. 2–3.
12. 'Afghan Militiamen Defect with Government Weapons', *JDW*, 9 Jan. 1988.
13. See AIC 88, July 1988, p. 34; AIC 93, Dec. 1988, pp. 8–9; AIC 94, Jan. 1989, pp. 29–31; Joseph Newman, Jr., 'The Future of Northern Afghanistan', *AS*, July 1988, p. 739.

Chapter 7. The Third Phase of the War, 1983–89

1. The Soviets claim to have controlled only 23% of Afghan territory: Colonel V G Safronov, 'Kak Eto Bylo' (How it Was), *ViZh*, No. 5, 1990, p. 69.
2. 'Afghanistan. The Struggle in Its Fifth Year', pamphlet (Washington, DC: US Information Agency, June 1984), p. 11. See also Khalilzad, p. 9.
3. Charles Dunbar, 'Afghanistan in 1987: A Year of Decision', *AS*, Feb. 1988, p. 151.
4. Charles Dunbar, 'Afghanistan in 1986: The Balance Endures', *AS* Feb. 1987, p. 128.
5. Safronov, p. 70.
6. Major A Oliinik, 'The Fiery Kilometers', *KZ*, 26 May 1985, p. 2 (FBIS translation JPRS-UMA-85-040, 15 July 1985, pp. 138–141).
7. Dunbar, 'Afghanistan in 1986', pp. 133–134.
8. Ibid.
9. AIC 60, Mar. 1986, p. 9; AIC 65, Aug. 1986, p. 14; AIC 69, Dec. 1986, p. 17.
10. 'Improvised Convoy Escort Vehicle', *JDR*, Vol. 2, No. 2, 1982, p. 99.
11. Captain O Bedular, 'Za Povorotum — Kabul' (Beyond the Turn — Kabul), *SV*, No. 6, 1983, p. 18.
12. Several disasters occurred in or near the tunnel. In October 1983, a fuel tanker

exploded when hit by another vehicle inside the tunnel. The ends of the tunnel were sealed. Most of the people inside suffocated, perhaps as many as 5–700 Soviets and 4–500 Afghans: AIC 23, Feb. 1983, p. 13. Then, in March 1985, in circumstances which are unclear, an explosion of ammunition on a truck in a convoy waiting at a checkpoint near the tunnel ignited vehicles in two other convoys, including one of oil tankers. Reportedly, all three convoys were consumed by fire. The highway was closed for four days. The cause of the explosion may have been a time bomb. AIC 48, Mar. 1985, p. 19; AIC 49, Apr. 1985, p. 6.

13. Oliinik, 'The Fiery Kilometers', p. 2.
14. Cardoza, p.87. (See also Chapter 9, Note 3.)
15. Senior Lieutenant V Sokirko, 'Oshibka Chernogo Uchitelya' (The Mistake of the Black Teacher), *VV*, No. 4, 1989, p. 42.
16. AIC 29, Aug. 1983, p. 9.
17. Gromov, 'Zashchishchali', p. 13. However, another authoritative Soviet source indicated that 60 per cent of the Soviet force was involved in the security and defence of fixed sites. The latter figure seems more reasonable: Safronov, p. 70.
18. Coldren, Leo, 'Afghanistan in 1985: The Sixth Year of the Afghan War', *AS*, Feb. 1985, pp. 236–237.
19. AIC 25, Apr. 1983, p. 6.
20. AIC 41, Aug. 1984, p. 15.
21. AIC 59, Feb. 1986, p. 3.
22. AIC 65, Aug. 1986, p. 15.
23. In July 1986, the *mujahedin* destroyed sixty outposts guarding the city and then held off an attack by a large Soviet MR column (said to include 800 combat vehicles — probably an exaggeration).
24. AIC 67, Oct. 1986, p. 10.
25. Major V Kutishchev, 'Ot Blagodarnogo Afganskogo Naroda' (From the Grateful Afghan People), *VV*, No. 8, 1989, pp. 40–43.
26. Alexiev, 'Inside the Soviet Army in Afghanistan', p. 22.
27. 'Soviet Spring', BBC Programme, Mar. 1990.
28. Gromov, 'Zashchishchali', p. 13.
29. Alexiev, 'Inside the Soviet Army in Afghanistan', p. 22.
30. Urban, *War in Afghanistan*, pp. 179, 190–195.

Chapter 8. The Soviet Counter-Insurgency Force

1. Major G Shevchuk, 'Manevr v Gorakh' (Manoeuvre in Mountains), *VV*, No. 12, 1985, pp. 29–31; Tretiak, pp. 42–49; Kozhbakhteyev, pp. 36–37.
2. Captain N Stepanov, 'Granatometchiki v Gorakh' (Grenadiers in the Mountains), *VV*, No. 9, 1985, p. 23.
3. The Soviet term used to denote self-sustainment and self-support is *samostoyatel'nost*.
4. N Stepanov, p. 23.
5. Virtually every account of a night operation conducted by Soviet troops in Afghanistan in the military press involved reconnaissance, airborne or air assault troops, not motorised rifle troops.
6. Steve Sego, 'US Experts Discuss Soviet Army in Afghanistan', RFE/RL,

Report 302/87, 24 July 1987; Alexander Alexiev, 'Inside the Soviet Army in Afghanistan', p. 26.

7. See Roger Bort, 'Air Assault Brigades: New Element in the Soviet Desant Force Structure', *Military Review*, Oct. 1983, pp. 21–37; FM 100-2-3, 4-131 to 4-132.

8. David C Isby, 'Soviet Special Operations Forces in Afghanistan, 1979–1985', *Report of Proceedings, Light Infantry Conference, 1985* (Seattle: Boeing Corporation, 1985), p. 187.

9. Ibid., pp. 185, 187.

10. Ibid., p. 194.

11. Colonel G Kochurov, 'Obkhodiashchii Otriad v Gorno-Tayezhnoi Mestnosti' (The Enveloping Detachment in Mountain-Taiga Terrain), *VV*, No. 6, 1986, pp. 20–23. The use of enveloping detachments is cited in almost every article dealing with manoeuvre in mountains, whether the article refers to Afghan operations or training exercises in the USSR. In addition, many articles which discuss Soviet special troops (engineers, communications troops, etc.) do so within the context of their attachment to an enveloping detachment.

12. A rare example of a MR unit used as an enveloping detachment is described in Senior Lieutenant A Shmatko, 'Bez Nastroya Net Pobedy' (Without the Right Attitude, There is no Victory), *VV*, No. 6, 1989, pp. 46–49.

13. Blokhin, pp. 76–77.

14. Major V Selivanov, 'Bo Flang i Tyl' (To the Flanks and Rear), *VV*, No. 12, 1989, pp. 44–46.

15. Senior Lieutenant A Kiselev, 'Skovz Dushmanskiye Zaslony' (Through Dushman Traps), *VV*, No. 7, 1989, pp. 42–46.

16. Senior Lieutenant A Kravchenko, 'Gruppa v Zacade' (The Group in an Ambush), *VV*, No. 7, 1989, pp. 45–48.

17. Ibid., p. 47.

18. Major S Tuayev, 'Zacada' (Ambush), *VV*, No. 2, 1989, pp. 68–71.

19. Ibid., p. 68.

20. See AIC 42, Sept. 1984, pp. 10 and 12; AIC 49, Apr. 1985, pp. 15–17; AIC 55, Oct. 1985, pp. 5–6; AIC 58, Jan. 1986, p. 12; AIC 74, May 1987, p. 19.

21. AIC 41, Aug. 1984, p. 6.

22. AIC 69, Dec. 86, p. 6.

23. Safronov, p. 70.

24. Colonel S Korobka, 'Razvedka v Gorakh' (Reconnaissance in the Mountains), *VV*, No. 10, 1985, pp. 13–15; Captain E Stepanov, 'Boi v Gorakh — Osobaya Usloviya' (Combat in the Mountains — Special Conditions), *VV*, No. 3, 1988, p. 22.

25. Lieutenant Colonel G Ivanov, 'Razvedka Gornogo Perevala' (Reconnaissance of a Mountain Pass), *VV*, No. 1, 1985, pp. 25–27.

26. See, for example, Major V Alekseyenko, 'Nepreryvno, Tshchatel'no, i Svoyevremenno' (Unceasingly, Carefully and Timely), *VV*, No. 5, 1989, pp. 42–44; Kiselev, p. 42; Kurochkin, p. 35.

27. Ibid., p. 42.

28. Isby, 'Soviet Special Operations Forces in Afghanistan, 1979–1985', p. 188.

29. Alekseyenko, p. 44.

Chapter 9. The Air War

1. Collins, p. 144, reported 240 Soviet gunships and 400 other models of helicopters in Afghanistan in 1985, plus an undetermined number of fixed-wing squadrons and regiments. Amstutz estimated the presence of 300 fixed-wing and 600 helicopters in 1985. Girardet, p. 42, guessed that there were 6–700 helicopters, of which 200 were Hinds, in 1982. In 1987, Aaron Karp asserted the presence of 270 helicopters (140 Hinds) and 150 fighters: 'Blowpipes and Stingers in Afghanistan: One Year Later', *Armed Forces Journal International*, Sept. 1987, p. 40. James Bruce suggested that the Soviets had 900 or so helicopters in the country in late 1986: 'Afghan Rebels "downing more Soviet helicopters"', *JDW*, 15 Nov. 1986, p. 1150. Many other conflicting estimates could be cited. Fixing the exact number of aircraft is not nearly so important as understanding how they were used.
2. John Gunston, 'Afghans Plan USSR Terror Attacks', *JDW*. 31 Mar. 1984, p. 481.
3. 'Special Report: Afghanistan War', *Aviation Week and Space Technology*, 29 Oct. 1984, p. 41. See also, Captain Anthony A Cardoza, 'Soviet Aviation in Afghanistan', *US Naval Institute Proceedings*, Feb. 1987, p. 85.
4. 'The Afghanistan Air War', *Warplane*, Vol. 1, Issue 1, 1985, pp. 5–6.
5. The testimony of John Gunston in 'Special Report: Afghanistan War', p. 41.
6. Colonel V Moroz, 'Letayushchii Tank' (The Flying Tank), *KZ*, 18 May 1989, p. 4.
7. Ibid.
8. Colonel V Tulkhov, 'Deistviya Bombardirovshchikov v Gorakh' (Actions of Fighter-Bombers in Mountains), *AK*, No. 10, 1989, pp. 24–25; Cardoza, p. 86; Gunston, p. 481.
9. Colonel M Konfindratov, 'Gory Uchat, Gory Zakaliayut' (The Mountains Teach, The Mountains Toughen), *AK*, No. 11, 1984, pp. 4–5.
10. Isby, 'Soviet Tactics in the War in Afghanistan', p. 685.
11. Jalali, p. 177.
12. AIC 72, Mar. 1987, p. 3.
13. FM 100-2-3, *The Soviet Army: Troops, Organization and Equipment* (Washington, D C: HQDA, July 1984), pp. 5–177.
14. Isby, 'Soviet Tactics in the War in Afghanistan', p. 683.
15. Ibid.
16. Yossef Bodansky, 'Afghanistan: The Soviet Air War', *Defense and Foreign Affairs*, Sept. 1985, p. 16. The discussion of desant raids is fully supported by a multitude of tactical accounts of desant raids in the Soviet press.
17. Lieutenant Colonel S Dovzhenko, 'Desantirovaniye v Gorakh' (Conducting *Desants* in Mountains), *AK*, No. 6, 1988, pp. 20–21.
18. James F Holcomb, 'Recent Developments in Soviet Helicopter Operations', *Soviet Military Studies*, No. 3, 1989, p. 269.
19. Major V Grechkin, 'Vizhu! Upravlayu! ...' (I See and I Direct ...), *AK*, No. 5, 1988, pp. 36–37; Galina Marchenko, 'Voyennyye Letchiki' (Military Pilots), *AK*, No. 3, 1990, pp. 28–29. Colonel Yu Protasov, 'Nad Gorami' (Above the Mountains), *AK*, No. 5, 1983, p. 17.

20. Lieutenant Colonel G Drugoveiko, 'Shirota 34 Gradusov i Yuzhneye' (Latitude 34 Degrees and South), *AK*, No. 10, 1988, pp. 12–13.
21. Marchenko, p. 29.
22. Major V Trusov and Captain V Maiorov, 'Ekho Salanga' (Echo of the Salang Pass), *AK*, No. 12, 1989, pp. 12–13; A Oliinik, 'Chas' (The Hour), *KR*, No. 2, 1990, p. 10; Colonel Ye Besschetnov, 'Chas Muzhestva' (The Hour of Courage), *AK*, No. 9, 1989, pp. 14–16.
23. Oliinik, 'Chas', p. 10.
24. 'Special Report: Afghanistan War', p. 41.
25. 'Helicopter Protection from IR Missiles', *JDW*, 5 Oct. 1985, p. 743.
26. AIC 90, Sept. 1988, p. 13; AIC 61, Apr. 1986, p. 5; Radek Sikorski, 'Moscow's Afghan War: Soviet Motives and Western Interests', *Occasional Paper No. 27* (London: Alliance Publishers for the Institute of European Defence and Strategic Studies, 1987), p. 26.
27. Charles Dunbar, 'Afghanistan in 1986: The Balance Endures', *AS*, Feb. 1987, p. 129.
28. AIC 75, June 1987, pp. 6–7.
29. David B Ottaway, 'Stingers were Key Weapon in Afghan War, Army Finds', *Washington Post*, 5 July 1989, p. A5. See also Karp, p. 40.
30. Yossef Bodansky, 'SAMs in Afghanistan: Assessing the Impact', *JDW*, 28 July 1987, p. 154.
31. Ibid., p. 132.
32. AIC 90, Sept. 1988, p. 7.
33. Giles Bertin, 'Stingers Change the Face of War in Afghanistan', *JDW*, 10 Oct. 1987, p. 785.
34. Karp, pp. 38–40.
35. Collins, Amstutz, Jalali, Girardet, *et al* . . . are all in general agreement as to the level of aircraft losses. Perhaps more authoritatively, Lieutenant General Peroots, then Commander of the US Defense Intelligence Agency, cited 500 as the number of Soviet aircraft losses through the summer of 1986.
36. AIC 90, Sept. 1988, p. 7.
37. Karp, p. 40.
38. AIC 63, June 1986, p. 9; Trusov, p. 13.
39. A Yarushenko, 'A Bright Hour: Even Today there is a Place for Heroic Deeds', *Soviet Patriot*, 15 Oct. 1986.
40. Drugoveiko, p. 13.
41. Colonel Ye Besschetnov, 'Geroi Afganistana' (Hero of Afghanistan), *KR*, No. 9, 1989, p. 7.
42. Dovzhenko, p. 20.
43. 'Vertolety Vysazhivayut Desant' (The Helicopters Carry Out an Assault Landing), *AK*, No. 12, 1982, p. 28.
44. Lieutenant Colonel N Shilovskii, 'Za Pobedy Otvechayu' (I am Responsible for Victory), *AK*, No. 12, 1989, p. 14.
45. Konfindratov, p. 5.
46. Shilovskii, p. 14.
47. Marchenko, p. 28.
48. Captain S Popov, 'S Chem Idesh' v Boi' (With What Should One Go Into

Battle?), *AK*, No. 7, 1988, pp. 20–21.

49. This deficiency has been reported almost unanimously by Western journalists who have visited the combat zone, and in the Soviet press as well.
50. Paul Moorcraft, 'Bloody Standoff in Afghanistan', *Military Review*, Apr. 1985, pp. 33–34.
51. AIC 68, Nov. 1986, p. 4.
52. General Lieutenant B V Gromov, 'Zashchishchali, Obuchali, Stroili' (We Defended, Trained and Built), *Vizh*, No. 3, 1989, p. 12.
53. Marchenko, p. 29; Besschetnov, 'Tovarisch za Tovarishcha', *AK*, No. 5, 1989, pp. 38–39.
54. Naturally, exceptions exist to this generalisation, but as usual, the exception proves the rule. See Popov, pp. 20–21.
55. Captain S Prokopenko, 'Prikaz Uzhe Podpisan!' (The Order Has Already Been Signed!), *AK*, No. 8, p. 19.
56. Lieutenant Colonel D Goldyrev, 'Uchit'sya Po-Novomu' (Train by New Methods), *AK*, No. 2, 1990, pp. 4–5.
57. General Major Posrednikov, 'Obstacles to Raising Pilots' Qualification Levels', *KZ*, 10 Jan. 1990, p. 2 (FBIS translation JPRS-UMA-90-008, 3 Apr. 1990, p. 34) (original title: 'Class and Proficiency Rating').

Chapter 10. Combat Support

1. 'Hind, 152-mm SP gun in Afghanistan', *JDW*, 14 Nov. 1987, p. 113.
2. Anthony Human, 'Soviet Advisors and Help for Afghanistan', RFE/RL, *Report on the USSR*, RL 97/90, pp. 3–4.
3. Robert H Scales, Jr., *Firepower in Limited War* (Washington: National Defense University Press, 1990), pp. 169–170.
4. See Major V Kurochkin, 'V Zelenoi Zone' (In the Green Zone), *VV*, No. 3, 1988, p. 36; Colonel Yu Churkin, '"Berkut" Vykhodit na Sviaz' ("Break, Break" — Come Up on the Air), *VV*, No. 5, 1988, p. 76.
5. Scales, pp. 182, 196.
6. Captain A Fedorov, 'Pri Vybore Ognevykh Positsii' (Concerning the Choice of Firing Positions), *VV*, No. 1, 1989, p. 57.
7. Colonel V Litvinenko, 'V Gornykh Usloviakh' (In Mountainous Conditions), *VV*, No. 4, 1989, p. 38; Fedorov, p. 55.
8. Ibid., p. 37.
9. Ottaway, p. A5.
10. Colonel V Isgarshev, 'Komandarm' (Army Commander), *Pravda*, 9 Aug. 1988, p. 3.
11. Major R Aushev, 'Bez Sviazi Net Nadezhnogo Upravleniye' (Without Communications There is nor Reliable Communication), *VV*, No. 8, 1986, p. 79.
12. For example, Major Yu Kuz'michev and Captain S Ponomarev, 'Perepriem i Retransliatsiya v Gorakh' (Receipt and Retransmission of Radio Messages in the Mountains), No. 12, *VV*, 1985, p. 74.
13. Captain V Isayev, 'Po Surovoi Shkale Boya' (By the Severe Scale of Combat), *VV*, No. 7, 1989, pp. 44–45; Captain V Kochnev, 'Initsiativa na Povodke' (Initiative on a Leash), *VV*, No. 9, 1989, pp. 49–50.

14. AIC 55, Oct. 1985, p. 6; AIC 41, Aug. 1984, p. 13; AIC 79–80, Oct.–Nov. 1987, p. 4.
15. 'PFM-1 Mine in Afghanistan', *JDW*, 26 May 1985, p. 920. FM 100-2-3, 5-122.
16. Ibid., p. 920.
17. Ibid. *Mujahedin* reports confirm the delivery of mines by all these means.
18. Major G D Shakaib, 'Soviet Military Problems', *WUFA*, July–Sept. 1987, p. 96.
19. For example, Major A Zel'tin 'Zagrazhdeniye v Gorakh' (Obstacles in the Mountains), *VV*, No. 4, 1986, p. 84.
20. AIC 48, Mar. 1985, p. 4. The number of 20,000 may be exaggerated, but the fact of the use of mines in this fashion has been widely reported.
21. According to the Soviets, the *mujahedin* obtained mines of American, British, Italian, Belgian, Chinese, and Egyptian manufacture.
22. Lieutenant Colonel V Martynov, 'Naiti i Obezvredit' (Find and Neutralise), *VV*, No. 12, 1986, p. 69.
23. Gromov, 'Zashchishchali', p. 14.
24. Martynov, p. 69.
25. This information is provided in a caption to a photograph on page 70 of *VV*, No. 2, 1989.,
26. 'New Soviet Mine-Clearing Vehicle', *JDW*, 7 Mar. 1987, p. 376; 'New Mine Clearing Vehicle in Action', *JDW*, 16 Jan, 1988, p. 90.
27. Lieutenant Colonel V Ostankhov, 'Ninnaya Opasnost' (Mine Danger), *VV*, No. 10, 1985, p. 63; Colonel V Lebedev, 'Vernost Internatsional'nomu Dolgu' (Faithfulness, to Internationalist Duty), *AK*, No. 7, 1983, p. 43.
28. Guards Lieutenant A Blokhin, 'Sapery Idut Pervymi' (Sappers Go First), *VV*, No. 11, 1985, p. 76.
29. AIC, 58, Jan. 1986, p. 20.
30. AIC 67, Oct. 1986, p. 17.
31. Yossef Bodansky, 'Soviets "Testing Chemical Agents in Afghanistan"', *JDW*, 7 Apr. 1984, p. 508.
32. Stuart J D Schwarzstein, 'Chemical Warfare in Afghanistan: An Independent Assessment', *World Affairs*, Winter 1982–83, p. 268. Also Amstutz, p. 172.
33. Amstutz, p. 172; according to Girardet, p. 33, the Soviet Army used chemical agents in its first operation in the Kunar Valley.
34. Ibid., pp. 172–173.
35. Schwartzstein, p. 268.
36. Bodansky, 'Soviets "Testing Chemical Agents in Afghanistan",' p. 508.
37. Ibid.
38. AIC 23, Feb. 1983, p. 4.
39. Yossef Bodansky, 'Soviets Use Afghanistan to Test "Liquid Fire",' *JDW*, 26 May 1984, p. 819.
40. 'A New Generation of CB Munitions', *JDW*, 30 Apr. 1988, p. 853.
41. Ibid., pp. 852–53.

Chapter 11. Troop Support

1. 'Afghanistan: The Soviet Army Will Stay', *The Army Quarterly and Defence Journal*, July 1986, p. 275.

2. 'Soviet Maintenance in Afghanistan: Part 1', *JDW*, 22 Feb. 1986, p. 316.
3. AIC No. 48, Mar. 1985, p. 18.
4. 'Soviet Maintenance in Afghanistan: Part 2', *JDW*, 1 Mar. 1986, p. 367.
5. Ibid.
6. Tukharinov, p. 127.
7. Steve Sego, 'US Experts Discuss Soviet Army in Afghanistan', RL 302/87, 24 July 1987.
8. Alexiev, 'Inside the Soviet Army', p. 48.
9. Natalie Gross, 'How Healthy is the Soviet Soldier?', *Soviet Analyst*, 16 Apr. 1986, pp. 3–5.
10. Ibid., p. 4.
11. Alexiev, 'Inside the Soviet Army', p. 44.
12. Revealed on Soviet Central Television on 2 June 1990. Quoted in Steven Foye, 'Murders of Soviet Military Officers', RFE/RL *Report on the USSR*, RL 282/90, 21 June 1990, p. 11.
13. Alexiev, 'Inside the Soviet Army', p. 45.
14. Ibid., p. 46.
15. Ibid.
16. Ibid., p. 47.
17. Svetlana Alekseivich, 'Don't Say You Have Not Been in That War', *IA*, Jan. 1990, pp. 135–137.
18. S Kushnerev, 'After Afghanistan', *Komsomolskaya Pravda*, 21 Dec. 1989, p. 2, reported in JPRS-UMA-90-006, 20 Mar. 1990, pp. 21–24.
19. Official Soviet statistics report 13,833 deaths in Afghanistan during the war, of which 82 per cent (11,381) were combat fatalities. The remainder died as a result of wounds, illness or accidents. The figures are not credible, given the quantity of personal testimony which suggests much higher casualties (as many as 50,000) and a much higher percentage of non-combat deaths.
20. Roger Frost, 'Plamya — the Soviet Flame', *IDR*, No. 12, 1984, p. 1881.
21. Ibid.
22. David C Isby, 'The Soviet AGS-17 Automatic Grenade Launcher' , *JDR*, Vol. 3, No. 5, 1982, p. 473.
23. Lieutenant Colonel V Chernyshov, 'Ognemetchiki v Shturmovom Otriade' (Flame-thrower Operators in an Assault Detachment), *VV*, No. 1, 1985, pp. 76–78; Major V Kurochkin, 'V Zelenoi Zone' (In the Green Zone), *VV*, No. 3, 1988, pp. 35–36; Lieutenant Colonel V Novikov, 'Ognemetchiki Deistvuyut v Gorakh' (Flame-thrower Operators Perform in Mountains), *VV*, No. 3, 1988, p. 44; 'New Soviet RPO-50 Flame Rocket Launcher', *JDR*, Vol. 3, No. 5, 1982, p. 437.
24. 'New LAW usd in Afghanistan', *JDW*, 3 Dec. 1988, p. 1425.
25. In the USSR, all young men undergo pre-military training in their high-school years. As a result, before enlisting, draftees should be proficient in a number of basic skills such as marksmanship, wear and care of the uniform, driving, radio operation, etc. In actuality, much of this training is poorly run, equipment is in short supply, and training objectives are often not achieved. Many recruits into the airborne and air assault units already have significant experience in sport parachute jumping before enlistment.

26. Technical specialists also go to technical training courses. However, only a minimum level of proficiency is attained bfore they are assigned to field units where they are to receive additional training and become fully qualified. See Harriet Fast Scott and William F Scott, *The Armed Forces of the USSR* (Boulder, COL: Westview Press, 1984), chapter 10, pp. 320–348.

27. Tukharinov, p. 127.

28. Mark Urban, *War in Afghanistan*, p. 130.

29. Ibid.

30. Alexiev, 'Inside the Soviet Army', p. 14.

31. 'Afghanistan Poses Training Problems', *JDW*, 12 Mar. 1988, p. 471; John Gunston, 'Afghans Plan USSR Terror Attacks', *JDW*, 31 Mar. 1984, p. 481.

32. Francesco Sartori, 'Afghanistan at War (2)', RL 290/84, 27 July 1984, p. 5.

33. Alexiev, 'Inside the Soviet Army', p. 15.

34. General Lieutenant V Kostylev, 'Sekrety Desnatnoi Zakalki' (Secrets of the Hardening of the Desant Troops), *VV*, No. 4, 1989, pp. 45–48.

35. Alexiev, 'Inside the Soviet Army', p. 17.

36. Tukharinov, p. 127.

37. The number of articles which cite deficiencies in physical fitness of Soviet troops in Afghanistan is surprising. Three of many examples which focus on this subject: Major N Kudrin, 'Reservy Vtorogo Eshelona' (Reserves of the Second Echelon), *KZ*, 1 Oct. 1989, p. 2; Guards Lieutenant Colonel A Soluyanov, 'Ya Protiv Damskogo Vospitaniya' (I Am Against Girlish Upbringing), *KZ*, 17 Sept. 1989, p. 2; Major G Pisukov, 'Gory Lubiat Sil'nikh' (The Mountains Love the Strong), *VV*, No. 11, 1985, p. 42.

38. In contrast, one journalist, Yossef Bodansky, who writes frequently for *Jane's Defence Weekly*, consistently characterised the Soviet leadership in Afghanistan as skilled, imaginative, flexible, and sure to achieve victory. Although his reports of events were generally reliable, his assessments of Soviet military performance were frequently overblown and out of touch with reality.

39. For example, Colonel Yu Protasov, 'Eto v Samom Cheloveke' (It's in the Person Himself), *VV* No. 7, 1985, pp. 52–54; Lieutenant Colonel V Roshchupki, 'Vyshe Gor — Tol'ko Lyudi' (Only People are Higher than Mountains), *VV*, No. 2, 1988, pp. 37–38; Major V Alekseenko, 'Nepreryvno, Tshchatel'no, i Svoyevremmeno' (Unceasingly, Carefully and Timely), *VV*, No. 5, 1989, pp. 42–44; Captain V Kochnev, 'Initsiativa na Povodke' (Initiative on a Leash), *VV*, No. 9, 1989, pp. 49–50; Major B Makarevich, 'Ne Po Shablonu, a Tvorcheski' (Not by Stereotype, but Creatively), *AK*, No. 1, 1983, p. 9; Lieutenant Colonel M Novikov, 'Shablon i Tvorchestvo Nesovmestimyu' (Stereotype and Creativity are Incompatible), *AK*, No. 11, 1983, p. 4; Lieutenant Colonel N Shilovski, 'Za Pobedu Otvechayu' (I am Responsible for Victory), *AK*, No. 12, 1989, p. 14; Captain Ya Cherenkov, 'Meroi Real'nogo'Boya' (By the Measure of Actual Combat), *KVS*, No. 21, 1984, pp. 64–67.

40. Captain V Lavrenyuk and Senior Lieutenant A Kutz, 'Chemu Nauchila Voina?' (What Did the War Teach?), *VV*, No. 1, 1989, p. 60.

41. 'Boyevaya Ucheba Glazami Afgantsev' (Combat Training with the Eyes of Afghan Veterans), *KVS*, No. 24, 1989, pp. 16–19.

42. For example, Shilovskii, p. 14.
43. Guards Major Yu Konobitskii, 'Serzhanty — Nadezhniye Pomoshchniki Ofitserov' (Sergeants — Reliable Assistants to Officers), *VV*, No. 9, 1985, pp. 30–32.
44. Ibid. See also Colonel N Goriachev, 'Ne Oprekat' Serzhantov, a Obuchat'' (Don't Patronise Sergeants, Teach Them), *VV*, No. 5, 1988, pp. 33–35.
45. Gromov, 'Zashchishchali', p. 13.
46. Alexiev, 'Inside the Soviet Army', pp. 35–44. One Soviet officer commented: 'Well, it is true that the officers beat the soldiers. Sometimes they beat them dreadfully. I saw it myself, though I didn't do it personally... Well, in rare cases, I did slap a soldier.'
47. Ibid., p. 40. See also, 'All I Wanted Was To Live', *Komsomolskaya Pravda*, 21 Dec. 1989, p. 2, reported in JPRS-UMA-90-006, 20 Mar. 1990, p. 24, under the title 'Hazing Leads to Desertion'.
48. Alexiev, 'Inside the Soviet Army', pp. 35–39.
49. Ibid., pp. 53–54. Many Western observers and almost every bulletin from the Afghan Information Centre cite Soviet atrocities.

Chapter 12. Conclusions

1. In the Soviet system, low-level commanders have virtually no authority to modify tactics or tactical plans. Even when the tactics in use are obviously unsuited to the situation, permission to alter procedures must be received from higher headquarters. Throughout the Second World War, for example, all important changes to tactical organisation and tactical procedures were driven by the General Staff and disseminated in mandatory directives. As a result, change comes slowly and often only after costly losses on the battlefield. See Scales, *Firepower*, pp. 166–168, for a good, short discussion on this issue.
2. Ian Kemp, 'Abdul Haq: Soviet Mistakes in Afghanistan', *JDW*, 5 Mar. 1988.
3. Gromov, 'Pravda Vyshe Sensatsii' (Truth is Higher than Sensation), p. 4.
4. Major N Babin, 'Voinoi Opalennyye Vedut Za Soboi' (Those Singed by the War Will Lead), *VV*, No. 5, 1990, p. 41.
5. Colonel Yu Protasov, 'V Takticheskom Vozdushnom Desante' (In a Tactical Desant), *VV*, No. 11, 1985, pp. 10–14; Jalali, p. 174.
6. 'Air Defence Soviet Priority', *JDW*, 30 July 1988, p. 177; 'Guard Battalions', *JDR*, Vol. 4, No. 4, 1983, p. 313.
7. Babin, pp. 41–43; Major P Drozdov, 'Boi Nachinayetsia s Rasvedki' (Battle Begins with Reconnaissance), *VV*, No. 5, 1990, p. 39; Fel'dt, pp. 25–28; Kochnev, p. 50.
8. For example, Goldyrev, pp. 4–5; Tkachev, pp. 4–5; Babin, p. 39; Lieutenant Colonel A Shevchuk, 'Sluchainost' ili Zakonomernost'?' (Chance or Regularity?), *VV*, No. 5, 1990, p. 49.
9. General Major (Ret.) I N Vorobyev, 'Why Did Tactics Stagnate?', *VM*, No. 1, 1990, pp. 37–44, as reported in JPRS-UMT-90-001-L, 22 Feb. 1990, pp. 21–26.
10. Ibid., p. 25.
11. Gromov, 'Pravda Vyshe Sensatsii' (Truth is Higher than Sensation), p. 3.
12. For example, Army General Varennikov, Commanding General, Soviet Ground

Forces, has made several public statements since 1989 in which he addresses the probable use of Army units in a CI role in the USSR. See Natalie Gross, 'Soviet Press Review', *Jane's Soviet Intelligence Review*, July 1989, p. 335. See also the Novosti Press Agency translation of Sergei Ignatyev, 'Low-Intensity Conflicts and Military Reform in the Soviet Union, *Military Bulletin*, Feb. 1990, No. 4 (82), pp. 8–11.

13. The question of the use of regular army troops in the maintenance of public order in the USSR is a contentious one which has been and is being debated in the Soviet press. For a good overview, see Stephen Foye, 'Domestic Role of Soviet Armed Forces Debated', *RL 27/90, Report on the USSR*, 19 Jan. 1990, pp. 7–9.

Bibliography

Soviet Sources

Journals

Aviatsiya i Kosmonavtika (Aviation and Cosmonautics)

Besschetnov, Colonel Ye, 'Tovarischch za Tovarishcha' (One Comrade for Another), No. 5, 1989, pp. 38–39.

— 'Chas Muzhestva' (The Hour of Courage), No. 9, 1989, pp.14–16.

Dovzhenko, Lieutenant Colonel S, 'Desantirovaniye v Gorakh' (Conducting Desants in Mountains), No. 6 1988, pp. 20–21.

Drugoveiko Lieutenant Colonel G, 'Shirota 34 Gradusov i Yuzhneye' (Latitude 34 degrees and South), No. 10, 1988, pp. 12–13.

Goldyrev, Lieutenant Colonel D, 'Uchit'sya Po-Novomu' (Train by New Methods), No. 2, 1990, pp. 4–5.

Grechkin, Major V, 'Vizhy! Upravlyayu ...' (I See and I Direct ...), No. 5, 1988, pp. 36–37.

Khorobrykh, Colonel A, 'Za Perevalom Pereval' (One Mountain Pass After Another), No. 10, 1980, pp. 8–9.

Konfindratov, Colonel M, 'Gory Uchat, Gory Zakaliayut' (The Mountains Teach, the Mountains Toughen), No. 11, 1984, pp.4–5.

Lebedev, Colonel V, 'Vernost' Internatsional'nomu Dolgu' (Faithfulness to International Duty), No. 7, 1983, p. 43.

Makarevich, Major B, 'Ne po Shablonu, a Tvorcheski' (Not by the Numbers, but Creatively), No. 1, 1983, p. 9.

Malashko, Captain A, 'Samolety Baziruyutsya v Gorakh' (Aircraft are Being Based in the Mountains), No. 12, 1982, p. 29.

Marchenko, Galina, 'Voyennyye Letchiki' (Military Pilots), No. 3, 1990, pp. 28–29.

Nadezhdin, Major A, 'Pobedu Obespechivayet Initsiativa' (Initiative Provides Victory), No. 7, 1989, pp. 22–23.

Novikov, Lieutenant Colonel M, 'Shablon i Tvorchestvo Nesovmestimy' (Stereotype and Creativity are Incompatible), No. 11, 1983, p. 4.

Popov, Captain S, 'S Chem Idesh v Boi?' (With What Should One Go into Battle?), No. 7, 1988, pp., 20–21.

Prokopenko, Captain S, 'Prikaz Uzhe Podpisan!' (The Order has Already Been Signed!), No. 8, 1989, p. 19.

— 'Traditsiyam Vernost' Khranya' (Faithfulness to Traditions), No. 5, 1988, pp. 30–32.

Protasov, Colonel Yu, 'Nad Gorami' (Above the Mountains), No. 5, 1983, pp. 16–17.

Rachko, Captain A, 'Rybok iz Kapkana' (Dash From the Trap), No. 1, 1990.

Shilovskii, Lieutenant Colonel N, 'Za Pobedu Otvechayu' (I am Responsible for Victory), No. 12, 1989, p. 14.

'Takticheskii Zamycel' Trebuyet Tvorchestva' (A Tactical Concept Requires Creativity), No. 3, 1989, p. 11.

'Taktika Predpolagayet Tvorchestvo' (Tactics Suggest Creativity), No. 6, 1989, pp. 14–15.

Tkachev Colonel V, 'Neobkhodim Novyi Podkhod' (A New Approach is Necessary), No. 1, 1990, pp. 4–5.

Tolkov, Colonel V, 'Deistviya Bombardirovshchikov v Gorakh' (Actions of Fighter-Bombers in Mountains), No. 10, 1989, pp. 24–25.

Trusov, Major V and Captain V Maiorov, 'Ekho Salanga' (Echo of the Salang Pass), No. 12, 1989, pp. 12–13.

'Vertolety Vysazhivayut Desant' (The Helicopters Carry Out an Assault Landing), No. 12, 1982, p. 28.

Zhilin, Major A, 'Zhizn' na Letu' (Life in the Air), No. 8, 1988, pp. 10–11.

International Affairs (published in English by the Soviet Ministry of Foreign Affairs)

'Afghanistan: One Year Later', Mar. 1990, pp. 88–93.

Alekseivich, Svetlana, 'Don't Say You Have Not Been in That War', Jan. 1990, pp. 132–140.

Prokhanov, A, 'Afghanistan', Aug. 1988, pp. 15–24.

Kommunist Vooruzhennikh Sil (Communist of the Armed Forces)

Aushev, Major P, 'Komandirskaya Zrelost' Proveriayetsia Boyem' (A Commander's Maturity is Tested by Combat), No. 2, 1986, pp. 45–50.

'Boyevaya Ucheba Glazami Afgantsev' (Combat Training with the Eyes of Afghan Veterans), No. 24, 1989, pp. 16–19 (interview).

Cherenkov, Captain Ye, 'Meroi Real'nogo Boya' (By the Measure of Actual Combat), No. 21, 1984, pp. 64–67.

Kniazev, Lieutenant Colonel V, 'Sluzhit' Tak Bol'she Ne Mogu' (I Can no Longer Serve This Way), No. 13, 1988, pp. 59–63.

Malyshev, Lieutenant Colonel, N, 'Meroi Real'nogo Boya' (By the Measure of Actual Combat), No. 8, 1988, pp. 34–39.

Mazyrin, Lieutenant Colonel L and Major N Moskalev, 'Na Linii Ognya' (On the Line of Fire), No. 23, 1986, pp. 57–62.

Moseichenok, Major I, 'Afganskiye Problemy' (Afghan Problems), No. 24, 1989, pp. 69–71.

Oliinik, Lieutenant Colonel O, 'Zarnitsi Nad Gindukyshem' (Heat Lightning Above the Hindu Kush), No. 8, 1988, pp. 77–81.

Kryl'ya Rodiny (Wings of the Motherland)

Besschetnov, Colonel Ye, 'Geroi Afganistana' (Hero of Afghanistan), No. 9, 1989, p. 7.
Oliinik, A, 'Chas' (The Hour), No. 2, 1990, p. 10.

SShA. Ekonomika, Politika, Ideologiya (United States of America. Economics, Politics, Ideology)

Mil'shtein, M A, 'Kak Prinimalos' Resheniye', No. 6, 1989, pp. 68–71.
Tsagolov, K M, 'Ne Vse Tak Prosto', No. 6, 1989, pp. 62–68.

Sovetskii Voin (Soviet Soldier)

Bedular, Captain O, 'Za Povorotum Kabul' (Beyond the Turn — Kabul), No. 6, 1983, p. 18.
Chefimova A, 'Afganistan: Starty Druzhby' (Afghanistan: The Beginnings of Friendship), No. 9, 1986, pp. 40–41.

Voenno-istoricheskii Zhurnal (Military History Journal)

Andrianov, Colonel V, 'Partizanskaya Voina i Voennaya Strategiya' (Guerrilla Warfare and Military Strategy), No. 7, 1975, pp. 29–38.
Chugunov, A, 'Deistviya Pogranichnikov na Zapadnoi Granitse v 20-kh godakh' (Actions of the Border Troops on the Western Border in the 1920s), No. 7, 1975, pp. 69–74.
Gromov, General Lieutenant B V (former Commander of Soviet troops in Afghanistan), 'Zashchishchali, Obuchali, Stroili', (We Defended, Trained, and Built), No. 3, 1989, pp. 11–15.
Kozhbakhteyev, General Lieutenant V (Chief of Central Group of Forces), 'Razvitiye Taktiki Deistvii Voisk v Gorno-Lesistoi Mestnosti' (Development of Tactics in Mountain-Forested Terrain), No. 2, 1981, pp. 36–43.
Larionov, General Major V, 'Nekotoryye Voprosy Voennogo Iskusstva po Opytu Lokal'nykh Voin' (Several Questions of Military Art from the Experience of Local Wars), No. 4, 1984, pp. 46–52.
Malinovskii, G, 'Lokal'nyye Voiny v Zone Natsional'no-Osvoboditel'nogo Dvizheniya' (Local Wars of the National-Liberation Movement), No. 5, 1974 pp. 91–98.
Matsulenko, General Major V, 'O Vnezapnnosti v Lokal'nykh Voinakh' (On Surprise in Local Wars), No. 4, 1979, pp. 54–65.
— 'O Nekotorykh Voprosakh Upravleniya Voiskami v Local'nykh Voinakh' (On Several Questions of Troop Control in Local Wars), No. 3, 1980, pp. 52–63.
Mikryukov, General Major L and Colonel V Vaitushko, 'Iz Opyta Boevogo Primeneniya Vertolety v Lokal'nykh Voinakh' (From the Experience of the Combat Employment of Helicopters in Local Wars), No. 11, 1983, pp. 74–81.
Nikitin, Colonel N, 'Nekotoryye Operativno-takticheskiye Uroki Lokal'nykh Voin Imperializma' (Several Operational-Tactical Lessons of the Local Wars of Imperialism), No. 12, 1978, pp. 60–66.
Odintsov, Colonel V, 'Tylovoye Obespecheniye Voisk s Primeneniem Aviatsii po Opytu Lokal'nykh Voin' (Rear Support of Forces Using Aviation according

to the Experience of Local Wars), No. 2, 1985, pp. 81–86.

Safronov, Colonel V G, 'Kak Eto Bylo' (How it Was), No. 5, 1990, pp. 66–71.

Shesterin, F, 'Protivo-vozdushnaya Oborona v Lokal'nykh Voinakh (Air Defence in Local Wars), No. 10, 1977, pp. 70–77.

Sinitskii A, 'Nekotoryye Takticheskiye Vyvody iz Opyta Agressivnoi Voiny SShA protiv V'etnama' (Several Tactical Observations from the Experience of the Aggressive War of the US Against Vietnam), No. 6, 1979, pp. 53–57.

Tretiak, Army General I (Commander, Far Eastern Military District), 'Organizatsiya i Vedeniye Nastupatel'nogo Boya v Gorno-Tayezhnoi Mestnosti' (Organisation and Conduct of Offensive Combat in Mountain-Taiga Terrain), No. 7, 1980, pp. 42–49.

Yeliseyev, Colonel V T, 'Iz Opyta Armeiskikh Nastupatel'nikh Operatsii Pri Gornym Usloviam' (From the Experience of Army Offensive Operations Conducted in Mountain Conditions), No. 1, 1986, pp. 16–23.

Voennyi Vestnik (Military Herald)

Alekseenko, Major V, 'Nepreryvno, Tshchatel'no, i Svoyevremenno' (Unceasingly, Carefully, and Timely), No. 5, 1989, pp. 42–44.

Aushev, Major R, 'Bez Sviazi Net Nedezhnogo Upravleniya' (Without Communications there is no Reliable Command and Control), No. 8, 1986, pp. 79–81.

Babin, Major N, 'Voinoi Opalennyye Vedut Za Soboi' (Those Singed by War Will Lead), No. 5, 1990, pp. 41–43.

Blokhin, Guards Lieutenant A, 'Sapery Idut Pervymi' (Sappers Go First), No. 11, 1985, pp. 76–77.

Chernyshov, Lieutenant Colonel V, 'Ognemetchiki v Shturmovom Otriade' (Flamethrower Operators in an Assault Detachment), No. 1, 1985, pp. 76–78.

Chumichev, Guards Major A, 'Oboroniayetsia Vzvod' (The Platoon Defends), No. 10, 1985, pp. 26–29.

Churkin, Colonel Yu, '"Berkut" Vykhodit na Sviaz' ('Break, break', Come Up on the Air), No. 5, 1988, pp. 76–78.

— 'Snaipery Efira — Besstrashnyye Boitsy' (Snipers of the Ether — Fearless Warriors), No. 10, 1986, pp. 69–71.

Danil'chenko, Colonel V, 'V Obkhodiashchem Otriade' (In an Enveloping Detachment), No. 4, 1983, pp. 23–27.

Drozdov, Major P, 'Boi Nachinayetsia s Razvedki' (Battle Begins With Reconnaissance), No. 5, 1990, p. 39.

Fedorov, Captain A, 'Pri Vybore Ognevykh Positsii' (Concerning the Choice of Firing Positions), No. 1, 1989, pp. 55–57.

Fel'dt, Captain A, 'Motostrelki Nastupayut v Gorakh' (Motorised Rifle Troops Attack in the Mountains), No. 11, 1985, pp. 25–28.

Goncharov, Major V, 'Sviaz' na Salange' (Communications at Salang Pass), No. 8, 1986, p. 82.

Goriachev, Colonel N, 'Ne Oprekat' Serzhantov, a Obuchat' (Do not Patronise Sergeants, Teach Them), No. 5, 1988, pp. 33–35.

Gordyi, Major Ya, 'Eto Bylo na Voine' (It Was in the War), No. 10, 1989, pp. 52–54.

Gul'ko, Captain S, 'Pervym Podniat'sia v Ataku' (First to Rush into the Attack), No. 5, 1989, pp. 45–46.

Il'iashenko, Colonel G, 'Krutoi Povorot' (Sharp Turnaround), No. 4, 1985, pp. 82–85.

Isayev, Captain V, 'Po Surovoi Shkale Boya' (By the Severe Scale of Battle), No. 7, 1989, pp. 44–45.

Ivanov, Lieutenant Colonel G, 'Razvedka Gornogo Perevala' (Reconnaissance of a Mountain Pass), pp. 25–27.

Kabatskii, Guards Lieutenant V, 'Kazhdyi Vystrel — v Tsel' (Every Bullet on Target), No. 5, 1990, pp. 51–52.

Kelpsh, Colonel V, 'Vosstanovleniye Putei v Gorakh' (Re-establishment of Routes in Mountains), No. 2, 1983, pp. 79–82.

Kirshin, Guards Lieutenant O, 'Na Poisk Dushmanskikh Skhronov' (In Search of the Dushmen Bandits), No. 11, 1985, pp. 79–80.

Kiselev, Senior Lieutenant A, 'Skvoz' Dushmanskiye Zaslony' (Through Dushman Traps), No. 7, 1989, pp. 42–44.

Kochnev, Captain V, 'Initsiativa na Povodke' (Initiative on a Leash), No. 9, 1989, pp. 49–50.

Kochurov, Colonel G, 'Obkhodiashchii Otriad v Gorno-Taezhnoi Mestnosti' (Enveloping Detachment in Mountain-Taiga Terrain), No. 6, 1986, pp. 20–23.

Kokhan, Senior Lieutenant M, 'Radisti v Gorakh Afganistana' (Radio Operators in the Mountains of Afghanistan), No. 5, 1986, pp. 81–82.

Konobritskii, Guards Major Yu, 'Serzhanty — Nadezhniye Pomoshchniki Ofitserov' (Sergeants — Reliable Assistants to Officers), No. 9, 1985, pp. 30–32.

Korobka, Colonel S, 'Razvedka v Gorakh' (Reconnaissance in the Mountains), No. 10, 1985, pp. 13–15.

Kostulev, General Lieutenant V (First Deputy Commander of Air-Desant Troops), 'Sekrety Desantnoi Zakalki' (Secrets of the Hardening of Desant Troops), No. 4, 1989, pp. 45–48.

Kravchenko, Guards Major N, 'Po Dolgy Internatsionalistov' (For Duty of Internationalists), No. 4, 1985, pp. 81–82.

Kravchenko, Senior Lieutenant A, 'Gruppa v Zasade' (The Group in Ambush), No. 7, 1989, pp. 45–48.

Kurochkin, Major V, 'V Zelenoi Zone' (In the Green Zone), No. 3, 1988, pp. 35–36.

Kutishchev, Major V, 'Ot Blagodarnogo Afganskogo Naroda' (From the Grateful Afghan People), No. 8, 1989, pp. 40–43.

Kuz'michev, Major Yu and Captain S Ponomaerv, 'Perepriem i Retransliatsiya v Gorakh' (Receipt of Radio Messages and Retransmission in Mountains), No. 12, 1985, pp. 74–75.

Lavrenyuk, Captain V and Senior Lieutenant A Kutz, 'Chemu Hauchila Voina?' (What Did the War Teach?), No. 1, 1989, pp. 58–61.

Litvinenko, Colonel V, 'V Gornikh Usloviakh' (In Mountainous Conditions), No. 4, 1989, pp., 37–39.

Martynov, Lieutenant Colonel V, 'Naiti i Obezvredit' (Find and Neutralise), No. 12, 1986, pp. 69–71.

Nefedov, Lieutenant Colonel A, 'Planirovaniye Svetovogo Obespecheniya v Gorakh' (Planning Illumination Support in the Mountains), No. 3, 1988, p. 44.

Noskov, General Major A, 'Takticheskaya Vnezapnost'' (Tactical Surprise), No. 1, 1985, pp. 22–24.

Novikov, Lieutenant Colonel V, 'Ognemetchiki Deistsvuyut v Gorakh' (Flamethrower

Operators Perform in Mountains), No. 2, 1983, pp. 83–85.

Novitskii, Guards Captain G, 'Provereno. Min Nyet.' (It Has Been Checked. There Are No Mines), No. 5, 1985, pp. 53–54.

Orel, Captain A, 'Svetovoye Obespecheniye Strel'by Vertoletov Ognevoi Podderzhki' (Illumination for the Fires of Fire Support Helicopters), No. 2, 1985, pp. 58–59.

Ostankov, Lieutenant Colonel V, 'Minnaya Opasnost' (Mine Danger), No. 10, 1985, pp. 63–65.

Perov, Guards Lieutenant Colonel V, 'V Gorno-Pustynnoi Mestnosti' (In Desert-Mountain Terrain), No. 5, 1985, pp. 52–53.

Pogorelyi, Senior Lieutenant Yu, 'Deistvuyut Telefonistry' (The Wiremen are Working), No. 6, 1986, pp. 81–82.

Pisukov, Major G, 'Gory Lyubiat Sil'nikh' (The Mountains Love the Strong), No. 11, 1985, p. 42.

'Primeneniye Artillerii v Gorakh' (Artillery Usage in the Mountains), No. 5, 1983, pp. 60–63.

'Pristrel 'ka Tseli v Gorakh' (Registration in Mountains), No. 9, 1989, pp. 48–49.

Protasov, Colonel Yu, 'Kombat Pimenov' (Battalion Commander Litenov), No. 8, 1985, pp. 39–41.

— 'Eto v Samom Cheloveke' (It is in the Person Himself), No. 7, 1985, pp. 52–54.

— 'Meroi Boya' (By the Measure of Combat), No. 4, 1983, pp. 31–32.

— 'V Takticheskom Vozdushnom Desante' (In a Tactical Air *Desant*), No. 11, 1985, pp. 10–14.

Protokovskii, Guards Senior Lieutenant A, 'V Poiske' (In Search), No. 5, 1985, pp. 50–51.

Putilov, Major O, 'Vnezapnost' Prinosit Uspekh' (Surprise will Bring Success), No. 5, 1990, pp. 40–41.

Roshchupki, Lieutenant Colonel V, 'Vyshe Gor — Tol'ko Lyudi' (Higher than Mountains — Only People), No. 2, 1988, pp. 37–38.

Salikhov, Colonel R, 'Batal'on Oboroniaetsia v Gorakh' (The Battalion Defending in the Mountains), No. 8, 1985, pp. 33–37.

— 'Reid Batal'ona' (Battalion Raid), No. 4, 1988, pp. 40–41.

Savilov, Guards Major Ye, 'Vzbod v Nastuplenii Noch'yu' (The Platoon in a Night Offensive), No. 6, 1986, pp. 27–29.

Selivanov, Major V, 'Vo Flang i Tyul' (To the Flank and Rear), No. 12, 1989, pp. 44–46.

Semenov, Colonel Yu and Lieutenant Colonel I Sobran, 'Opredeleniye Zon Obstrela iz Tankov v Gorakh' (Determination of the Zones of Fire of Tanks in the Mountains), No. 6, 1983, pp. 77–79.

Shcherbakov, Lieutenant Colonel V, 'Turetskii Batl'on Nastupayet v Gorakh' (A Turkish Battalion Attacks in the Mountains), No. 11, 1988, pp. 83–84.

Shepilov, Guards Senior Lieutenant M, 'V Boyevom Podvizhnom Okhranenii' (In a Mobile Security Detachment), No. 3, 1986, pp. 34–36.

Shevchuk, Major G, 'Manevr v Gorakh' (Manoeuvre in Mountains), No. 12, 1985, pp. 29–31.

Shevchuk, Lieutenant Colonel A, 'Sluchainost' ili Zakonomernost'?' (Chance or Regularity?), No. 5, 1990, pp. 49–50.

Shmatko, Senior Lieutenant A, 'Bez Nastroya Net Pobedy' (Without the Right

Attitude, There is no Victory), No. 6, 1989, pp. 46–49.

Shumilov, Guards Senior Lieutenant P, 'V Gruppe Razvedki i Razgrazhdeniye' (In a Reconnaissance and Mine Clearance Group), No. 11, 1985, pp. 77–79.

Sokirko, Senior Lieutenant V, 'Oshibka Chernogo Uchitelya' (The Mistake of the Black Teacher), No. 4, 1989, pp. 40–42. Sosnitskii, Guards Captain V, 'Desantniki v Atake' (*Desantniks* in the Attack), No. 10, 1985, pp. 29–30. Starodymov, Guards Captain N, 'Obespecheniye Prodvizheniye Kolonn' (Insuring the Progress of Columns), No. 10, 1985, pp. 66–68.

Stepanov, Captain E, 'Boi v Gorakh: Osobaya Usloviya' (Battle in the Mountains: Special Conditions), No. 3, 1988, pp. 22–24.

Stepanov, Captain N and Senior Lieutenant V Matienko, 'Granatometchicki v Gorakh' (Grenadiers in the Mountains), No. 9, 1985, pp. 23–25.

Tuayev, Major S, 'Zacada' (Ambush), No. 2, 1989, pp. 68–71.

Tunitskii, Guards Major V, 'Chtoby Upravleniye Bylo Nadezhnym' (So That Command and Control Will Be Reliable), No. 5, 1985, pp. 54–55.

Usmanov, Major T, 'Gory ne Proshchayut Nebrezhnost' (The Mountains Do Not Forgive Carelessness), No. 5, 1990, pp. 36–37.

Yeremeyev, Major N, 'Karasu, Chernaya Voda' (The Black Waters of the Karasu River), No. 9, 1986, pp. 14–15.

Zaitsevskii, Guards Senior Lieutenant N, 'Ne Chislom, a Umeniym' (Not by the Number but the Skill), No. 4, 1986, pp. 28–29.

Zel'tin, Major A, 'Zagrazhdeniye v Gorakh' (Obstacles in the Mountains), No. 8, 1985, pp. 82–84.

Newspapers

Krasnaya Zvezda (Red Star)

Belichenko, Colonel Yu, 'Ushchel'ye' (Canyon), 8 Nov. 1986, p. 4.

Borsukov, General Lieutenant of Aviation A, 'Kto Tvorit Taktiky?' (Who is Devising Tactics?), 5 Apr. 1987, p. 2.

Burbyga, Captain N, 'Kupola v Nebe' (Cupola in the Sky), 24 Aug. 1983, p. 4.

Bystrov, Captain 1st Rank S, 'Front Bez Linii Fronta' (A Front Without Front Lines), 2 Feb. 1989, p. 1.

Filatov, Colonel V, 'Tsement' (Cement), 3 Mar. 1984, p. 4.

Khazikov, General-Lieutenant V, 'Vozrodit' Kak Iskusstvo' (To Revive [*Tactics*] as an Art), 7 Jan. 1989, pp. 1–2.

Kovalov, Colonel V, Lieutenant Colonel I Esyutin and Lieutenant Colonel A Oliinik, 'Chas Vozvrashcheniye' (The Hour of Return), 2 Feb. 1984, pp. 1–2.

Kudrin, Major N, 'Rezervy Vtorogo Eshelona' (Reserves of the Second Echelon), 1 Oct. 1989, p. 2.

Markushin, Lieutenant Colonel V, 'Vyrazhayu Glubochaishee Nedoumeniye' (I Express the Deepest Perplexity), 28 Feb. 1989, p. 3.

Oliinik, Major A, 'Muzhestvo' (Courage), 24 Mar. 1984, p. 3.

— 'Posty v Gorakh' (Guardposts in the Mountains), 17 July 1986, p. 1.

— 'Spravedlivoye Vozmezdiye' (A Just Retribution), 31 May 1987, p. 3.

Otmakhov, Lieutenant Colonel S, 'U Nashikh Voyennikh Medikov' (With Our Military Medics), 17 July 1983, p. 2.

Polyakov, Colonel A, 'General Gromov', 22 July 1989, p. 4.

— 'Mezhdu Armiei i Narodom Net Mezhi' (There is no Boundary Between the
   Army and the People), 19 Mar. 1989, p. 1.
Skrizhalin, Lieutenant Colonel V, 'Lyudi Velikogo Dolga' (People of Great Duty),
   27 Aug. 1983, p. 3.
Sukhodolskii, Lieutenant Colonel V, 'Razvedchik' (Reconnaissance Officer), 31
   Dec. 1983, p. 4.
Soloyanov, Lieutenant Colonel A, 'Ya Protiv Damskogo Vospitaniya' (I am Against
   Girlish Upbringing), 17 Sept. 1989, p. 2.
Vorobev, General Major I, 'Iz Plena Zauchennikh Skhem' (From the Captivity of
   Blindly Memorised Scenarios), 2 Feb. 1989, p. 2.
'Vystupleniye General-Leitenanta Gromova B V' (General Lieutenant Gromov's
   Speech), 2 July 1988, p. 3.
Yefanov, Major V, 'V Nochnom Rukapashnom' (In Hand-to-Hand Combat at
   Night), 4 Aug. 1983, p. 1.
Ziemin'sh, Lieutenant Colonel M, 'Rana' (The Wound), 30 May 1987, p. 2.

Sovetskaya Rossiya (Soviet Russia)

Gromov, General Colonel B V (former Commander of Soviet Troops in
   Afghanistan), 'Pravda Vyshe Sensatsii' (Truth is Higher than Sensation), 15
   Nov. 1989, p. 4.

Miscellaneous Soviet Journals and Newspapers

Borovik, Artem, 'Bstretimcia u Trekh Shuravlei' (We Will Meet at the Three
   Cranes), *Ogonek*, No. 30, 1987, pp. 18–21.
Ignatyev, Sergei, 'Low-Intensity Conflicts and Military Reform in the Soviet
   Union', *Military Bulletin*, Feb. 1990, No. 4 (82), pp. 8–11, translated into
   English by the Novosti Press Agency.
Izgarshev, Colonel V, 'Komandarm' (Army Commander), *Pravda*, 9 Aug. 1988, p. 3.
Maximov, Army General Yu, 'Mountain Training', *Soviet Military Review*, No. 12,
   1984.
Nazarov, V, 'Kontrapartizanskaya' Programma Voinstvuyushchego Kolonializma'
   (The Counter-Insurgency Programme of Militant Colonialism), *Vestnik
   Voyennoi Istorii (Herald of Military History)*, No. 2, 1971, pp. 121–153.
Tukhachevskii, M, 'Bor'ba s Kontrrevolyutsionnymi Vosstaniyami. Iskoreneniye
   Tipichnogo Banditizma' (The Struggle Against Counter-revolutionary Uprisings.
   Rooting Out a Typical Case of Banditism), *Voina i Revolyutsiya (War and
   Revolution)*, Aug. 1926, pp. 4–15.

Books

Afghanistan: *Bor'ba i Sozidaniye*. Moscow: Voenizdat, 1984
Lunin, B, editor, *Basmachestvo. Sotsial'no-Politicheskaya Sushnost'*. Tashkent: Fan,
   1984. Institute of History, Academy of Sciences, Uzbek SSR.
Malinkovich, V, *Afganistan v Ogne. Dokumenty i Svidetel'stva o voine v Afganistane*.
   Sugasnist, 1985.
Shavrov, Army General I Ye, *Lokal'niye Voiny. Istoriya i Sovremennost'*. Moscow:

Voyenizdat, 1981.

Translations of Soviet Sources by FBIS (Foreign Broadcast Information Service)

'An Assault Landing Force Captures an Objective'. *Znamenosets*, No. 10, 1980, pp. 4–5. (JPRS 77548, 2 Jan. 1981, pp. 32–36.)

Avakyan, Warrant Officer S, 'In a Flanking Detachment', *Znamenosets*, No. 10, 1980, p. 11 (JPRS 77548, 2 Jan. 1981, pp. 50–52.)

Bacconier, Beatrix and Jean-Jose Puig, 'The Soviet Offensive in Afghanistan', *Liberation*, 2 May 1984, pp. 2–6. (JPRS-NEA-84-089, 6 June 1984, pp. 36–49.)

'The Cliffs Submit to the Bold', *Znamenosets*, No. 10, 1980, pp. 10–11. (JPRS 77548, 2 Jan. 1981, pp. 47–50.)

'Defence of an Entrance to a Gorge', *Znamenosets*, No. 10, 1980, pp. 12–13. (JPRS 77548, 2 Jan. 1981, pp. 52–55.)

'For Battle, For Victory', *Znamenosets*, No. 10, 1980, p. 5. (JPRS 77548, 2 Jan. 1981, pp. 36–37.)

'From Helicopters — Into the Attack', *Znamenosets*, No. 10, 1980, p. 6. (JPRS 77548, 2 Jan. 1981, pp. 37–39.)

Gromadskii, L, 'Dzholoy Chyntemirov's Red Star', *Sovetskaya Kirgizia*, 23 Mar. 1984, p. 3. (JPRS-UMA-84-045, 13 June 1985, pp. 50–55.)

Ivanov, Lieutenant Colonel N, 'Former 1st Deputy Commander, Turkestan MD on Invastion', *Sovetskaya Rossiya*, 20 Dec. 1989, originally entitled 'H-Hour'. (JPRS-UMA-90-007, 23 Mar. 1990.)

Kulishev, General Colonel O (Commander, Transcaucasus Military District), 'Small Unit Mountain Training — to the Foreground', *Znamenosets*, No. 10, 1980, pp. 2–3. (JPRS 77548, 2 Jan. 1981, pp. 28–32.)

Kushnerev, S, 'After Afghanistan', *Komsomolskaya Pravda*, 21 Dec. 1989, p. 2. (JPRS-UMA-90-006, 20 Mar. 1990, under the title 'Interpretation and Results of Survey'.)

Levin, V and V Khachirashvili, 'He Wears the Red Star, Discharging International Duty', *Sovetskaya Belorussiya*, 16 Nov. 1984, p. 4. (JPRS-UMA-85-010, 11 Feb. 1985, pp. 102–104.)

Meschaninov, D, 'A Powerful Blow by the Afghan Army: A Major Insurgent Base Destroyed', *Izvestiya*, 26 Nov. 1986. (JPRS-UMA-87-006, 30 Jan. 1987.)

Mkhitaryan, Warrant Officer L, 'Before a March', *Znamenosets*, No. 10, 1980, p. 8. (JPRS 77548, 2 Jan. 1981, pp. 42–44.)

Nefedov, Senior Sergeant V, 'School of Soldierly Skill', *Znamenosets*, No. 10, 1980, pp. 14–15. (JPRS 77548, 2 Jan. 1981, pp. 55–57.)

Oliinik, Major A, 'The Fiery Kilometers', *Krasnaya Zvezda*, 26 May 1985, p. 2. (JPRS-UMA-85-040, 15 July 1985, pp. 136–41.)

— 'Dushmans Routed in Their Lair', *Krasnaya Zvezda*, 26 Nov. 1986. (JPRS-UMA-87-002, 9 Jan. 1987.)

Rotashnyuk, Sergeant A, 'Across a Swift River', *Znamenosets*, No. 10, 1980, p. 9. (JPRS 77548, 2 Jan. 1981, pp. 44–46.)

Solovyev, Major V and Captain V Sokolov, 'The T-72 Tank: Maintenance in Mountains', *Tekhnika i Vooruzheniye*, No. 11, 1989, 10–11. (JPRS-UMA-90-007, 23 Mar. 1990, pp. 51–2.)

'Snipers in the Sight', *Znamenosets*, No. 10, 1980, p. 7. (JPRS 77548, 2 Jan. 1981, pp. 39–41.)

Sosnovskii, L V, 'The Concept of Counterguerrilla Operations', *SShA*, No. 5, 1971, pp. 118–123. (JPRS 53268, 6 Feb. 1971, pp. 146–55.)

Stalovskii, Colonel V, 'Stationed in Afghanistan', *Voyennoye Znaniye*, No. 3, 1981, pp. 4–5. (JPRS-79678, 17 Dec. 1981, pp. 1–7.)

de Villoutreys, Armand, 'Three Months with the Afghan Resistance', *Geopolitique*, Winter 1984–85, pp. 81–84. (JPRS-NEA-85-022, 11 Feb. 1985, pp. 76–79.)

Vorobyev, General Major I N, 'Why Did Tactics Stagnate?', *Voyennaya Mysl'* *(Military Thought)*, No. 1, 1990, pp. 37–44. (JPRS-UMT-90-001-L, 22 Feb. 1990, pp. 21–26.)

Yarushenko, A, 'A Bright Hour: Even Today There is a Place for Heroic Deeds', *Soviet Patriot*, 15 Oct. 1986.

Yermolina, O and A Zubkov, 'Lieutenant General Varennikov Interviewed on Entry Into Afghanistan', *Soviet Patriot*, 27 Dec. 1989, pp. 1–2, originally entitled 'We Were not Preaching Evil'. (JPRS-UMA-90-007, 23 Mar. 1990.)

Afghan Sources

Monthly Bulletin, Afghan Information Centre, University Town, Peshawar, Pakistan. Each issue discusses activities of the *mujahedin* and special subjects, in the space of about 20–30 pages, as reported by *mujahedin* leaders and other journalists travelling in Afghan combat zones.

No. 17, Sept. 1982.	No. 65, Aug. 1986.
No. 20, Dec. 1982.	No. 66, Sept. 1986.
No. 21, Dec. 1982.	No. 67, Oct. 1986.
No. 23, Feb. 1983.	No. 68, Nov. 1986.
No. 24, Mar. 1983.	No. 69, Dec. 1986.
No. 25, Apr. 1983.	No. 70, Jan. 1987.
No. 27, June 1983.	No. 72, Mar. 1987.
No. 28, July 1983.	No. 73, Apr, 1987.
No. 29, Aug. 1983.	No. 74, May 1987.
No. 30, Sept. 1983.	No. 75, June 1987.
No. 31, Oct. 1983.	No. 76, July 1987.
No. 41, Aug. 1984.	No. 77, Aug. 1987.
No. 42, Sept. 1984.	No. 78, Sept. 1987.
No. 43, Oct. 1984.	Nos. 79–80, Oct.–Nov. 1987.
No. 48, Mar. 1985.	No. 81, Dec. 1987.
No. 49, Apr. 1985.	No. 84, Mar. 1988.
No. 52, July 1985.	No. 87, June 1988.
No. 53, Aug. 1985.	No. 88, July 1988.
No. 55, Oct. 1985.	No. 89, Aug. 1988.
No. 58, Jan. 1986.	No. 90, Sept. 1988.
No. 59, Feb. 1986.	No. 91, Oct. 1988.
No. 60, Mar. 1986.	No. 92, Nov. 1988.
No. 61, Apr. 1986.	No. 93, Dec. 1988.
No. 63, June 1986.	No. 94, Jan. 1989.
No. 64, July 1986.	No. 95, Feb. 1989.

Writers' Union of Free Afghanistan (WUFA) (Afghan Journal)

Amin, A Rasul, 'Unity is the Remedy', Vol. 1, No. 1, 1985, pp. 9–15.
— 'Interview with Dr J H Grevemeyer', Vol. 4, No. 1, Jan.–Mar. 1989, pp. 64–75.
Dupree, Louis, 'Afghanistan 1987: The "Bleeding Wound" and the Tourniquet', Vol. 2, No. 3, July–Sept. 1987, pp. 26–44.
Ikram, M Asef, 'Russo-Afghanistan Relations', Vol. 1, No. 1, 1985, pp. 51–60.
— 'Liberation of Eastern Afghanistan', Vol. 4, No. 1, Jan.–Mar. 1989, pp. 29–41.
'Interview with Afghan Professors', Vol. 4, No. 1, Jan.–Mar. 1989, pp. 76–84.
Kaimur, Dr Sarzamin, 'Afghanistan: Yet Another Victim of Sovietisation', Vol. 2, No. 1, Jan.–Mar. 1987, pp. 61–86.
Kamrany, Nake M, 'The Effect of Soviet War on the Afghan Economy', Vol. 2, No. 1, Jan.–Mar. 1987, pp. 43–57.
Khan, Azmat Hayat, 'Causes of Soviet Invasion', Vol. 2, No. 2, Apr.–June 1987, pp. 51–60.
Mumtaz, Dr Z A, 'Soviet Aggression of Afghanistan', Vol. 1, No. 1, pp. 16–24.
— 'Islam as a Binding Force in Afghanistan', Vol. 2, No. 2, Apr.–June 1987, pp. 61–77.
Noorzay, M Siddieq, 'Some Observations on and Assessment of the Population Losses in Afghanistan', Vol. 3, No. 3, July–Sept. 1988, pp. 6–14.
Rezburg, Jack, 'Why Soviets Invaded, Why They Stay?', Vol. 2, No. 1, Jan.–Mar. 1987, pp. 25–42.
Safi, Major Nasrullah, 'Soviet Military Tactics in Afghanistan', Vol. 1, No. 1, pp. 1–8.
— 'A Brief Appraisal of War in Jalalabad', Vol. 4, No. 2, Apr.–June, 1989, pp. 12–21.
Samin, Prof Dr, 'War Impacts on Afghan Agriculture', Vol. 4, No. 2, Apr.–June 1989, pp. 22–33.
Shakaib, Major Ghulam Dastagir, 'Soviet Military Problems', Vol. 2, No. 3, July–Sept. 1987, pp. 90–102.
Taniwal, Hakim and Ahmad Yusuf Nuristani, 'Pashtun Tribes and the Afghan Resistance', Vol. 1, No. 1, pp. 35–49.

Other Sources

Unpublished Manuscripts

Doan, Douglas C, 'Study of Soviet Foreign Policy: An Empirical Approach Based Upon Content Analysis of Red Star', 1988.
Erickson, John, 'Afghanistan. A Review of Current Developments'. 1980.

Journals

Asian Survey

Amin, Tahir, 'Afghan Resistance: Past, Present, and Future', Apr. 1984, pp. 373–399.
Cheema, Pervaiz Iqbal, 'The Afghan Crisis and Pakistan's Security Dilemma', Mar. 1983, pp. 227–243.

Coldren, Lee O, 'Afghanistan in 1984. The Fifth Year of the Afghan War', Feb. 1985, pp. 169–179.
— Afghanistan in 1985. The Sixth Year of the Afghan War', Feb. 1986, pp. 235–245.
Dunbar, Charles, 'Afghanistan in 1986: The Balance Endures', Feb. 1987, pp. 127–142.
— 'Afghanistan in 1987: A Year of Decision?', Feb. 1988, pp. 148–162.
Dupree, Louis, 'Afghanistan in 1982: Still No Solution', Feb. 1983, pp. 133–142.
— 'Afghanistan in 1983: And Still No Solution', Feb. 1984, pp. 229–239.
Naby, Eden, 'The Ethnic Factor in Soviet-Afghan Relations', Mar. 1980, pp. 237–256.
Newman, Joseph Jr., 'The Future of Northern Afghanistan', July 1988, pp. 729–739.
Rubin, Barnett R, 'Lineages of the State in Afghanistan', Nov. 1988, pp. 1188–1209.
Wafadar, K, 'Afghanistan in 1980: The Struggle Continues', Feb. 1981, pp. 172–180.
— 'Afghanistan in 1981: The Struggle Intensifies', Feb. 1982, pp. 147–154.

Jane's Defence Review

'BRDM-2 in close-up', Vol. 4, No. 8, 1983, p. 717.
'Guard Battalions', Vol. 4, No. 4, 1983, p. 313.
'Hind Tactics Change', Vol. 2, No. 5, 1981, p. 390.
Isby, David C, 'The Soviet AGS-17 automatic grenade launcher', Vol. 3, No. 5, 1982, pp. 473–474.
— 'Soviet Tactics in the War in Afghanistan', Vol. 4, No. 7, 1983, pp. 681–691.
'New Soviet RPO-50 flame rocket launcher', Vol. 3, No. 5, 1982, p. 437.
'Soviet Chemical Warfare in Afghanistan', Vol. 3, No. 4, 1982.
'Sukhoi Su-24 'Fencer'', Vol. 2, No. 5, 1981, p. 387.

Jane's Defence Weekly

'A new generation of CB munitions', 30 Apr. 1988, pp. 852–853.
'A Soviet view of duty in Afghanistan', 18 Oct. 1986, p. 887.
'Abdul Haq: My fight with the Red Army', 7 Feb. 1987, p. 181.
'Afghan Army can cope, says Vostrov', 10 Sept. 1988, p. 585.
'Afghan commando brigade decimated by *mujahideen*', 20 July 1985, p. 109.
'Afghan militiamen defected with government weapons', 8 Jan. 1988.
'Afghan protest to China', 16 Feb. 1985, p. 249.
'Afghanistan poses training problems', 12 Mar. 1988, p. 471.
'Airbase defence Soviet priority', 30 July 1988, p. 177.
'BM-27 MLRS in Afghanistan', 17 May 1986, p. 886.
'The BMD-2 air assault transporter', 9 Aug. 1986, p. 205.
'BMP infantry combat vehicle — Part 2', 6 Oct. 1984, p. 580.
'BTR-70 in Afghanistan', 16 June 1984, p. 956.
Bertin, Giles, 'Stingers change the face of war in Afghanistan', 10 Oct. 1987, p. 785.
Bodansky, Yossef, 'Afghan defector talks of Soviet insults', 24 Mar. 1984, p. 430.
— 'Learning Afghanistan's lesson', 20 Feb. 1988, pp. 310–311.

— 'Most feared aircraft in Afghanistan is Frogfoot', 19 May 1984, p. 768.

— 'New weapons in Afghanistan', 9 Mar. 1985, p. 412.

— 'SAMS in Afghanistan: assessing the impact', 25 July 1987, pp. 153–154.

— 'Soviet net closes in on Afghan resistance', 2 Aug. 1986, pp. 173–176.

— 'Soviets reduce troop levels in Afghanistan', 9 Aug. 1988, p. 204.

— 'Soviets "testing chemical agents in Afghanistan",' 7 Apr. 1984, p. 508.

— 'Soviets use Afghanistan to test "liquid fire",' 25 May 1984, p. 819.

Bruce, James, 'Afghan rebels "downing more helicopters",' 15 Nov. 1986, p. 1150.

— 'Afghan guerrillas pound Kabul to divert Soviets', 30 Aug. 1986, p. 348.

— 'Major Soviet offensive expected in Afghanistan', 19 Apr. 1986, p. 693.

— 'Soviet and Afghan troops pound rebel forces', 27 Sept. 1986, p. 670.

Cloughley, Brian, 'Watchdog of the Afghanistan border: duties of Pakistan's Frontier Corps', 30 Nov. 1985, p. 1190.

'Combat helicopter emerges as major battlefield system', 6 Apr. 1985, pp. 583–584.

Eaks, Louis, 'Afghan Protest to China', 16 Feb. 1985, p. 249.

'Grid Chart for encoding signals', 18 Oct. 1986, p. 889.

Gross, Richard C, 'Stinger in use by *mujahideen*', 16 Nov. 1986, p. 1151.

Gunston, John, 'Afghanistan plan USSR terror attacks', 31 Mar. 1984, pp. 481–484.

'Heavy civilian casualties in assault on Afghan villages', 5 Dec. 1987, p. 1311.

'Helicopter protection from IR missiles', 5 Oct. 1985, p. 743.

'Identified roles of MIL Mi-24 Hind', 1 Aug. 1987, p. 187.

Isby, David C, 'Soviet airmobile and air assault brigades', 14 Sept. 1985, pp. 561–565.

Jacobs, G. 'Afghanistan forces: how many Soviets are there?', 22 June 1985, pp. 1228–1233.

Kemp, Ian, 'Abdul Haq: Soviet mistakes in Afghanistan', 5 Mar. 1988.

'Learning the lessons of the Afghan war', 3 July 1988, p. 47.

'Map pinpoints rebel positions, training areas', 18 Oct. 1986, p. 889.

'*Mujahideen* in major offensive against Kabul', 20 Sept. 1986, p. 501.

'*Mujahideen* leaders disabled by mine blast', 31 Oct. 1987, p. 977.

'New claims of CW in Afghanistan', 25 Nov. 1986, p. 1205.

'New LAW used in Afghanistan', 3 Dec. 1988, p. 1425.

O'Dwyer-Russell, Simon, 'Afghan rebels supplied with British-built SAMS', 23 Aug. 1986.

'PKPE-1 multiple grenade launcher', 4 Oct. 1986, p. 731.

'Six Soviet helicopters shot down in Afghanistan', 16 Mar. 1985, p. 439.

'Soviet Air Force in Afghanistan', 7 July 1984, pp. 1104–1105.

'Soviet aircraft destroyed in *mujahideen* attacks', 2 Feb. 1985, p. 167.

'Soviet BMP-2 increases battlefield threat', 20 July 1985, p. 127.

'Soviet forces mass for Kandahar attack', 18 Feb. 1984, p. 223.

'Soviet 40th Army headquarters', 31 Mar. 1984, p. 479.

'Soviet "killing zone" strategy', 19 May 1984, p. 769.

'Soviet losses limited in Panjshir offensive', 12 May 1984, p. 715.

'Soviet maintenance in Afghanistan. Part 1', 22 Feb. 1986, pp. 316–317.

'Soviet maintenance in Afghanistan. Part 2', 1 Mar. 1986, pp. 367–368.

'A Soviet view of duty in Afghanistan', 18 Oct. 1986, p. 887.

'Sukhoi SU-25 Frogfoot', 2 Mar. 1985, p. 362.

'240 Soviet troops die in Afghan aircrash', 10 Nov. 1984, p. 824.

Urban, Mark, 'A more competent Afghan Army?', 23 Nov. 1985, p. 1147.

— 'Afghanistan: a new horizon for Soviets', 8 Feb. 1986, pp. 209–210.

'Vostrov to head training shake-up', 8 Oct. 1988, p. 832.

Wrixon, Tim, 'Frogfoot's cannon firing — first pictures', 13 Oct. 1984, p. 611.

'Warfare in Special Conditions', 10 Nov. 1984, pp. 840–841.

Miscellaneous Journals and Newspapers

'Afghanistan: The Soviet Army will Stay', *The Army Quarterly and Defence Journal*, July 1986, pp. 268–278.

Bort, Roger, 'Air Assault Brigades: New Element in Soviet Desant Force Structure', *Military Review*, Oct. 1983, pp. 21–37.

Bodansky, Yossef, 'Afghanistan: The Soviet Air War', *Defense & Foreign Affairs*, Sept. 1985, pp. 12–16.

Cardoza, Captain Anthony A, 'Soviet Aviation in Afghanistan', *US Naval Institute Proceedings*, Feb. 1987, pp. 85–88.

Collins, Joseph J, 'Soviet Military Performance in Afghanistan', *Comparative Strategy*, Vol. 4, No. 2, 1983.

Dickson, Captain Keith D, 'The Basmachi and the Mujahedin: Soviet Responses to Insurgency Movements', *Military Review*, Feb. 1985, pp. 29–44.

Frost, Roger, 'Plamya — the Soviet Flame', *International Defence Review*, No. 12, 1984, p. 1881.

Gross, Natalie, 'How Healthy is the Soviet Soldier?', *Soviet Analyst*, 16 Apr. 1986, pp. 3–5.

— 'Soviet Press Review', *Jane's Soviet Intelligence Review*, July 1989, pp. 335–336.

Holcomb, James F, 'Recent Developments in Soviet Helicopter Operations', *Journal of Soviet Military Studies*, No. 3, 1989, pp. 266–287.

Holden, Constance, 'Unequivocal Evidence of Soviet Toxin Use', *Science*, No. 216, 9 Apr. 1982, pp. 154–155.

Karp, Aaron, 'Blowpipes and Stingers in Afghanistan: One Year Later', *Armed Forces Journal International*, Sept. 1987, pp. 36–40.

Khalilzad, Zalmay, 'Moscow's Afghan War', *Problems of Communism*, Jan.–Feb. 1986, pp. 1–20.

'Kremlin Assails its Afghan Role', *International Herald Tribune*, 24 Oct. 1989, p. 1.

Mackenzie, Richard, 'Afghan Rebels Never Say Die', *Insight*, 25 Jan. 1988, pp. 8–16.

McDermott, Captain David F, 'The Invasion of Afghanistan', *Infantry*, Jan.–Feb. 1985, pp. 19–23.

Moorcraft, Paul L, 'Bloody Standoff in Afghanistan', *Military Review*, Apr. 1985, pp. 26–36.

Ottaway, David B, 'Stingers Were Key Weapon in Afghan War, Army Finds', *Washington Post*, 5 July 1989, p. A5.

Richards, Martin, 'Afghanistan: Stalemate or Climb Down?', *The Army Quarterly and Defence Journal*, July 1983, pp. 262–265.

Schwartzstein, Stuart J D, 'Chemical Warfare in Afghanistan: An Independent

Assessment', *World Affairs,*Winter 1982–83, pp. 267–272.

'Special Report: Afghanistan War', *Aviation Week & Space Technology*, 29 Oct. 1984, pp. 39–43.

Yardley, Michael, 'Afghanistan: A First Hand View', *International Defence Review*, No. 3, 1987, p. 27.

Radio Free Europe/Radio Liberty Reports (Munich, FRG)

Foye, Stephen, 'Murders of Soviet Military Officers', RL 282/90, *Report on the USSR*, 21 June 1990, p.11.

— 'Domestic Role of Soviet Armed Forces Debated', RL 27/90, *Report on the USSR*, 19 Jan. 1990, pp. 7–9.

Hyman, Anthony, 'Towards a Settlement in Afghanistan', RL 3/90, *Report on the USSR*, 5 Jan. 1990, pp. 5–6.

— 'Afghanistan's Uncertain Future', RL 137/90, *Report on USSR*, 23 Mar. 1990.

— 'Soviet Advisors and Help for Afghanistan', RL 97/90, *Report on USSR*, 2 Mar. 1990.

Konovalov, Valerii, 'Legacy of the Afghan War: Some Statistics', RL 157/89, *Report on the USSR*, 7 Apr. 1989.

Kruzhin, Peter, 'Soviet Army Places Emphasis on Training for Mountain Warfare', RL 252/83, 30 June 1983.

— 'Afghanistan: Soviet Troops Under Fire', RL 513/81, 23 Dec. 1981.

— 'Afghanistan: A Training Exercise', RL 514/81, 28 Dec. 1981.

Roberts, Cynthia, 'Glasnost' in Soviet Foreign Policy: Setting the Record Straight', *Report on the USSR*, 15 Dec. 1989, pp. 4–12.

Sartori, Francesco, 'Afghanistan at War', RL 270/84, 12 July 1984.

— 'Afghanistan at War', RL 290/84, 27 July 1984.

Sego, Steve, 'US Experts Discuss Soviet Army in Afghanistan', RL 302/87, 24 July 1987.

Monographs

Sikorskii, Radek. Moscow's Afghan War: Soviet Motives and Western Interests. Occasional Paper No. 27. Alliance Publishers, for the Institute of European Defence and Strategic Studies, London, 1987.

RAND Reports (RAND Corporation, Santa Monica, CA)

Alexiev,Alexander, 'Inside the Soviet Army in Afghanistan', R-3627-A, May 1988.

— 'The United States and the War in Afghanistan', P-7395, Jan. 1988.

Bennigsen, Alexandre, 'The Soviet Union and Muslim Guerrilla Wars, 1920–1981: The Lessons for Afghanistan'. N-1707/1, Aug. 1981.

Daley, Ted. 'Afghanistan and Gorbachev's Global Foreign Policy'. OPS-015, May 1989.

Fukuyama, Francis. 'Soviet Civil-Military Relations and the Power Projection Mission'. R-3504-AF, Apr. 1987.

— 'The Future of the Soviet Role in Afghanistan: A Trip Report.' N-1579-RC,

Sept. 1980.

Gelman, Harry. 'The Soviet Military Leadership and the Question of Soviet Deployment Retreats'. R-3664-AF, Nov. 1988.

Wimbush, S Enders and Alex Alexiev. 'Soviet Central Asian Soldiers in Afghanistan'. N-1634/1, Jan. 1981.

Books

Amstutz, J Bruce. *Afghanistan. The First Five Years of Soviet Occupation.* Washington, D C: National Defense University Press, 1986.

Arney, George. *Afghanistan.* London: Mandarin Paperbacks, 1990.

Bonner, Arthur. *Among the Afghans.* London: Duke University Press, 1987.

Collins, Joseph J. *The Soviet Invasion of Afghanistan.* Lexington, MA: Lexington Books, 1986.

Girardet, Edward. *Afghanistan: The Soviet War.* London: Croom Helm, 1985.

Huldt, Bo and Erland Jansson, editors. *The Tragedy of Afghanistan: The Social, Cultural and Political Impact of the Soviet Invasion.* London: Croom Helm, 1988.

Nyrop, Richard F, editor. *Afghanistan. A Country Study.* Prepared by Foreign Area Studies, The American University for the Department of the Army, Washington D C, 1986.

Scales, Robert H Jr. *Firepower in Limited War.* Washington: National Defense University Press, 1990.

Urban, Mark. *War in Afghanistan.* London: Macmillan Press, 1988.

Miscellaneous

Military Thought. 1937–1973. Chronological, Author, and Title Index. Edition 4, Defense Intelligence College, Washington D C, 1981.

'Soviet Spring'. BBC Television Special. Mar. 1990.

US Army Field Manual 100-2-3. *The Soviet Army: Troops, Organization and Equipment.* Washington: HQDA, July 1984.

APPENDIX A

Mujahedin Organisations

(*Caveat: for simplicity, the present tense has been used extensively throughout this chapter, as it refers to the situation extant during the period of the Soviet occupation. In some respects, changes will have taken place since, but the concern of this book is with the Soviet occupation and involvement.*)

The Seven Peshawar-Based Parties of the Islamic Union

Fundamentalist Groups (All Sunni Muslim, not Shiite as in Iran)

Hezb-i-Islami (Islamic Party - Engineer Gulbuddin Hekmatyr faction)

History: This group is the oldest, one of the largest, the most radically fundamentalist, and possibly the most influential of the *mujahedin* groups. The founder, Gulbuddin Hekmatyr, is a Pushtun and former engineering student at Kabul University. He founded the group in 1968 as an anti-Daoud organisation. In 1979, *Hezb-i-Islami* split into two factions. The second one, described below, is led by Younis Khalis. The Hekmatyr faction is larger and more fundamentalist. The primary goal of the group is the establishment of a one-party Islamic state similar to Iran. The group rejects Western values and ideas and favours strong relations and solidarity with the Muslim world. *Hezb-i-Islami* is also anti-traditionalist in several respects: it desires to institute land reform, nationalisation of industries and compulsory military training. This group has been the most xenophobic and intolerant and is the least co-operative by far. Hekmatyr claimed to have a large following serving within the DRA Army.

Structure: The organisation is run by nine separate committees. The most important committee is the Religious (*sharia*) Committee, which supervises several military functions, such as training, procurement and resupply. Hekmatyr and his advisers formulate military policy. Its constituent fighting groups are organised on a regional basis with two key leaders in each 40-man group, the commander and his religious commissar.

Manpower: Strength is estimated to be 15–20,000, of which about 4,000 are full-time. *Hezb-i-Islami* has been active in south-eastern Afghanistan, but it has a strong

165

presence as well in Konduz, Laghman, Baghlan, Kunar, and Nangarhar, and cells in all the major cities and in the north.

Hezb-i-Islami (Islamic Party - Younis Khalis faction)

History: The second of the fundamentalist parties, Younis Khalis broke from the main organisation because he favoured a more liberal attitude toward association with the West. Still, this faction also supports the goal of the establishment of a state based on Islamic law. Its policy positions differ in a number of other respects from Hekmatyr. Like the main organisation, the membership of this faction is largely Pushtun. Militarily, it has been more active and more effective than Hekmatyr, despite the fact that it is slightly smaller.

Structure: Khalis is the key figure, but he exercises little centralised control over the fighting groups. Regional commanders have been established and committees have been created to provide non-military administrative services. Its most well-known commander is Jallaladin Haqqani of Paktia.

Manpower: Approximately 15–20,000 men, with 3,500 full-time fighters. Its centre of power is in eastern Afghanistan in Paktia, Paktika, Nangarhar, Kunar provinces and Jalalabad.

Jamiat-i-Islami (Islamic Society of Afghanistan)

History: Jamiat was formed in the early 1970s by Ustad Burhanuddin Rabani, a former professor of Islamic law at Kabul University. The primary goal of the organisation is the transformation of Afghanistan into a fundamentalist Islamic state. *Jamiat-i-Islami* is more moderate in its interpretation of Islamic law and in its tolerance for other *mujahedin* parties than is *Hezb-i-Islami*. The group has attracted many professional and educated persons to leadership positions. Regionally, the organisation is centred in north-east Afghanistan, drawing most of its support from non-Pushtun (Pathan) Tajiks and Uzbeks. Jamiat maintains offices in both Iran and Peshawar. The most well-known Jamiat commander is Ahmad Shah Massoud of the Panjsher Valley, who has survived more large-scale offensives than any other commander.

Structure: Jamiat is one of the most coherent and integrated groups of the seven. Rabani is accepted by all as the leader and arbiter of disputes. The political apparatus of the organisation has well-defined functions and appears to run smoothly without dissension. The Military Committee has made attempts to co-ordinate operational plans by the autonomous field groups.

Manpower: In the late 1980s, the strength of the organisation was estimated to be 60,000, of which 12–15,000 are full-time fighters. Fighting groups have been most active in Konduz, Baghlan, Badakhshan, Takhar, Balkh, Samangan provinces, as well as in Faryab, Jozjan, Kabul, Herat, and Farah.

Moderate Groups

Harakat-i-Inqilabe-i-Islam (Revolutionary Islamic Movement)

History: Maulvi Muhammed Nabi Muhammadi, a former member of the Afghan Parliament founded the movement, following the PDPA coup of 1978. The primary goals of the movement are: to establish democratic government while retaining many features of the traditional society; to hold free elections following a period of martial law, during which the political situation would be normalised; to introduce some measures of agricultural reform; to maintain international non-alignment. The group draws its membership from the Uzbek and Pathan populations and has attracted students, moderate religious leaders and teachers, tribal chiefs, and former officers as members.

Structure: Muhammadi is the most important figure in the group. The rural mullahs have had significant influence in the past in decision-making by the Political Committee, the most important one. In general, the movement is quite decentralised. Qari Taj Mohammed of Ghazni is one of its best-known commanders.

Manpower: The largest of the moderate groups, Harikat is said to have suffered a decline in membership (possibly as a result of a general decline in the influence of the rural clergy). The strength of the movement has been estimated to be about 30,000 permanent and part-time fighters. Harakat is most active in Logar, Ghazni, Kabul, Farah and Herat provinces with some activity in Paktia, Kandahar, and Helmand.

Mahaz-i-Milli-Islami (National Islamic Front for Afghanistan)

History: Milli-Islami was initially brought into being by Pir Sayid Ahmed Gailani in 1979 as an attempt to bring several different, disputing groups together under one umbrella. Despite the high respect in which his family is held within the country, this effort failed and Gailani wound up forming his own separate group. Considered to be the most moderate group, Milli-Islami advocates the creation of a constitutional monarchy with an elected legislature. The group is based primarily in southeastern Afghanistan (Paktia province), but it is also active in Kandahar and the Kabul region.

Structure: Milli-Islami lacks a structure to fulfil a full range of pseudo-governmental functions. Gailani makes most decisions personally. The military organisation is quite tight with seemingly good leadership. Special ranger/raider units apparently exist.

Manpower: Estimated to have 2,000 full-time members and up to 15,000 supporters, largely among the Pushtun tribes.

Jabha-i-Najat-i-Milli-Afghanistan (Afghan National Liberation Front)

History: A small organisation based in southern Afghanistan, the front formed in

December 1978, with Sibghat-Ullah Mojadidi, an Islamic spiritual leader at its head. The primary goal is to establish representative government based on Islamic principles, Afghan traditions, and democracy. They are favourably disposed toward relations with the West. This group has clashed frequently with the Hekmatyr faction of Hezb-i-Islami.

Structure: Several committees exist to oversee the policy process, but Mojadidi retains strong personal influence over decisions. Major operational decisions are made by the Military Committee (e.g. whether or not to participate with other groups in a siege) but the regional commanders enjoy a high degree of autonomy as in other groups.

Manpower: Strength is estimated to be between 8,000 and 15,000 persons. Provinces where active: Kunar, Kandahar.

Ittehad-i-Islami (Islamic Alliance)

History: Ittehad was one of the later groups to form, its origins dating to January 1980. Professor Ghulam Sayaf, an Islamic fundamentalist, established it as a coalition of several different groups; it later split into moderate and fundamentalist factions. As a result, Ittehad eventually evolved into a small organisation under the personal leadership of Sayaf. The group is strongest in Paghman province, where it has been the focus of severe attacks by the régime. It is also active in Parwan, Nangarhar, Paktia, and Kabul provinces.

Structure: There are Political and Military Committees, but Sayaf retains primary control over decisions. Local commanders run their own operations but also respond to overall strategy determined by the Military Committee.

Manpower: Estimated strength is 6–15,000 men.

Other *Mujahedin* Groups

Note: These organisations are all small Shiite groups, with some ties to Iran. They are not members of the Islamic Union of Afghan *Mujahedin*, better known as the Group of Seven. The majority of the population of Afghanistan is Sunni, so these parties have relatively smaller followings and less influence than the Sunni groups described above. They also have received less support from outside sources who legitimately see them as irreconcilable Iranian proxies.

Hezbollah

(Party of God). A Shiite group closely aligned with Iran, this group actually backs unity with Iran. It comprises 1,500 cadre and 3,000 total supporters and is most active in the western provinces where Afghanistan shares a border with Iran.

Shura

Shura is led by Sayed Ali Beheshti. Its strength is 4–8,000 and it operates in Bamiyan, Baghlan, Balkh, and Ghazni provinces. It advocates an autonomous

Hazara region, presumably based on Islamic law.

Harakat Islami

(Islamic Movement). Sheikh Muhsini leads this Shiite group, which operates in the north in Faryab, Jozjan, Balkh, and Badakhshan provinces. The group is fighting for the establishment of a fundamentalist, Islamic state. Its strength is thought to be about 2,000 cadre with more than 10,000 supporters.

Sepha-i-Pasdara

(Revolutionary Guards). Led by Mohsen Reza'i, the Revolutionary Guards also favour union with Iran. Strength, estimated at 3–8,000, is concerned in Ghour, Jozjan, Helmand, Bamiyan, and Herat. They have been strongly backed by Iran.

In the Nuristan region of eastern Afghanistan, two other groups are active — the *Free Resistance Front* and the *Free Government Group* — about which little is known.

The Panjshir 7 Offensive

THE Panjshir 7 operation (Apr–Jun 1984) was selected for description as a typical offensive for several reasons. First, all the main features of a major operation are depicted. Second, the operation was larger than many of the others, but it was not the largest (this was probably Operation Magistral' in November and December of 1987). Third, Panjshir 7 incorporated some tactical innovations, thus, it shows how the Soviets adapted tactically to previous operational failures. The strengths and weaknesses of both sides can also be seen. Finally, the Soviets ran more offensives into the Panjshir Valley than any other area, so it is fitting that one of them should be used to illustrate a 'model' Soviet offensive in Afghanistan.

Lying 65 kilometres to the north of Kabul, the Panjshir Valley extends north-easterly across the Hindu Kush range for 150 kilometres. Next to the Salang Highway, the Panjshir is the best access route to the north and north-east of the country from Kabul. Tributaries of the Panjshir River form smaller, higher valleys and canyons to either side of the main valley. The mouth of the valley opens onto the Salang Highway, hence the frequent attacks of the Panjshir insurgents, commanded by Ahmed Shah Massoud, against convoys, outposts, and the Pol-i-Khomri logistics centre. The valley narrows at its upper end, making it difficult for motor traffic. The valley can be entered in force from one direction only — the south-western end — but there are many plateaux and passes suitable for heliborne *desants*.

For the six months prior to the initiation of Panjshir 7, the valley had been quite peaceful, owing to a controversial cease-fire between Massoud and the Soviets. Massoud had used the respite well. Residents had returned, rebuilt their villages, and started farming once more. The rebels reconstituted and reorganised. More fighters had joined and new stocks of weapons and ammunition had been brought in. Caches had been fortified, stocks of food put up, and the rebels had enjoyed a time of rest and recuperation, coupled with military training. In addition, Massoud had renewed and solidified his command organisation.

By the end of the truce, the *mujahedin* within the valley numbered 5,000 rested, trained, well-armed fighting men, plus as many as 200 heavy machine-guns, several tanks, and three D-30 howitzers.[1] When Massoud refused to extend the cease-fire, he knew it was only a matter of time until the Soviets launched a new attack. His intelligence sources gave him a good idea of when it would occur. The two failed attempts at his assassination by KHAD agents in late March had also undoubtedly served as early warning.[2]

The Soviet offensive plan contained all the characteristic features of past plans, plus a few important operational innovations. The goal of the operation was to deal a major blow to the Panjshir rebel groups which were growing in size and influence. Utter destruction was unrealistic, but the Soviets did hope to inflict enough damage to force a long recovery period on the *mujahedin*. Essentially, the operation was carried out in five phases:

1. Logistical build-up.
2. Pre-attack bombardment and assembly of manoeuvre forces.
3. Ground offensive into the valley.
4. Insertion of large *desant* forces into side valleys and exit passages.
5. Establishment of manned outposts to hold the lower half of the valley.

During phases 1 and 2, the Soviets assembled the men and materials needed to conduct a four-to-five week operation without pause. Thirty-six TU-16 Badger bombers moved from other areas of the Soviet Union to airfields in Turkestan from which they could fly daily sorties into the objective area. Helicopter units redeployed temporarily to concentrate at Bagram and points northward. As usual, the motorised rifle force used in the operation came from several different formations, assembled under one headquarters, probably the 108th MR Division. One battalion came from the 66th MR Brigade near Jalalabad, a second from the 191st Independent MR Regiment in Ghazni. The 180th MR Regiment, comprising the largest ground element in the task-force, deployed from its camp at Khair Khana in northern Kabul.[3] At least one other unidentified MR regiment was probably involved as well. Undoubtedly, smaller numbers of supporting troops, especially engineers and long-range artillery from the army artillery brigade in Khair Khana were also deployed northward. The total Soviet ground force probably numbered about 7,500 troops.

In addition, the task force included air assault and airborne battalions and regiments of the CI force, perhaps 2–3,000 in all. Finally, 5,000 Afghan soldiers from the undermanned 8th and 20th Divisions and the 37th Commando Brigade also took part. Although the total number of troops involved was relatively small for modern war, it is evident that the task of mounting the operation involved a great deal of co-ordination, as combat power was assembled from all over Afghanistan as well as the Soviet Union.

Knowing that the attack was coming, Massoud decided to strike first in order to interfere with the assembly and advance of the ground force. First, having evacuated the civilian population, he ordered all the main thoroughfares in the valley to be mined. On 16 April, his guerrillas destroyed three bridges on the Salang Highway, cutting traffic for three days until Soviet engineers repaired the damage. Four days later, a huge convoy of fuel trucks was hit. However, the Soviets responded very quickly to this attack, sending in a large *desant* force which harried the rebel raiders quite effectively, and drove them off with unusually high losses. On 20 April, Massoud ordered yet another pre-emptive strike against a Soviet-Afghan garrison in Onawa in the mouth of the valley; several hundred prisoners are said to have been taken. Finally, a raid was mounted to destroy helicopters at Bagram on the 21st, but without success.[4]

The Soviet offensive began on 21 April with high-altitude bombardment by

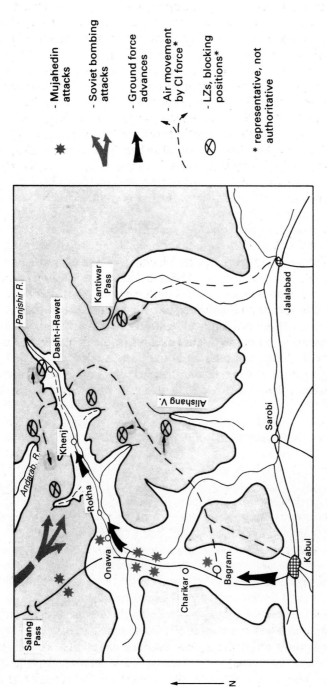

- Mujahedin attacks
- Soviet bombing attacks
- Ground force advances
- Air movement by CI force*
- LZs, blocking positions*

* representative, not authoritative

Phases 1 and 2

1. Soviets assemble air and ground forces from various garrisons to Kabul-Bagram region.
2. Long-range bombers (TU-16) from USSR conduct preparatory strikes throughout the valley.
3. Mujahedin conduct spoiling attacks along the Salang highway, at Bagram airbase and Onawa and mine roads in the valley.

Phases 3 - 5

1. Conventional forces move slowly and deliberately into the valley, advancing cautiously for 1 week.
2. Heliborne battalion occupies Dasht-i-Rawat at valley's end.
3. Heliborne CI forces occupy key terrain and passes vic of side canyons to seal off the valley.
4. After several weeks, CI and ground units withdraw but leave lower half of valley occupied by strongpoints.

Figure B.1 The Panjshir 7 Operation

Badgers and air strikes by Flogger and Fencers. During the course of the offensive, the Badgers allegedly averaged 30 sorties a day, completely saturating the objective area. The total daily fixed-wing sortie rate may have been as high as 100.[5]

The MR task force began to move into the valley a day or two later, accompanied by continuous, planned artillery and air strikes on the flanks and to the front. In keeping with his previous strategy of avoiding contact with such a large force until it had spread itself out thoroughly, Massoud retreated into the side valleys and kept watch. The armoured columns moved deliberately, slowed by the hundreds of mines which had to be cleared. No effort was made to explore the side valleys at this time. After the better part of a week, the MR force reached Khenj, where it had to halt because of deep, unthawed snow. A heliborne battalion occupied Dasht-i-Rawat, farther on, approximately 80–90 kilometres from the mouth of the valley. According to a rebel source, casualties during this period amounted to 200 Soviet/ Afghan troops and 150 guerrillas, an exchange ratio more unfavourable to the insurgents than past operations.[6]

Then, at the beginning of May, the Soviets surprised the *mujahedin* by attempting to seal off the entire valley by means of large *desants*. Several battalions occupied key passes within the Panjshir Valley system, and blocking positions were established by the CI force in the passages to the Andarab Valley to the north and Alishang Valley and Kantiwar pass to the south.[7] Simultaneously, the mechanised units pushed their way up into the smaller canyons, as artillery and fixed-wing aircraft conducted barrier/denial bombardments to restrict rebel movement. The *mujahedin* found themselves squeezed and scattered as a result. They had expected the eventual advance of the MR units into the side valleys, coupled with limited *desants*, but not on the scale experienced. Now, with so many *desant* units mixed into the operational area and many of their usual routes blocked, the rebels had to watch every step.

According to the insurgents, even though they were surprised by the new tactics, they applied some effective 'anti-commando' tactics of their own:

> The Russians sent their élite commandos to Panjshir; the troops were the best, well-trained, knowing how to operate in mountainous terrain. The units were dropped in six places on the hill tops and the valley floor. Each time when a commando would land, the *mujahedin* would retreat, no frontal clash, no shooting at their helicopters. The commandos, finding no resistance, nobody to shoot, would settle down and slowly relax. Small groups would form, smoking or opening food cans to eat. At that moment, groups of four or five *mujahedin* would go and sit in a hidden position near the unit and wait. Individuals or groups roaming around detached from the main body of the commandos were shot dead. All the commandos were harassed in the same manner. The enemy could not hold out for more than four or five days. In the end, the units were carried away, half of them dead and wounded, without having fought or killed or wounded a single *mujahedin*.[8]

Naturally, this kind of report always puts the best light on the ability of the rebels to react to the *desant* threat. The level of complete success described above must be considered as only one example of a tactic, not as a standard outcome of the many confrontations between the rebels and the CI force during the operation. It is quite clear that the heavy use of *desant* troops in Panjshir 7 reduced the mobility and aggressiveness of the insurgents.

There are no reports of excessive losses of personnel on either side as a result of the offensive. Despite the use of larger numbers of *desantniks*, the valley was not closed off and the rebel strongholds in the valley were not destroyed. Eventually, the operation outran its logistic support and both the Soviet and régime forces were withdrawn. This time, however, the lower half of the valley was garrisoned as far up as Pechgur, just below Khenj, primarily by Afghan units.

The Soviets did achieve one important objective; for the better part of the rest of 1984, Massoud's men were occupied with attacks against the valley garrisons (i.e. against other Afghans), leaving the Salang Highway in that sector free from their ambushes and raids. By the end of the year, however, the Panjshir insurgents reasserted their full control over the valley, notwithstanding the existence of a few unreduced forts. Thus, even though the operation showed tactical refinement and improved performance, the ultimate outcome of the Panjshir 7 offensive was the same as the first six. Soviet and régime forces established temporary control in the region, but relinquished it after the passage of a few months. The rebels were held at bay for a longer period of time, but they were not crippled. From this point of view, the operation must be considered to have been a failure.

Notes

1. Mark Urban, *War in Afghanistan* (London: Macmillan Press, 1988, p. 145.
2. 'Soviet Long Range Occupation Dilemma Examined', JPRS-NEA-84-089, 6 June 1984, p. 49. This source contains several news excerpts translated from the French (Paris) newspaper *Liberation*, 2 May 1984. This information comes from a report by Beatrice Bacconier entitled 'Commander Mas'ud: The Lion of Panjshir', p. 6.
3. Urban, *War in Afghanistan*, pp. 144–45.
4. JPRS-NEA-84-089, p. 38.
5. Yossef Bodansky, 'Afghanistan: The Soviet Air War', *Defense & Foreign Affairs*, Sept. 1985, p. 14.
6. Quoted in Urban, *War in Afghanistan*, p. 147.
7. Ibid.
8. AIC 43, Oct. 1984, p. 10.

APPENDIX C

Soviet Planning for an Ambush

Sequence and Time Requirement for Scheduled Preparations

1.	Meal	15 min.
2.	Personal Time	20 min.
3.	Receipt of mission order from higher commander	1 hr. 20 min.
4.	Issuing mission order to subordinates	1 hr. 20 min.
5.	Physical training and exercise	
	— Loosening up	10 min.
	— 2 kilometre run	10 min.
	— strength exercises	30 min.
	— hand-to-hand combat practice	25 min.
	— cool-down run	5 min.
6.	Washing up	10 min.
7.	Meal	15 min.
8.	Cleaning, preparation of weapons, ammunition, supplies	1 hr.
9.	Rest	6 hrs.
10.	Physical exercise, washing up	20 min.
11.	Light meal (tea, coffee, sandwiches)	15 min.
12.	Loading up	20 min.
13.	Final instructions to sub-group leaders	15 min.

TOTAL: 13 hours and 10 minutes

Note: It is quite clear that this schedule could be stretched out over several days and incorporate within it additional events such as: weapons zeroing, ambush rehearsal, specialist training (review), and inspections.

	Commander	Deputy Cdr	Radio Operator	Machine-gunner	Asst Machine-gunner	AGS-17 Grenadier	Asst Grenadier	Medic	Total
AKS-74	1		1		1		1	1	5
RPK-74[1]		1							1
PK MG[2]				1					1
AGS-17[3]						1			1
Rifle magazines[4]	9	9	9		9		9	5	50
Ammunition boxes[5]				1	2	1	2		6
Smoke-pots		1							1
Bayonets	1	1	1	1	1	1	1	1	8
Silencers	1	1							2
Special bullets[6]	1								1
Signal flares	2	2	2	1	1	1	1		10
Illuminating rockets	2	2	2	2	2	2	2	3	17
Flak vests	1	1	1	1	1	1	1	1	8
Dry ration	1	1	1	1	1	1	1	1	8

Combat Loads for Key Members of Ambush Group

1. 5.56 light machine-gun
2. 7.62 machine-gun
3. Automatic grenade launcher
4. Each magazine loaded with 45 rounds
5. Machine-gun box — 250 rounds; AGS-17 box — 28 rounds.
6. Ten rounds total, type unclear

Source: Senior Lieutenant A Kravchenko, 'Gruppa v Zacade' (The Group in an Ambush), *VV*, No. 7, 1989, p. 48.

Force Structure Tables for Primary Soviet Formations Used in the War

The Motorised Rifle Division

Motorised rifle divisions formed the backbone of the Soviet occupation forces in Afghanistan. Initially, elements of up to five MRDs invaded Afghanistan. Later, the MR force structure was modified, breaking some of the divisions up into separate

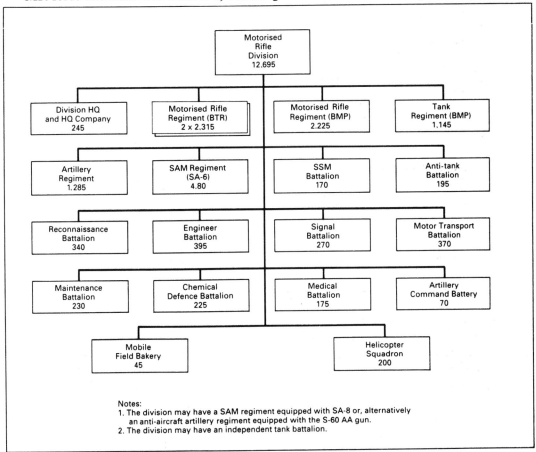

Table D.1. Structure of the Motorised Rifle Division showing unit strength.

brigades and regiments. Tank regiments, finding little utility in the DRA, were sent home, as were the SAM regiment, SSM battalion, AT battalion, and regimental AT companies and AA batteries, and at least part of the chemical defence units. MRDs normally did not operate as divisions, since their regiments were often garrisoned at separate locations. Instead, a changing combination of MR regiments and battalions from different manoeuvre headquarters were assembled under a divisional headquarters for periodic, conventional operations. Individual battalions within regiments usually remained behind to defend home garrisons.

The Airborne Division

Unlike most of their Western counterparts, Soviet airborne divisions are completely mechanised with light armoured vehicles (BMDs) which can be, and often were, deployed by helicopter. Only one airborne divisional headquarters was maintained in Afghanistan but regiments from at least two divisions based in the Soviet Union were deployed there. Used initially in the *coup de main* which opened the war and then as security forces in Kabul and other important localities, the airborne units eventually became a component of the CI force which carried out most of the

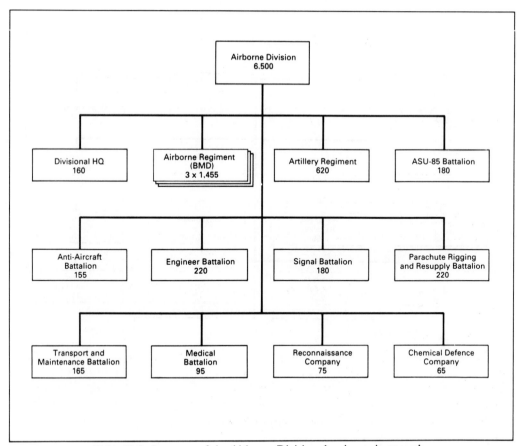

Table D.2. Structure of the Airborne Division showing unit strength.

direct action against the insurgents. They seldom conducted parachute assaults, the most common means of deployment into action being by helicopter. Divisional and regimental AA and AT elements were not sent to Afghanistan.

The Airborne Regiment

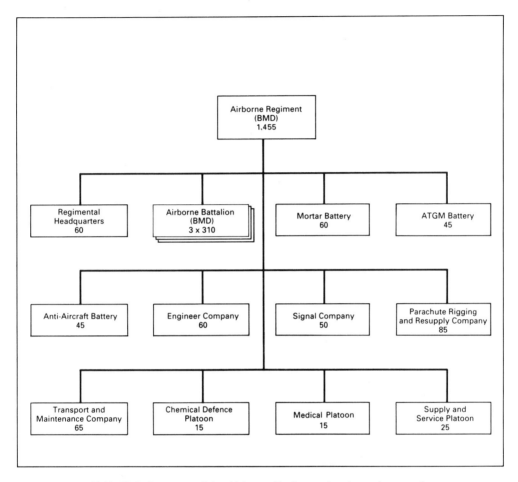

Table D.3. Structure of the Airborne Regiment showing unit strength.

Air Assault Brigade

The air assault brigade includes two parachute-trained battalions and two heli-borne battalions. The brigade has no helicopters organic to its organisations. Helicopters are provided by the Soviet Air Force (VVS). As a result, the infantry-helicopter co-ordination link can sometimes be fragile or unsatisfactory. Like the airborne forces, these heliborne units are equipped with BMDs. Most air assault operations were conducted at battalion-level and lower. Self-propelled assault guns, SAMs, and most of the AT weapons systems were not deployed to Afghanistan.

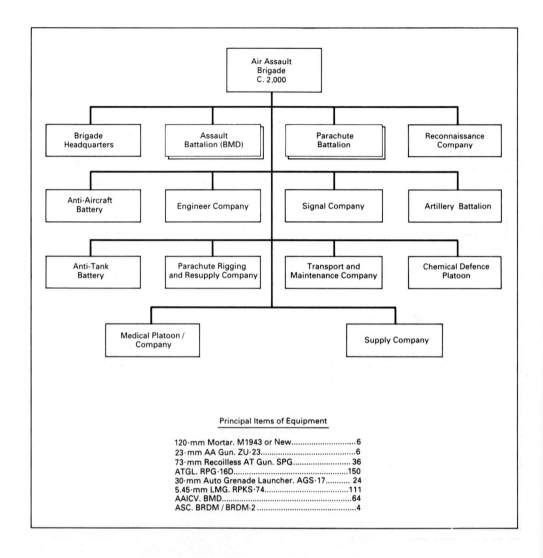

Table D.4. Structure of the Air Assault Brigade showing estimated unit strength and list of principal items of equipment.

Airmobile Assault Brigade

The airmobile assault brigades are quite similar in composition to the air assault brigades, the principal difference being the absence of parachute trained sub-units and the reduced numerical strength. Air assault and airmobile units formed an important part of the CI force. As both wear the same uniforms, it is quite difficult to distinguish between them. Both were used in the same way in Afghanistan and the *mujahedin* refer to them all as 'commandos'.

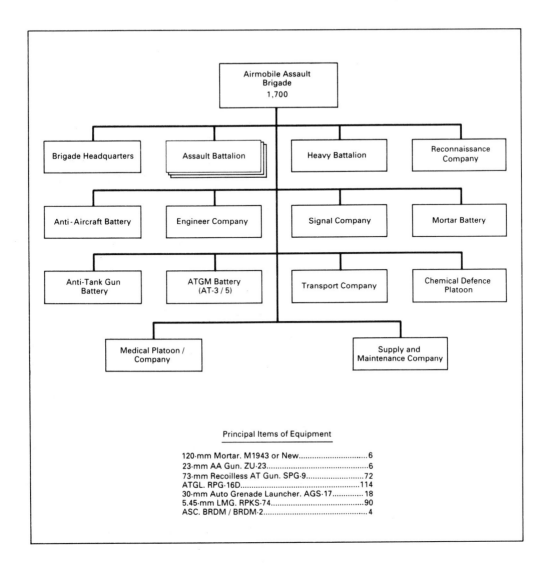

Table D.5. Structure of the Airmobile Assault Brigade showing estimated
unit strength and list of principal items of equipment.

Reconnaissance Battalion

Reconnaissance battalions are found in all MR and tank divisions. They usually are composed of the most able and best trained soldiers and officers. Reconnaissance companies are found in airborne divisions, air assault/airmobile brigades and manoeuvre regiments. MR units used in heliborne operations in Afghanistan almost always came from the reconnaissance organisations. Recon units formed another important component of the CI force.

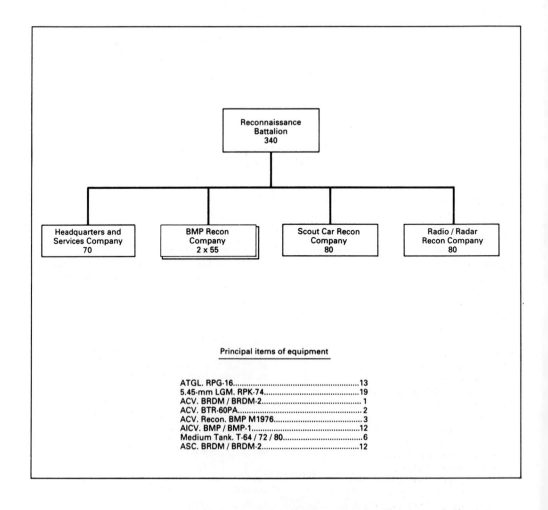

Table D.6. Structure of the Reconnaissance Battalion showing unit
strength and list of principal items of equipment.

Source: US Army Field Manual 100-2-3, *The Soviet Army: Troops, Organization and
Equipment.* Washington: HQDA, July 1984.

Index